C H I A R E N Z A

L A N D S C A P E S   O F   T H E   M I N D

CHIARENZA

LANDSCAPES OF THE MIND

Preface by Carl Chiarenza

Introduction by Estelle Jussim

Afterword by Charles W. Millard

DGR

DAVID R. GODINE, PUBLISHER, BOSTON

Original photographs separated as tritones
by Richard Benson

Printed in U.S.A. by Acme Printing Co.
Wilmington, Massachusetts

Production coordinated by Greg Graalfs

Designed by Carl Zahn

Library of Congress Cataloging-in-Publication Data

Chiarenza, Carl.
Chiarenza : landscapes of the mind.

1. Photography, Artistic. 2. Chiarenza, Carl.
I. Title.
TR654.C4836 1988 779'.092'4 87-46284
ISBN 0-87923-724-4

David R. Godine, Publisher
Horticultural Hall
300 Massachusetts Avenue
Boston, Massachusetts 02115

FOR HEIDI

ACKNOWLEDGEMENTS

This book has been made possible by the considerable contributions of several people whose faith in me and my work is unceasing. Eelco Wolf has been the prime mover in the making possible of this project. His support for many years and in many ways is beyond acknowledgement. Estelle Jussim and Charles Millard, longtime friends and supporters, have put together the words that make this publication more than an exhibition between covers. Susan Cohen and William Johnson made order out of the chaos of information at the "back of the book."

To Tobie Atlas I owe the clarity of my words. Once again she has been co-author as well as editor. For the remarkable design I thank Carl Zahn. And I thank Greg Graalfs of Polaroid Corporation, Fran Canzano of Acme Printing Company, and Richard Benson for the superb production.

David Godine has acted on his commitment to my work as he has for so many others. As a publisher he is unique in overseeing quality at every step of the way.

Cornell Capa made the exhibition of this work possible and I thank him and the staff of the International Center of Photography as well as Barbara Hitchcock of Polaroid Corporation.

To Hall Peterson I owe a great deal. He has been a major supporter for years and I thank him for his continued encouragement. I thank also my long-time friend and original representative, Carl Siembab, and my current dealer, Brent Sikkema of Vision Gallery in Boston.

I am indebted to many people not mentioned elsewhere in these pages, among them Richard Albright, Morton C. (Bob) Bradley, Eileen Heaney, Peter Laytin, Joy Neimanas, and Lynn Sternbergh, who have, through their friendship, given me unique and important support.

To Heidi Katz I continue to be indebted for unending faith and love, for a fulfilling and creative environment, and for all the things that make it possible to work and live. She has contributed directly and critically to the production of my photographs.

Some of the work included here was made under artist's fellowships from the Massachusetts Arts and Humanities Foundation and from the National Endowment for the Arts, and from an artist-in-residence grant from the Massachusetts Council of the Arts and the Boston Museum of Fine Arts.

I am grateful to Polaroid Corporation for years of support. In addition to Eelco Wolf, Barbara Hitchcock and Greg Graalfs, I'd like to thank Rosetta Tarantino, John Reuter, Sam Yanes, Constance Sullivan and Jon Holmes.

C.C.

CONTENTS

P R E F A C E

There is a riddle that overtakes me when I am asked to talk about my pictures. It's the one about the chicken and the egg. Words come when I can stand at a distance, when, out of compassion for an audience, I can propose a beginning, a middle, and an end to a discussion of art. But such deference to logic escapes me when I turn to discuss my own work.

What I know when I am making a picture is that I am on a journey into the unknown. Just that. How the journey began, I have no idea. Why I have become part of its momentum, I can't say. Where it will leave me to begin again and where it will take the viewer of my work are questions I can't answer. Pictures come from pictures. We do not know who gave birth to the first – or why or how. We can speculate on the cave or on its source of inspiration; we can speculate on how the first pictures were perceived. But we can't be sure. We cannot be sure what makes this picture *this* picture, though as artists and viewers we struggle to discover the what, where, why, how, and who of its reality. No application of theories of language, of post-modernism, of post-structuralism, of semiotics, of any ideology holds promise of yielding the sought-after definition. It's the enigma of the chicken and the egg, the question of cause and effect, the force of creativity, the force of the unknown.

I am captive to the photographic process. For me it is magical-alchemical. Each step in the making of a picture is guided by intrigue, the intrigue that comes from watching the real and unreal interact. Through the control of light an artist can probe space and surface. It is fascinating for me to watch how deep space becomes flat surface, and vice-versa, to see how space and surface fluctuate as I change my angle of viewing. It fascinates me to be swept up by the movement of source materials into field or space, to see the tangible transformed into a wholly unique visual event.

The potion that brews when I make a picture is made up of many ingredients, only some of which I determine. This is very different from what we have learned about photographs, from what we have come to believe we see through windows. The photographic process pushes me through the frame, through the window, into the reality of the unknown. I want my pictures to provide evidence of the existence of this reality, to testify to its significance, and to impel its pursuit.

We all experience from time to time forces that refuse logical explanation. Reason fails at these times. We wonder, get side-tracked by life, go on, forget, until another extraordinary moment returns to remind us of our own waywardness. Once in a while these experiences haunt us for days with a felt reality beyond our grasp. Photographs are rich with these extraordinary moments for both artist and viewer. "The image educates emotion where reason never reaches," in the words of Dorothea Blom. "The significant image held, recalled, has the power to transform. No one knows why this is so. One can only know that it works."[1] I want the viewer of my work to sense this power, to feel the presence of the unknown. All photographs share this life force, this force of their own individuality. Somewhere between the making and the viewing of the picture, we experience this force, though our experience remains forever beyond satisfactory explanation. This is what drives creativity – the unknown. It is the single most important force in being human. For me, it is the most vital life force. I want my pictures to attest to how little we know and how much we feel. I want the viewer of my work to move, moment to moment, from within the accessible and familiar to the realm of the unknown, to reality beyond.

The settings for my early work were the buildings, streets, railroads, and junkyards of the city, occasionally the passageways between city and country, and later the country and seashore. Eventually I went back to the city, then returned to the country and seashore for an extended period, and finally back again to the city to concentrate on its industrial and technological areas. In 1979, I was invited to use the Polaroid 20 x 24 camera in color. That changed everything, except my preference for black and white. Suddenly I had to find a way to bring the city, the junkyard, the industrial debris to the camera. I had to reverse my method of work. I had to reconstrue my sense of the process of making a picture. It was hard, very hard. But since 1979, I have not left the studio. I now know that it holds more possibilities for me than I ever could have discovered or created in the world outside its walls. It's an exciting place, and out of it, I believe, has come my best work.

What I do in the studio is build and modify constructions. The modifying evolves from the physical manipulation of light. I use Polaroid materials to make changes in each negative and print along the way. The final set of negatives results in a series of variations on a theme. The printing continues this process in the darkroom. I have never been able to work with an assistant (except when working on the 20 x 24 camera). Sometimes I think that most of my creativity takes place in the darkroom (Heidi, my wife, often reminds me how different the finished print is from the Polaroid print and negative). While each final print can stand alone, the process I use has led me to mount and frame two or more prints as a single work to reveal how variations, formally arranged, can expand the meaning of the idea that produced the first negative. What I have in mind is presenting how perceptual changes in time, space, light, and configuration mirror contemporary thought, feeling, memory, and speculation. Though the single print continues to be of interest, the process of juxtaposition has allowed me to enlarge my work not only in scale, but in presentation of idea and method. The early examples of this idea, in comparison, were simple, easy, calm. My recent works reveal more conflict; there is more about falling off the edge of the world. In a space that plays with the photograph's ability to collide macro and micro, the cosmos and its particles, shallowness and deep space, there now appears a hint of the shape of the future. That hint acknowledges the possibility of nuclear war.

Since my pictures draw from what happens in

the blacks, I begin with a paper that gives me the most flexibility in terms of response to light, time, temperature, developers, and selenium toner. I control the amount of light that reaches various parts of the paper. I control the dilution, temperature, and time of developers. I will use any additive that helps me get what I want. The most extensive activity, however, takes place between the enlarging lens and the paper. Here I play with my hands – sometimes with my arms and shoulders – and use a variety of custom-made dodging and burning tools and masks. I will use bare light, I will use anything I can to push the recalcitrant materials to produce the emotional resonance I am seeking. It is very difficult for me to make two identical prints.

The landscapes that appear in my photographs are about ideas about the land throughout time; they are, for me, landscapes of the mind. The mind today survives in an environment which is neither the natural one of the nineteenth century and earlier, nor the urban one of the first half of the twentieth century. Today's environment is a more thoroughly technological and informational one, one geared to focus us away from the land toward the visual and verbal promises of a better life through consumable products. This landscape of the mind, nevertheless, remains as mysterious and as full of unknown forces as it has throughout history. I work to expose this mental-emotional construct in my pictures, to present a reaction to, rather than a depiction or even an interpretation of, the material world. By allowing thought and feeling to interact with the physical world, abstraction and perception become compatible. But there is a paradox here: it is modern technology that has given me an edge. The Polaroid positive/negative materials I use let me consider possibilities and variations almost instantaneously. Both the print and the negative direct me immediately to the changes needed in an individual picture or in a sequence of pictures. And to enliven the paradox, I have, in some instances, used nothing other than Polaroid packaging materials to construct the object to be illuminated and photographed.

Control is something that has always escaped me, for better or for worse. Working in the studio has allowed me to harness some control, and I welcome it, not because it lets me define the limits of my subject matter, but because it lets me eliminate the boundaries of my subject matter. I still wait for chance, for accident, for discovery, but unlike before, when I would set out for a new or familiar place in search of who-knows-what, I now can prepare the way for encountering the unexpected. It is like putting together a puzzle that has yet to be made. The viewer of the finished product, of the picture, takes the unfinished puzzle and, in much the same way I do, puts it together by adding his or her own ideas, experiences, hopes, and fantasies.

As for the chicken and the egg, they persist in keeping me humble. Many who share this virtue know that it gets its life force from persistent self-doubt. That is certainly the case for me. Over the years I have found myself comforted and crippled by self-doubt; it has made me see the world as a place of possibilities and as an unapproachable fiasco. But through it all, for as long as I care to remember, my goal has been to make pictures. For over twenty-five years I have forced a continuation of two careers; one pays for the other. I still look forward to the day when I will be a full-time artist.

Recently I have become aware of a change in my approach. I now can enter the studio or darkroom and build, modify, construct, regardless of whether I am feeling confident or confused. Heidi believes that I have accepted the "constant availability of the Muses which seemed fickle and elusive before." That may well be. I feel my work is changing and growing. I continue to be driven by the desire to make pictures about things invisible in the world, honoring and exploiting what I feel are the essential characteristics of the medium.

Making a picture remains for me an extraordinarily intimate process. It is confrontational, it is elusive, and it is demanding, but it is also my way of coexisting with the force of reality. What Baziotes wrote about his painting answers many questions one might ask of me today:

> It is the mysterious that I love in painting.
> It is the stillness and the silence.
> I want my pictures to take effect very slowly, to
> Obsess and to haunt.[2]

CARL CHIARENZA
March, 1987

1. Dorothea Blom, *Encounters with Art,* Lebanon, PA: Pendle Hill, 1963, p. 13.
2. William Baziotes, quoted in *It Is,* Autumn, 1959.

MYSTERIES AND TRANSFORMATIONS:

The Art of Carl Chiarenza

If you could look into a kaleidoscope that revealed the major facets of Carl Chiarenza's career, you would find recurring motifs and transformations. Music would metamorphose into photography. Spiritual search would coalesce into image-making. Dark nights of the soul would shift into exuberant joy. Chance and discovery would intermingle with formal certainties. All these, however, would be dominated by the enigmatic and mysterious landscapes he expresses in the chords of blacks, grays, and reflected whites of his superb prints. For Carl Chiarenza is obsessed by the changing landscape, the poignant transformation of nature into urban and technological environments.

There are many other facets of his distinguished career. He is an art historian who has contributed significant publications on the theory of photographic images and their relationship to painting. He is a much revered teacher of the history of photography and visual art. His prints adorn the collections of major museums and private connoisseurs. As one of a group including Paul Caponigro, Walter Chappell, and Nicholas Dean, he was among the first to test the artistic potential of new Polaroid films. Chiarenza's critical essays, reviews, and reprints of his lectures, are widely read and anthologized. In short, the present American scene in photography and education in the visual arts probably would not be the same without him. This first substantial monograph on his work has been long overdue.

Beginnings

Born in Rochester, New York, on September 5, 1935, Chiarenza is a first-generation American of Sicilian parentage. In his childhood, the Sicilian population of Rochester suffered the usual fate of recent immigrants. Carl recalls being made to feel like a second-class citizen. His father, Charles, earned his living as a cabinet-maker. His mother, Mary, was a gifted seamstress employed by a fine men's clothier. Mary was also a strict Catholic, with an obsessive concern for the health and safety of her four sons. Her husband was a loner, an artist manqué who painted nudes, propagandistic urbanscapes, and mythical subjects after Dante. An idealist and utopian socialist, he hated priests and all organized religion. Carl went through all the appropriate rites of Catholicism, including confirmation, but he was thoroughly disillusioned by the discovery that priests were only human.

Carl recalls two seemingly trivial incidents. Visiting the rectory one day, he discovered the priests eating meat on a Friday at a time when church dogma insisted that only fish could be consumed. Having quit religious instruction, he was pursued home by a priest who wanted to inquire why he was continually absent. Noting several of his father's paintings of nudes hanging in the living room, the scandalized priest commented on the deleterious influence the parent was obviously having on the son. Whereupon his father threw the priest bodily out the front door. To Carl, these incidents symbolized a loss of a comforting faith. That loss has haunted him. Much of his subsequent life has been spent in a search for a meaningful spirituality. Certainly, if his father's secularism seemed a healthy balance to his mother's insistent religiousity, the young boy was left with the difficulty, often unconscious, of having to reconcile two powerful and contradictory ideologies.

Despite constant squabbling between the parents, the Chiarenza family was united by a passion for music. It was perhaps the only religion they shared, as each Saturday afternoon they would gather to listen reverently to the Texaco broadcasts from the Metropolitan Opera. Father Chiarenza played the mandolin and guitar with gusto; Mother and all the boys sang. (One brother had such a good voice that he was about to depart for an audition with Beniamino Gigli, a famous Metropolitan Opera star, when he was drafted into the Army.) By the time he was eight, Carl was taking lessons on the clarinet, and added the saxophone later in high school.

Not only did all the Chiarenzas love music, play instruments, and worship opera, but they also painted, drew, and designed. It was an intensely artistic family, yet the father was adamantly against his sons pursuing any career in the arts. He knew all too well the practical problems of supporting oneself as an artist. There were strenuous arguments about careers. Typically for immigrant parents of that generation, the emphasis was on careers that would make substantial amounts of money. Torn by a desire to please his father, young Carl nevertheless rejected any notion of becoming a doctor or lawyer. He was persuaded that his own calling was music. The constant turmoil of the family drama laid the groundwork for Carl's temperament to be forged into a passionate and despairing cynicism, an attitude he later enjoyed in the writings of H.L. Mencken, a journalist and essayist of a singularly acerbic disposition. It has been said that only an unabashed idealist and romantic can become a cynic. Idealist and romantic that Carl was, the defensive shell he erected against the harsh realities and disappointments of living never managed to obscure his essential sweetness, gentleness, and spirituality.

Carl was active in grammar and high school bands and orchestras. Later, he managed to pay his way through the Rochester Institute of Technology playing jazz for college dances. He worked in small combos as well as in big bands, in the Stan Kenton style of the 1950s. At the same time, through an accident of destiny understandable for anyone born in Rochester – home of the enormous Kodak enterprises – he was also becoming more and more intrigued with photography. In his eighth year, Carl had the curious fortune of receiving both a clarinet and a camera. The director of a playground he frequented encouraged his photography when he put together a darkroom for the neighborhood kids. His father's brother, Anthony, a painter, illustrator, and decorator, gave him an excellent lens for a Speed Graphic camera that Carl had purchased second-hand, and introduced him to the more complex rituals of darkroom practice. He even helped Carl build his own enlarger. Then, in high school, he took a photography course. Soon he was the newspaper and yearbook photographer. He wrote for the newspaper, too, took the advanced English writing course, and began to recognize his love of words and ideas. For all its raptures, music, which remained supremely important to him, did not offer a life style he was willing to pursue. He envisioned a future as a writer, artist, and photographer.

Since he was keenly interested in image-making, and since he knew he would shortly have to earn his own living, Carl decided that the practical courses at the Rochester Institute of Technology would satisfy both needs. Over the initial objections of his parents, he applied to R.I.T., was accepted, and embarked on what he thought would be an uneventful two-year Associate Degree program in Applied Science.

Unexpected Encounters

In 1953, all R.I.T. students had to take the same fundamental courses whether they wanted eventually to pursue careers in science, optics, portraiture, illustration, or photochemistry. During his first two years, Carl studied sensitometry, lighting, dye transfer and other color techniques, advertising set-ups – all subjects intended to give him a firm ground in professional practice. What he had not anticipated was that the Institute was in the process of formulating a new curriculum program that would lead to the Bachelor of Fine Arts in photography.

Initiated by Ralph Hattersley, an inspired teacher with decidedly unconventional methods and goals, the program managed to acquire the influential presence of the photographer Minor White, who had arrived at George Eastman House only the year before. White's charismatic personality offered an approach to artistic image-making that went straight back to Alfred Stieglitz and the early Paul Strand. The essence of the approach was that the photograph was an independent entity free of simple representational values. Like his personal god, the awesome Edward Weston, Minor promulgated the belief that photographs were to be looked at not for what they were, but for what else they might be. Stieglitz had established the Equivalent, a concept about the metaphoric content of a picture, and White expended much energy in trying to illuminate what the idea of Equivalence might include. If he did not entirely succeed in this ambition, he firmly demonstrated that photography could engage in symbolism, metaphor, and mystical resonances. His images, mysterious and enigmatic as they were, always connected to nature, a nature viewed as Mallarmé expressed it in his theory of correspondences taken from Swedenborgianism. As Jonathan Green, a noted photographer and historian, put it, "every fact of visible reality corresponds to a fact of mental or spiritual consciousness."

Minor was still exploring the potential of the

teaching methods that later made him such a controversial figure. At the same time, he was searching for a spiritual center to his own life. He was demanding, sometimes irascible, profoundly moving, difficult. Unlike many of his classmates, who found Minor's exercises in "reading" photographs irritating and exhausting, Chiarenza often enjoyed being forced to study a single photograph for two hours at a time. One of Minor White's aphorisms, set down as early as 1955, made a permanent impact on him: "Photographing is the transforming art of the photographer." Carl was making his own discoveries along these lines, to the effect that it is in the very nature of the medium of photography to be transformative. The phenomenological world is transformed into the artifact; nature is transformed into picture. Chiarenza would later devote much of his intellectual energy into investigating the implications of such transformations.

In his own way, Ralph Hattersley was far more innovative than Minor White, although, like White, he was intent on shattering his students' stereotypical responses to photography. As Carl reports, Hattersley once hired a nude model and, among other strange settings, wrapped her in ropes for the students to photograph. At other times, he could counter White's insistence on the straight, beautiful print, insisting that they deliberately try to make muddy images just to see what would happen to form and value. Hattersley took groups of students on exciting field trips, to New York City, to meet famous *Life* photographers and fashion greats like Irving Penn, Richard Avedon, and Alexey Brodovitch, later Diane Arbus's mentor. The students even went to Chicago's Institute of Design, where the Bauhaus influence of Moholy-Nagy had created a center of modernist art.

Many students in the program felt like guinea pigs as they were bounced back and forth between Minor's fervently mystical sessions and Ralph's surprises. Yet Hattersley was nothing if not a mystic himself. Later, in Minor White's publication called *Octave of Prayer* (1972), he wrote, "A great many people are aware that in some mysterious way photography is a kind of religion for them. They would not express themselves in such words, of course, nor would they equate photography with say, Christianity, Buddhism, or Vedanta. Nevertheless, photography has come closer to being a religion than anything else they've ever had." For all that Chiarenza occasionally found Minor's emphasis on the spiritual somewhat excessive – "we were trying to figure out how to make a living" – it seems inescapable that he found Minor's approach and the observations of Hattersley very close to his own soul. One could even venture to say that of all of Minor's famous students who were at R.I.T. when Carl was there – Ken Josephson, Jerry Uelsmann, Bruce Davidson – it is Carl who, consciously or unconsciously, remained the foremost exponent of Minor's philosophy in his own images, without incorporating any of Minor's lifestyle, his need to be a guru, or his imposition

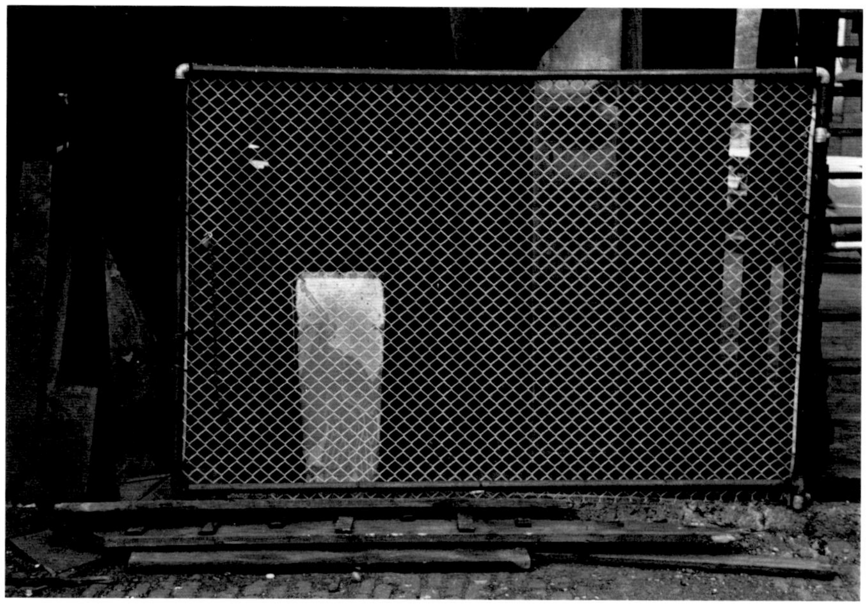

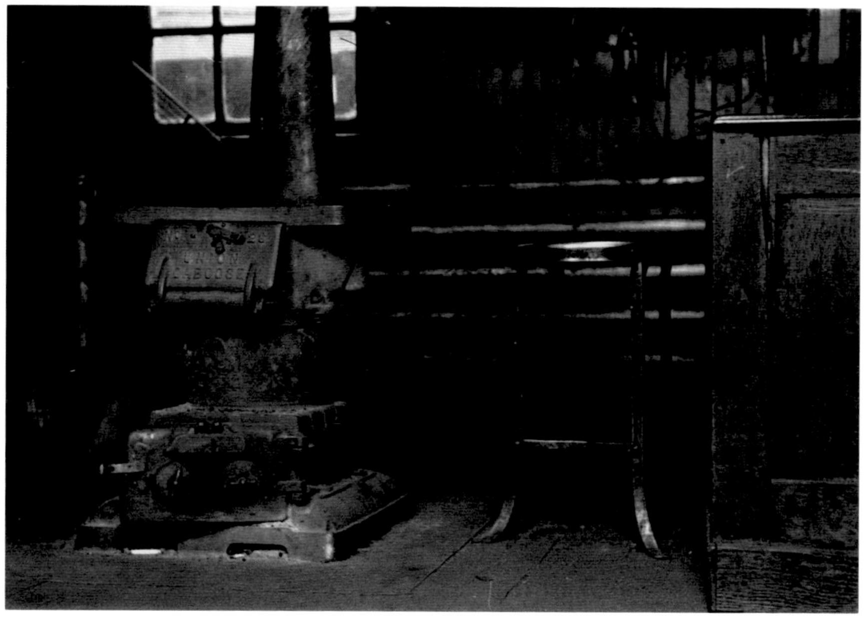

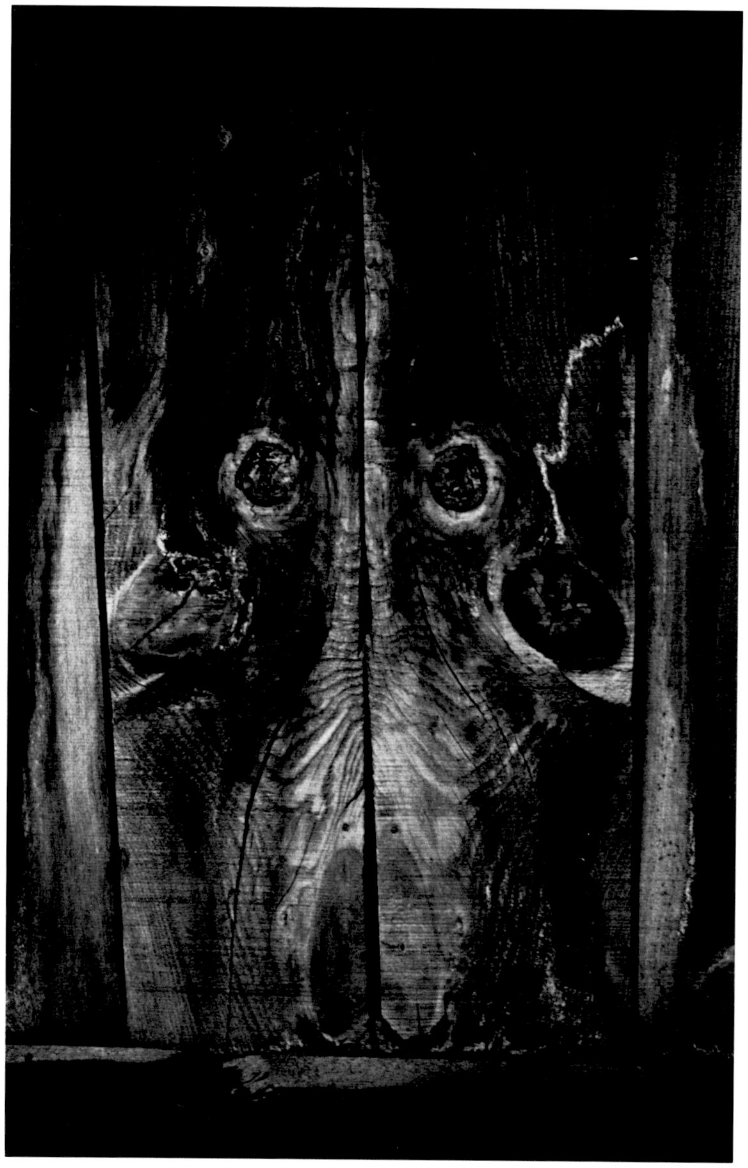

All photographs pages 17-18, Untitled, 1956-57
(from Interaction – Verbal/Visual)

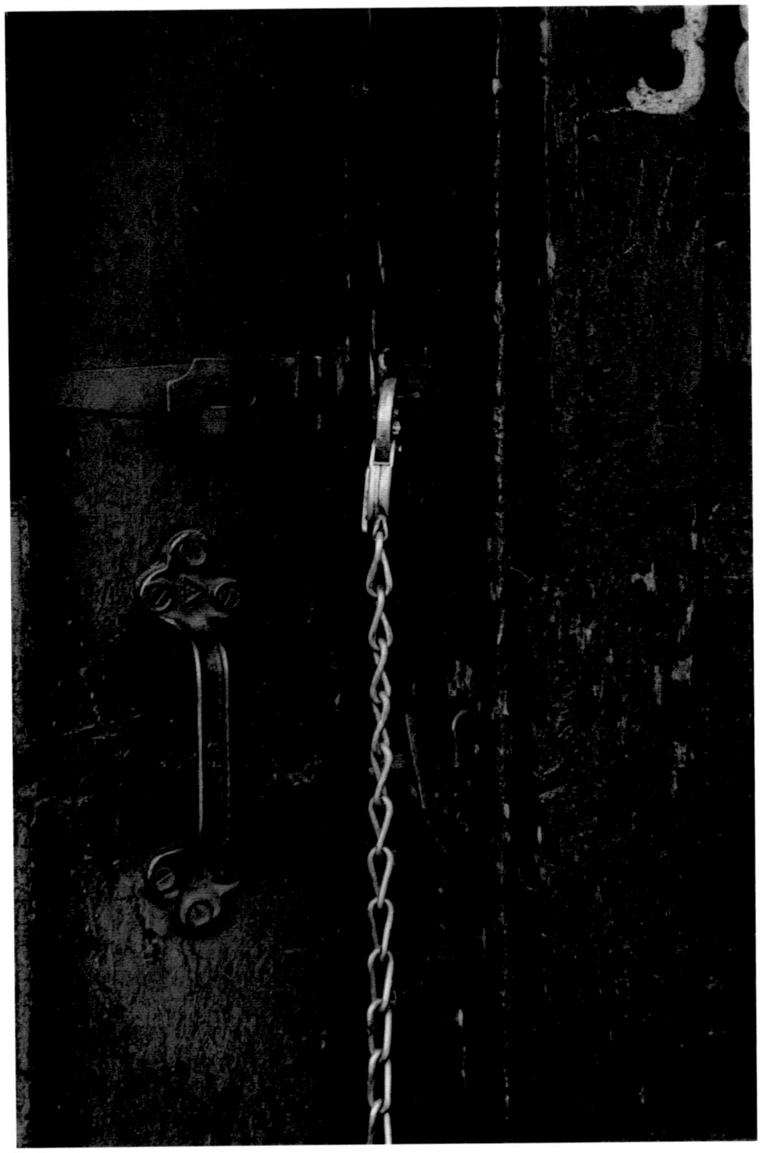

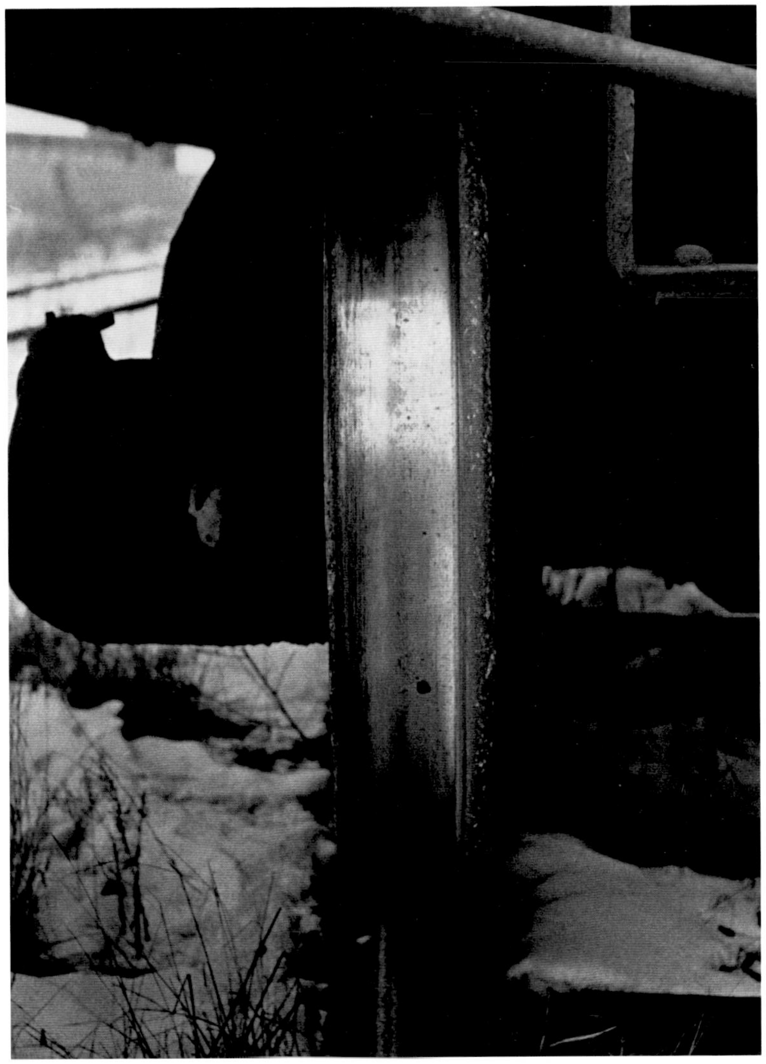

of his opinions on others. Looking at Carl's images, it would seem that he has tried always to answer some of the questions Minor posed: "How far can camerawork go toward making manifest the invisible? That is its work, but how far can it go? How much can camera bring to others of my own experiences of light and darkness, Christ or Lucifer?"

Both Minor White and Ralph Hattersley made lasting impressions. But they were not the only influences on Chiarenza. In fact, he claims that Robert Koch, a professor of English and American literatures and creative writing, may have made as profound an impact. Koch, a warm and sympathetic individual, had long discussions with his classes on the nature of both written and visual languages. He inspired Carl to investigate the relationships between these two forms of expression. Minor, of course, was also interested in such relationships, especially in the way that what he called "Sequences" reflected a similar structure to narrative form and poetic phrasing.

Carl was also much impressed with what W. Eugene Smith was doing with his photo essays in *Life*, with a style of photojournalism that was not only different from what appeared in the daily newspapers but that often reached profound emotional effect. It was particularly Smith's use of black as color, evoking both mystery and dramatic mood, that Chiarenza sought to emulate. Later, when he came to do his master's thesis at Boston University, Carl produced an essay, "City Hospital," which revealed his burgeoning love of richly complex images based on black. He still reveres Gene Smith.

Beaumont Newhall, then Director of George Eastman House, came over to R.I.T. to teach a course in the history of photography, which Carl attended with interest. Beaumont's wife, Nancy, had written an article called "The Caption," which appeared in the first issue of the journal, *Aperture*, begun in 1952, and edited by Minor White. With Minor's approval and under his supervision, Carl produced his R.I.T. thesis as a direct response to Nancy Newhall's article. His thesis was called *Interaction: Verbal/Visual;* its visual subject was aspects of railroads. Relying heavily on synecdoche, Carl created a series of poetic images of parts of wheels, railroad cars, and the technological detritus that accompanies rail transport. "I loved the railroad and I loved sequencing," Carl comments. The thesis was a hand-made and bound book; it exists in three copies, one of which is at George Eastman house.

Minor was clearly impressed with Carl. For many years afterward, Carl's photographs were reproduced either within the pages of *Aperture* or as a feature of its back cover. Carl's writing also appeared in *Aperture*. One early essay, "Stereotypes: Barriers to the Experience of Photographs," however, proved to be a turning point in their relationship. Minor accepted the essay with enthusiasm, yet when it appeared Carl discovered that more than half of it had been cut without Minor's having consulted him. He still recalls the incident with bitterness. It seemed more urgent than ever to remove himself entirely from Minor's overwhelming influence, and to find his own way. Minor had been such a force in his students' lives that many continued for the rest of their careers, and the rest of his life, to be intimately connected with the guru. But while Carl and Minor continued to have cordial relations, the younger man was determined to achieve artistic and personal independence.

"It is impossible to isolate exactly what Minor did for me," Carl has commented. "But two things seem clear: he provided support for a belief in the photograph as an object worthy of intense effort in the making, and in the photograph as an object in and of itself, apart from anything else in the world, that could be as expressive as music, poetry, or painting in relating the individual to the world." Purely on formal grounds, any study of Chiarenza's brooding prints reveals not only mysteries that Minor White could have approved, but transformations that are not dissimilar from several of Minor's ideologies and pictorial strategies.

If one were to construct a litany of transformations evident in Chiarenza's work and developed with content far different from Minor White's, that litany might be:

. . . Transforming the accidental and chance into composition and formal structure . . .

. . . Transforming the biomorphic and geomorphic into passionate visual music . . .

. . . Transforming the horizontal reality into vertical pattern . . .

. . . Transforming the jagged, brutalizing detritus of a technological civilization into negative/positive spaces of a beauty reminiscent of Oriental painting . . .

. . . Transforming texture, reflection, shape, modulations of three-dimensions, into mystery and enigma . . .

Where Carl's transformations differ most radically from his early mentor's are in their commentary on urban landscapes, rather than on what Carl calls the "unmolested landscape" of the countryside. His most recent works, of the past five years especially, have become more and more different from anyone else's, richer, more symphonic, with a confidence in his own personal visual language.

New Connections

In 1957, Carl Chiarenza had his B.F.A., a circle of friends he had met in Rochester, and no job prospects. Offered a fellowship as a teaching assistant, with a stipend, in the photo lab at Boston University, he accepted with alacrity. A master's degree in journalism seemed a reasonable route to gainful employment, something he could pursue without compromising his creative work. Unfortunately, the program deeply disappointed him. It seemed hardly the environment for a would-be Mencken, Ambrose Bierce, or W. Eugene Smith. Yet during the two years he was in

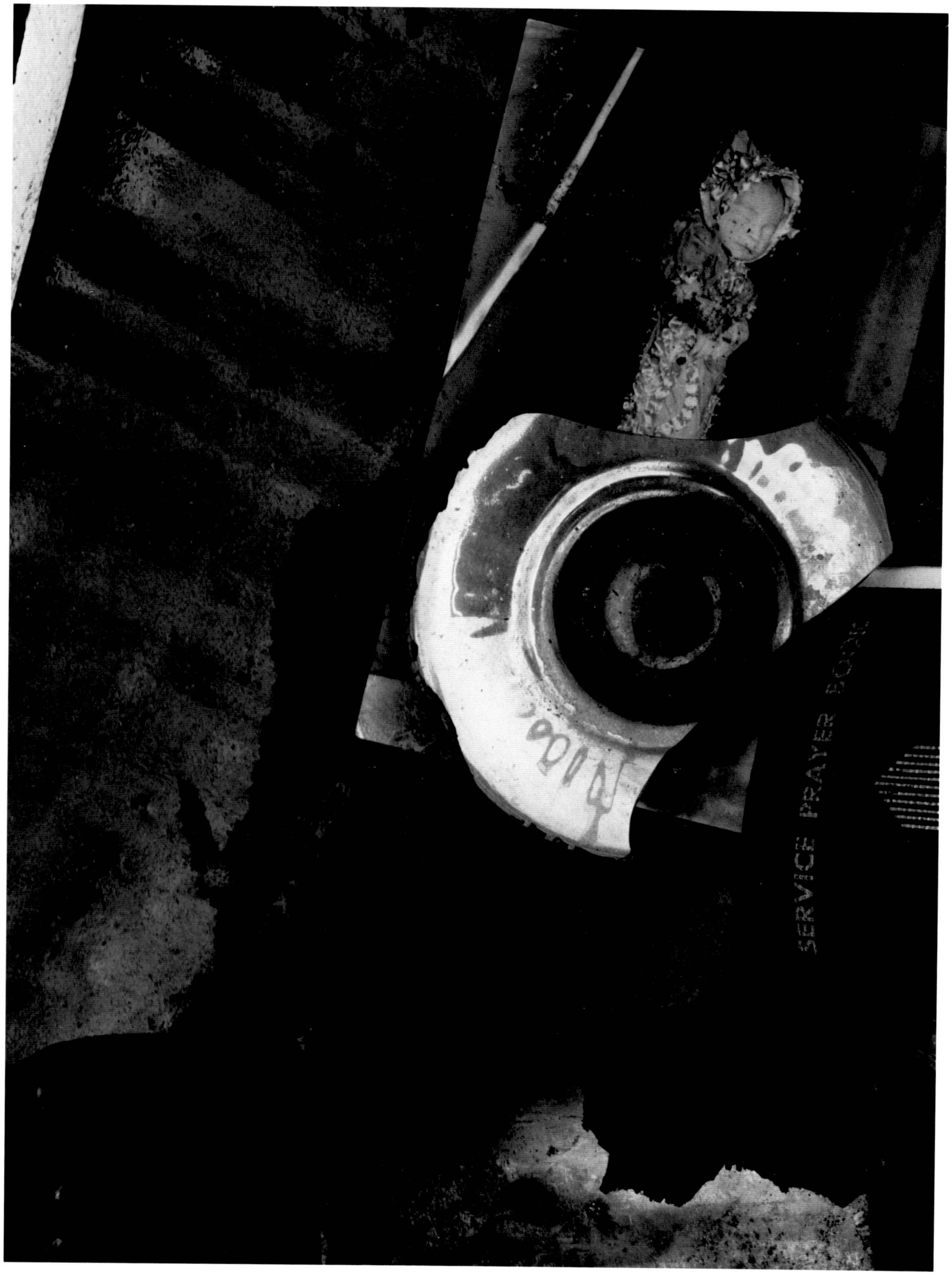

Untitled, c. 1958

the journalism program, Chiarenza found himself involved with more activities than he can remember. Photography, friends, photojournalism, working on occasional assignments for a commercial photography company, and making his presence known in the Boston community kept him busy.

His first major step was to establish a gallery in the basement of the photo lab. Called *Image Study,* the gallery helped to bring the visual ideologies of the Rochester group to Boston, as Chiarenza exhibited Minor White, Paul Caponigro, and Nathan Lyons, an innovative artist and educator who would soon capture naional attention. A recent article in *Boston* magazine called Chiarenza's activities at this time nothing less than the beginning of "the modern saga of Boston photography." Certainly, he was one of the prime catalysts in the invigoration of Boston photography, along with talented photographers like Walter Chappell, Nicholas Dean, Paul Caponigro, Irene Schwachman, Stephen Trefonides, John Brook, and the dealer Carl Siembab.

What histories of the 1950s photography scene do not stress sufficiently is the strong connection between Boston and Rochester. Chiarenza, Caponigro, and Chappell would think nothing of driving back and forth between the two cities, an eight hour drive each way. The Rochester group found a willing listener in the person of the Boston dealer, Carl Siembab, who had been exhibiting photographs along with paintings, sculpture, and graphic arts prints. Urged on by Irene Schwachman, other Boston photographers, and the newcomers, Siembab began to exhibit the prints of Edward Weston, Paul Strand, and other modern masters, as well as the work of younger unknowns. The Siembab Gallery became the site for weekly gatherings, and later for Minor White's workshops even before Minor moved to Boston permanently in the 1960s, when he became the controversial guru for a new program at the Massachusetts Institute of Technology. Siembab organized a one-man show for Aaron Siskind, and was for many years the East Coast dealer for Ansel Adams.

There was another crucial supporter for photographic innovation in the Boston area. This was Polaroid Corporation, based in Cambridge, where forward-looking executives had recognized the urgency of involving creative photographers in the testing of its new instant materials. Ansel Adams was serving as a consultant, and would publish his detailed handbook on the Polaroid processes in 1963. During the early sixties, Chiarenza, Caponigro, Nicholas Dean, among others, were invited to experiment with both positive and negative/positive films. Chiarenza's Polaroid-based abstractions began to appear on the back covers of *Aperture,* even as his poems were being published on its pages. It was the beginning of a long and productive association with Polaroid. More importantly, it was the start of Chiarenza's infatuation with the unusually rich blacks and silver tones of the

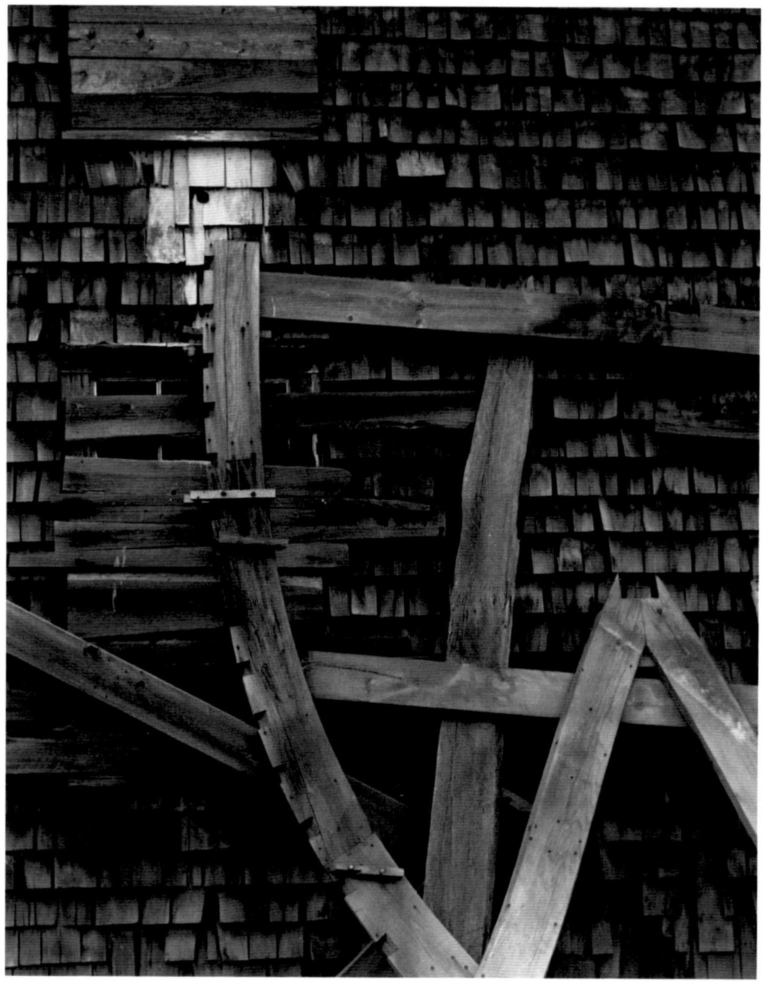

Untitled, 1958

Polaroid prints and of prints he made from Polaroid negatives. The instant feedback of the Polaroid process served him well as a kind of sketching dynamic that helped him make moment-to-moment transformations in his compositions and exposures. The exceptional versatility of the Polaroid medium has been the basis of his pictorial strategies since then.

Paul Caponigro, who had been studying privately with Minor White, met Carl during the period when Chiarenza was ostensibly pursuing his journalism degree. Both Italian in origin, they felt an immediate empathy, chummed around, went on photography jaunts together to Maine, Ipswich, Gloucester, and through the Northeast, becoming fast friends. Paul had also felt the need for some kind of spiritual center in his life. There was a Gurdjieff group in Boston which Paul and the printmaker George Lockwood persuaded Carl to join for a few months. Their meetings were held at Impressions Workshop, an important artists' space run by Lockwood. The group had no connection to the Gurdjieffians sanctioned by Minor White, but followed the same essential teachings: that human beings should recognize their interdependence with the universe; that they contemplate their lives to find their place within Creation; and that they follow certain procedures – dance, meditation, strenuous labor – to achieve freedom of psyche. Carl found himself unprepared for what he swiftly decided was not a route to salvation for himself.

He also discovered fairly soon that the life of a

photojournalist was not for him. Assigned by the Sickles Photo Company, for whom he had been writing as well as photographing, to record the newly shingled roof of a local high school, Carl was asked to climb into the lift bucket of a fire truck. There was no other way to see the shingles. But there was also no earthly way that Carl could or would oblige. A long-time sufferer from vertigo, it was looking at that bucket that convinced Carl he did not care for commercial photography. Besides, the idea of photographing shingles was excruciatingly boring.

In a manner of speaking, he was saved by being drafted into the Infantry no sooner than he had received his master's degree. From late 1959 to late 1961, Carl endured both the hell of an accidentally prolonged basic training and the joys of an unexpected shift into a new area of interest: he began to read art history. During his tour of duty, he was courting the daughter of Howard Thurman, then a dean at Boston University. He was fortunate to be sent eventually to Fort Devens in Massachusetts, within commuting distance to his future wife's apartment.

Chiarenza had met Anne Spencer Thurman on the steps of the Boston University chapel sometime in 1958. In 1961, they married. Anne had finished law school, and later worked for Eliot Richardson and other notables as a speech writer. In 1967, they adopted a five months old baby girl, Suzanne Mari. Unfortunately, the marriage deteriorated. In 1972, they underwent a painful divorce exacerbated by Carl's new academic commitments.

Just before Carl had been drafted, Boston University invited him to teach photography in the School of Journalism. The Army interrupted that opportunity. He was about to complete his tour of duty when the Berlin crisis exploded, with President John Kennedy immediately imposing an extension on all Armed Forces commitments. Chiarenza was able to escape this unwanted extension by a curious circumstance. There was a law that provided inductees with release from an extension of time in the Armed Forces if they were offered a scholarship they would lose if they could not take it immediately. It was a tremendous relief to Carl when he was offered such a scholarship back to Boston University. This time it was to take courses in art history while he continued his photographic activities.

In 1963, a group consisting of Paul Caponigro, Walter Chappell, William Clift, Marie Cosindas, Carl Chiarenza, Nicholas Dean, and Paul Petricone formed the Society of Heliographers, with the intention of making their talents known to the international art market in New York City. The group attracted much public notice with a major exhibition at Lever House. They had also formed a cooperative gallery. Unfortunately, there was contention over several members not abiding by the bylaws of the Heliographers, and questions of financial management coupled with the distance from the gallery prompted the withdrawal of the Boston group after one year. It was an important adventure for like-minded artists of the camera, but in terms of the fickle photography market, it was undoubtedly before its time. Ulti-

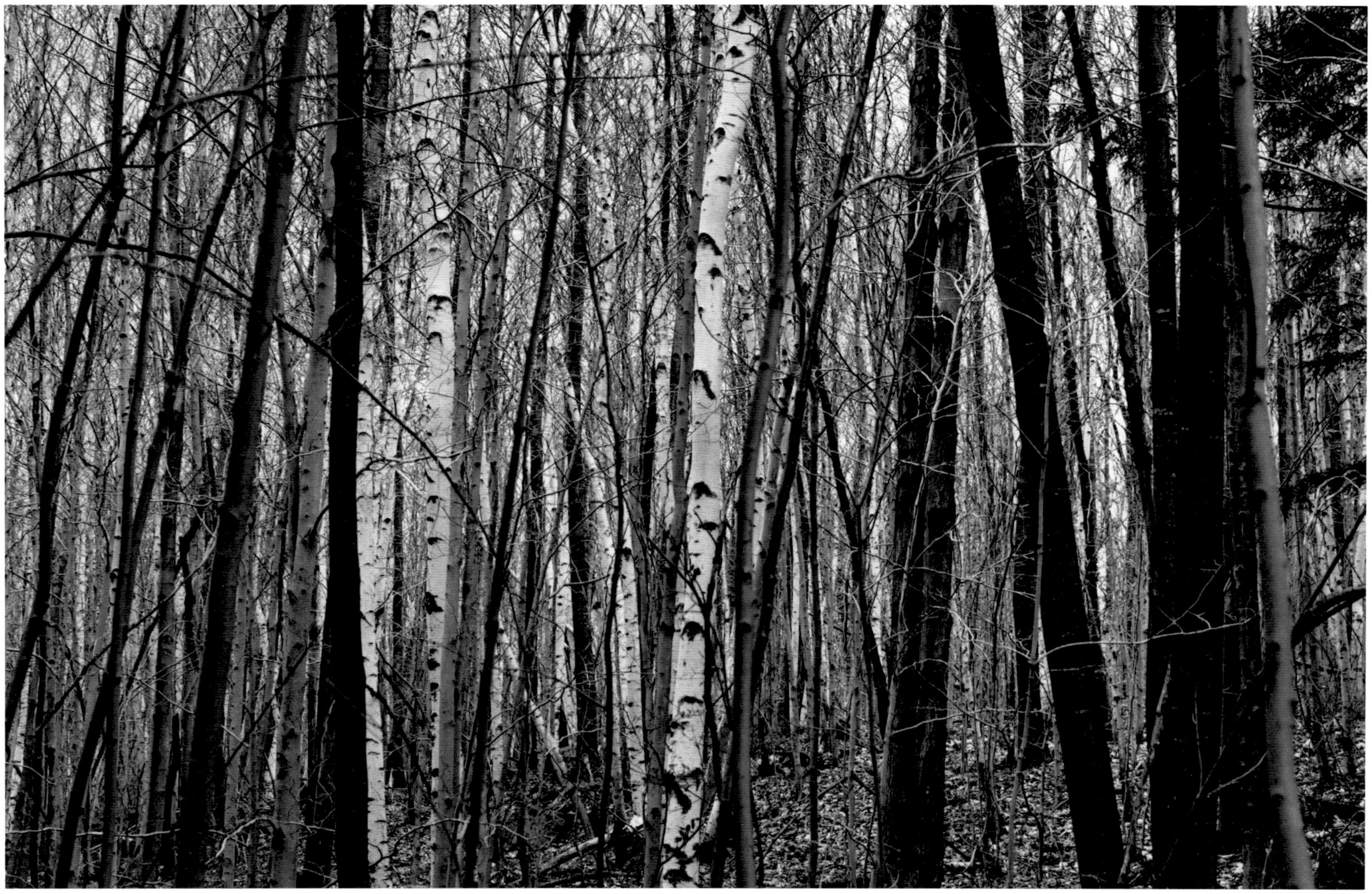

Berkshires, 1958

mately, although the Heliographers continued for some years, the original group scattered, with Clift and Caponigro later migrating to Santa Fe and Nick Dean moving to Maine. Chiarenza, Cosindas, and Petricone remained in Boston.

It was in 1964 also that Chiarenza, who was keenly devoted to the betterment of the photographic community, became an active leader in the Society for Photographic Education, a national organization founded by Nathan Lyons a year earlier. In 1963, Carl was asked by the Department of Fine Arts at Boston University to teach some basic courses. In 1964, he was officially appointed Instructor. Two years later, when he came up for renewal of contract, the Dean of the College advised him that if he wanted to continue teaching there, he would need a Ph.D. He was so well respected that the Dean not only granted him an extended leave, but nominated him for a Danforth teaching fellowship so that he could attend Harvard University.

As Carl describes it, Harvard was an almost unendurable experience. Finishing his residence and course work in 1968, he wanted to proceed with a doctoral dissertation on a contemporary photographer. No: the department envisioned a book about the relationship between painting and photography. As it happened, Aaron Scharf chose that moment to publish his own major book on that subject. Carl then proposed to his original thesis adviser, who shall remain nameless, that he write a biography of the highly respected photographer, Aaron Siskind. Siskind was, without question, one of the most important living artists working in the photography medium. With a mixture of incredulity and anger, barely diminished over the years, Carl reports that he received a letter from his adviser, then in London, to the effect that "I can't become excited about a living artist."

With heroic persistence, Carl managed to overcome the objections of the traditional art historians, and was finally permitted to begin his thesis on Siskind. Between 1969 and 1972, Chiarenza flew back and forth between Boston and Chicago, where Siskind was an influential professor at the Institute of Design, and made many side trips to New York to talk with painters considered to be Abstract Expressionists, to whose work Siskind's image had often been likened. Carl was increasingly intrigued by his subject, with whom he began to identify in terms of both being abstractionists – although of a very different order – both being first generation Americans, both from persecuted minorities, both having difficulties with marriages. Although Siskind was much older and already an established world figure in photography, and although he was generally temperamental and impatient, the two became good friends. It was a relationship that would have both vitalizing and discouraging aspects.

The critic Thomas Hess wrote a description of Aaron Siskind's pictures, which have included found graffiti, the ambiguous residues of torn and disintegrating posters, and patterns in nature, as their subjects. "It's in a formalist area that Siskind's particular genius obtains – his ability to make photography a matter of transcendent aesthetic import. The finished prints should be considered as pure phenomena, matters of inter-relationships, of parts to a whole, the whole to the medium, the medium to its particular state of technological and philosophical awareness at the moment in art-historical time." Hess emphasized that Siskind "talks to us through our humanity – through his feel for the tragic." It was Siskind's tragic view of life, as well as his abstract and formalist style, to which Chiarenza could relate directly.

At one point in his turbulent career, Siskind placed himself firmly at the antipodes from Minor White. He emphatically rejected Eastern philosophies, with their ideas of oneness and their technique of contemplation. He felt the essential problem for an artist was to deal with "the conflicting forces within us. That is what the Christian religion is. This is our culture." Chiarenza, who had been successfully freeing himself from what he perceived as Minor White's domination and strict dogmas, found Siskind's idea of conflict close to his own heart. Yet, for all that he was attracted to Siskind's art and philosophies, writing about him in many essays and in a definitive biography based on his thesis, Chiarenza soon found himself in a peculiar predicament. Because he had written so much about Siskind, and, more importantly, because the uninitiated tended to confuse the distinctions between one kind of abstraction and another, Chiarenza's own work became identified with that of Siskind. With his own art proceeding in a vastly different direction, he was made to feel as if he were living in Siskind's shadow. It was a difficult situation for a proud, articulate man.

Chiarenza had been longing for a non-traditional school for photographers, on the order of Nathan Lyons' Visual Studies Workshop in Rochester. With Warren Hill, a Cambridge fashion photographer, and the material support of Don Perrin, he cofounded in 1971 an ambitious enterprise called *Imageworks,* which offered itself as a center for all aspects of photography, from gallery space to education. Unfortunately, he was once again ahead of his time, and *Imageworks* foundered in 1973, after two years of far too rapid expansion. It was not until the founding of the *Photographic Resource Center,* largely through the efforts of Carl's good friend, the photographer Chris Enos, Carl himself, and Eelco Wolf of Polaroid Corporation, that Chiarenza's vision of a true center for New England photography was accomplished later in the 70s. He managed to persuade Boston University to offer a substantial space for the activities of the PRC, and, as one of the directors of the center, he encouraged the funding of numerous activities of interest, including lectures by, and grants for, renowned photographers and critics.

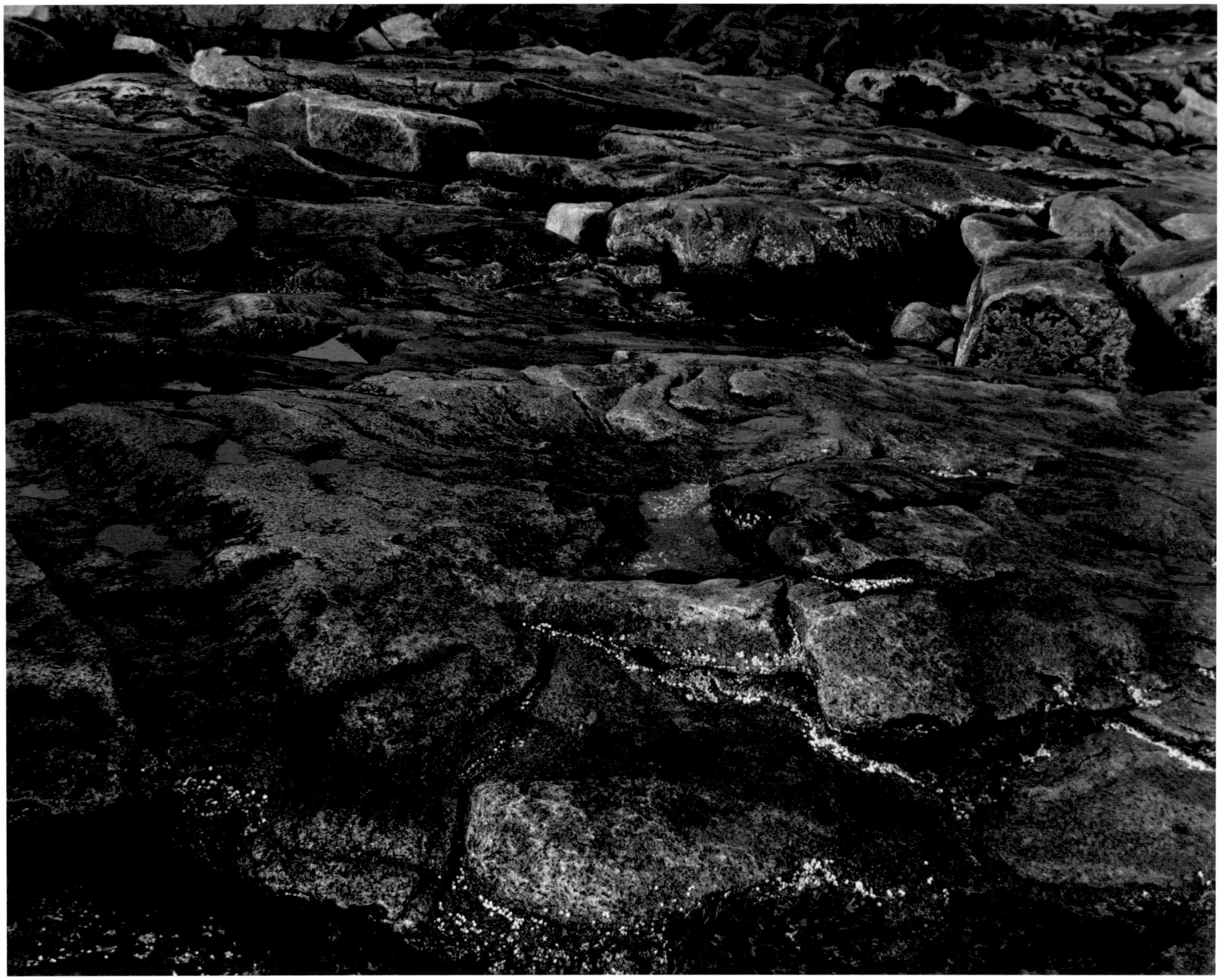

Untitled, c. 1970

Menotomy

Among his many activities, Chiarenza was on the lecture and workshop circuit in the early seventies. In August, 1974, he was teaching one of the Ansel Adams summer workshops at Yosemite, along with Jerry Uelsmann and Robert Heinecken, a photographer whom he had met in 1963 and who became one of his closest friends. Among the assistants assigned to the workshop was a young woman with cropped blond hair and a quiet but very energetic personality. Heidi Katz had been Heinecken's graduate student and teaching assistant at UCLA. She was both filmmaker and photographer, and would later teach at the University of Hartford. Carl recalls that he paid little attention to her at first. By that Christmas, however, he had succumbed entirely. He sent her a plane ticket to come east to spend the holidays. They have been inseparable ever since.

Carl and Heidi bought a house in Arlington, Massachusetts, not far from Boston, in 1976. In 1978, they made their marriage official. Son Jonah was born in 1980, by some curious circumstance on the same day as the birthday of Ansel Adams. Gabriella followed in 1983, born on the same day as Carl's first daughter, Suzanne. If asked to sum up his feelings about his second wife, Carl says, "Heidi is fantastic!" She has been, in fact, a source of tremendous emotional support during some trying years. With her excellent visual training and professional experience, she has also helped Carl through some aesthetic decisions, including encouraging his recent creation of diptychs and triptychs.

Arlington was originally called *Menotomy,* its Indian name. It is a name that has meant a great deal to Chiarenza, as he used it for many of his prints in homage to an area known as Menotomy Rocks, a park nearby where he took many long walks, both for relaxation and inspiration, although he never brought along a camera. Chiarenza has profound feelings about landscape. Nature is for him "a sustaining structure," a source for connection, both an idea and a reality. As he observes, "Our landscape is indeed in the mind, but the mind now survives in an environment which is neither the natural one of the nineteenth century and earlier, nor the urban one of the first half of the twentieth century. It is a more thoroughly technological environment, yet it remains as mysterious and as full of unknown forces as it has been throughout its tradition." He believes strongly that landscape is an idea, a construct out of which he makes his art. He sees that art as being imbued with both traditional concepts of landscape and a response to the new environment.

In 1979, Polaroid Corporation invited Carl, along with several other well-known photographers, to try his hand at using a powerful new tool: its 20 x 24 camera. Chiarenza had already experimented with the SX70 color film in the mid 1970s. The 20 x 24 experiment was to have a profound effect on him; not that it turned him from black and white photography to color. Carl had been used to taking his 4 x 5 camera outdoors with positive/negative Polaroid film. Suddenly he found that working exclusively in the studio was much to his liking. Since 1979, many of his prints have as their subjects imaginary landscapes created in the studio, all photographs of collages fabricated to be photographed, all based on Polaroid positive/negative film elaborately manipulated in the darkroom.

Philosophically, Chiarenza has always been attuned to the idea of an "unfixed, indeterminate, changing and fluctuating world." To watch him at work is a revelation of his intuitive approaches to this world of flux. He allows chance to operate in this construction of his subject. What is so surprising is that while his prints are large, his collages are relatively tiny, sometimes no more than five inches by three inches. They are composed of discarded materials, often from film wrappings, scraps of paper, torn strips. He roughly previsualizes the negative, but given the flexibility of the Polaroid negative, he freely rephotographs, moving a feathery piece of scrap here, crumpling silver paper, knowing that the darkroom will offer even greater opportunities for control. Unlike Ansel Adams, for example, who produced more than 800 prints of his famous *Moonrise over Hernandez,* Chiarenza, in the tradition of the print-maker even more than the photographer, sees no value in attempting to make perfectly equal replications of a print. He tends to limit himself to editions of no more than five to ten large prints, and his essential approach is not far different from that of a painter-etcher's manipulation of successive states of a plate.

Like an etcher, too, Chiarenza is infatuated with the potential densities of black. In the many variations of black, he expresses his sense of mystery and the unknown. Recently, he finds that the pictures coming back from satellites and interplanetary probes, as well as from science fiction, have greatly attracted him. Many of his prints now reflect an increasing obsession with the mysteries of the physical universe. In typical fashion, he comments briefly about his use of blacks and silvers as a reflection of the unknowable universe: "We have no answers." Pause. "There are stars in it." The blacks, which he says can be obtained in no medium other than photography, and which depend greatly on the paper he uses – Medalist, when it was available, now Galerie – are a symbol for a fundamental existential anxiety he experiences, while he sees his modulations towards grays and lighter silvers as a kind of optimistic counterpoint.

The idea of musical counterpoint is always present. Chiarenza admits to a longing to make pictures with the expressive qualities of Beethoven quartets. More than the polyphony he loves in Bach, he has a passion for the drama of Beethoven. As he works in his studio, he listens to a wide range of music, from the baroque to modern jazz. Beethoven's late quartets, Schumann, Mozart, Haydn, and Shubert's outpourings, all match his own romanticism. The separate phases of his diptychs and triptychs resemble the movements of a quartet, a sonata, or the variations of a concerto.

Curiously, perhaps, for a musician who has

played the Mozart Clarinet Concerto, as well as intensely personal jazz, it is only photography that has come to satisfy both his creative needs and his highly sophisticated aesthetic. That aesthetic, like music, includes the use of tones, motion, time, and space. He recognizes that many photographers have felt a close bond between music and the camera image. Frederick Sommer, a surrealist photographer and collagist, made abstract drawings that he invited friends to try to play as music. Paul Caponigro claimed recently that he was temporarily renouncing photography to return to his piano. Ansel Adams was a musician before becoming a photographer. Alfred Stieglitz called his pictures of clouds *Songs of the Sky.* Younger contemporaries like Michael A. Smith, who once tried to make pictures like the diagrams of bird song, and Barbara Crane, who attended concerts with a sketchpad to draw the patterns that music evoke, acknowledge their debt to music. For a medium that once promised to supply the closest possible representation of the natural world in all its material details, it may seem odd that photography has been trying to emulate the thrust of Walter Pater's dictum: "All art approaches the condition of music." Music, the most abstract, non-representational of all the arts, nevertheless conjures up visions.

Chiarenza admits a kinship with the Abstract Expressionists, but does not recall being thoroughly exposed to their work until he knew Siskind. His statements often resemble the philosophy of that art movement: "The transformations which take place in my photographs suggest a vital life force which, while unknown, insists forcefully on its presence. It lives in a space that often defies definition. Its shapes hover in a richly palpable blackness and appear as temptations composed of sensuous silver grays and whites. The photographic presence is magical-alchemical. In a sense my photographs attempt to present evidence of the unknown, to testify to its significance, and to suggest the importance of its pursuit."

Noumenon

The neo-Platonic aspect of Chiarenza's spiritual vision might be epitomized by his series called *Woods,* in which only the idea of trees is expressed. And in the pictures he titles *Noumenon* can perhaps be found his personal idea of spirit and his evocation of the unknown. His profoundly mystical and poetic approach to photography does not preclude his continuing admiration for artists like Goya or prophets like Nietzsche, nor does he forego a habitual, palpable and despairing cynicism, clearly the indication of an idealist's soul that has found no lasting peace.

The well-known photographer and educator, Jerome Liebling, has observed, "Carl Chiarenza's photographs are private dramas. They are not simple relationships, but tensions trying to reach an equilibrium. A slight push or shove and the pictures will come crashing." Liebling also considers that Chiarenza creates a visual terrain in which he knows where he is situated, and which he tightly controls to keep out intrusions. It is the tensions created by this control that increase the similarity of Chiarenza's prints to the passions of the late Beethoven quartets, profoundly internalized revelations of the artist's personal despairs.

One of the most fascinating prints Chiarenza made in 1975 is the abstraction *Somerville 17* (p. 51). Like a vision of a moonrise amidst the ruins of a modern city, the combination of biomorphic forms and the austerity of repeated verticals create a mysterious mood, mysterious but not at all pessimistic. It is like observing the creation of a new world.

In *Rockland 2,* 1979 (p. 63), one of Chiarenza's best known prints, the division of the surface of the print has an insistent rhythm, with the flame-like central black shape the beating heart of the structure. What is astonishing about this picture is that its content is simply the exposed ends of some warped plywoods he found in his perambulations, a typical example of Chiarenza's transformations.

The shift from the vibrating structure of *Rockland 2* to *Arlington 2* of that same year (p. 65) introduces the new phase of Chiarenza's work occasioned by the interaction with the Polaroid 20 x 24 and his discovery of the delights of working in the studio, fabricating imaginary landscapes. Manipulating both light in the studio and the printing in the darkroom, Chiarenza manages to offer a rocky, somewhat inimical landscape such as one might find on a desolate plateau, whether of this world or another it is hard to say. The mood is that of deep night, a night in which no stars appear, yet in which mysterious light plays on its surfaces.

Menotomy 382, 1983 (p. 93) is another dream landscape, closely resembling real landscapes through which a brilliant river might course, the distant mountains shimmering with reflected light and the foreground impossibly distant, as if the viewer were flying over the terrain toward the eerie light emanating from behind the mountains. This tension between unreality and reality demands resolution, an equilibrium which only the viewer can establish and which requires contemplation to achieve. All of Chiarenza's work requires close attention, like the complex and dissonant chords of modern music.

Woods 529, 1983 (p. 97) suggests not trees and leaves, but vegetation growing in deep woods, with the dappled light of such a glade expertly transmitted by Chiarenza's control of the direction of his highlights. This is nature revealed as a not unfriendly but hardly welcoming entity, with a life evolving out of some unfathomable principles. It is a wood in which arcane sacrifices might occur, where implacable gods announce their unique powers.

The term "noumenon" signifies ineffable spirit, and in *Noumenon 180,* 1984-85 (p. 108) can be found a vision of the heavens, primordial matter coalescing into cloud-like shapes. In *Noumenon 304/305,* 1984-85 (p. 113), Chiarenza moves out of the single photograph into a vertical diptych in which creative spirit now includes time as well as matter. The forms shift, like the transformations of evolution. An equilibrium may be reached, but the implication is that the forms will continue to shift. This continued growth and change is strongly demonstrated in the horizontal triptych, *Noumenon 245/249/247,* worked on from 1984 to 1985 (pp. 122-123). Eons seem to pass between each of the three images, almost as if we are watching the origin of mountains. In an elegant diptych, *Noumenon 444/441,* also from 1984 to 1985 (pp. 128-129), the transformation is not as violent, yet it has a decisiveness to it that matches Chiarenza's firm belief in the evanescence of the material world. Everything changes. Everything endures phases of an eternal flux. Such continual transformations, moment-to-moment, are perhaps best epitomized in the monumental *Menotomy Sextet,* 1982 (pp. 88-89), in which forms attract, repel, grow, collapse, ceaselessly experiencing a never-ending creation.

Chiarenza has noted an increasing desire to shift the direction of his photography, but he knows how slowly such change might come, if ever. He seeks new textures, new resonances for his collages. As an artist who relies upon the mysteries of chance, and on the moment-to-moment changes in his aesthetic and emotional responses to the landscape, he knows that inevitably his own conceptual strategies, even his fundamental ideologies, will continue to grow and to be transformed.

ESTELLE JUSSIM

December 1987

PORTFOLIO OF PHOTOGRAPHS 1958–1986

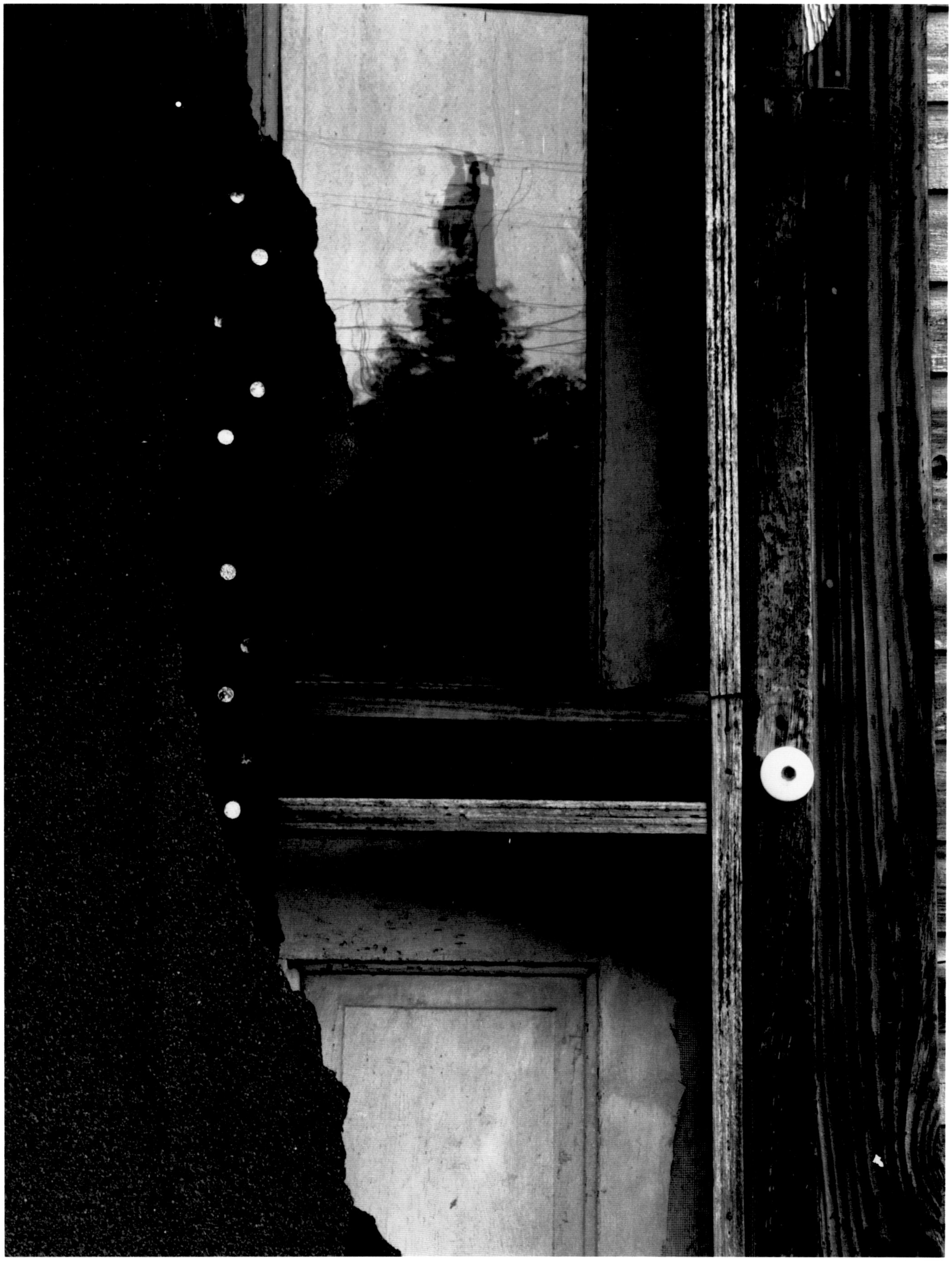

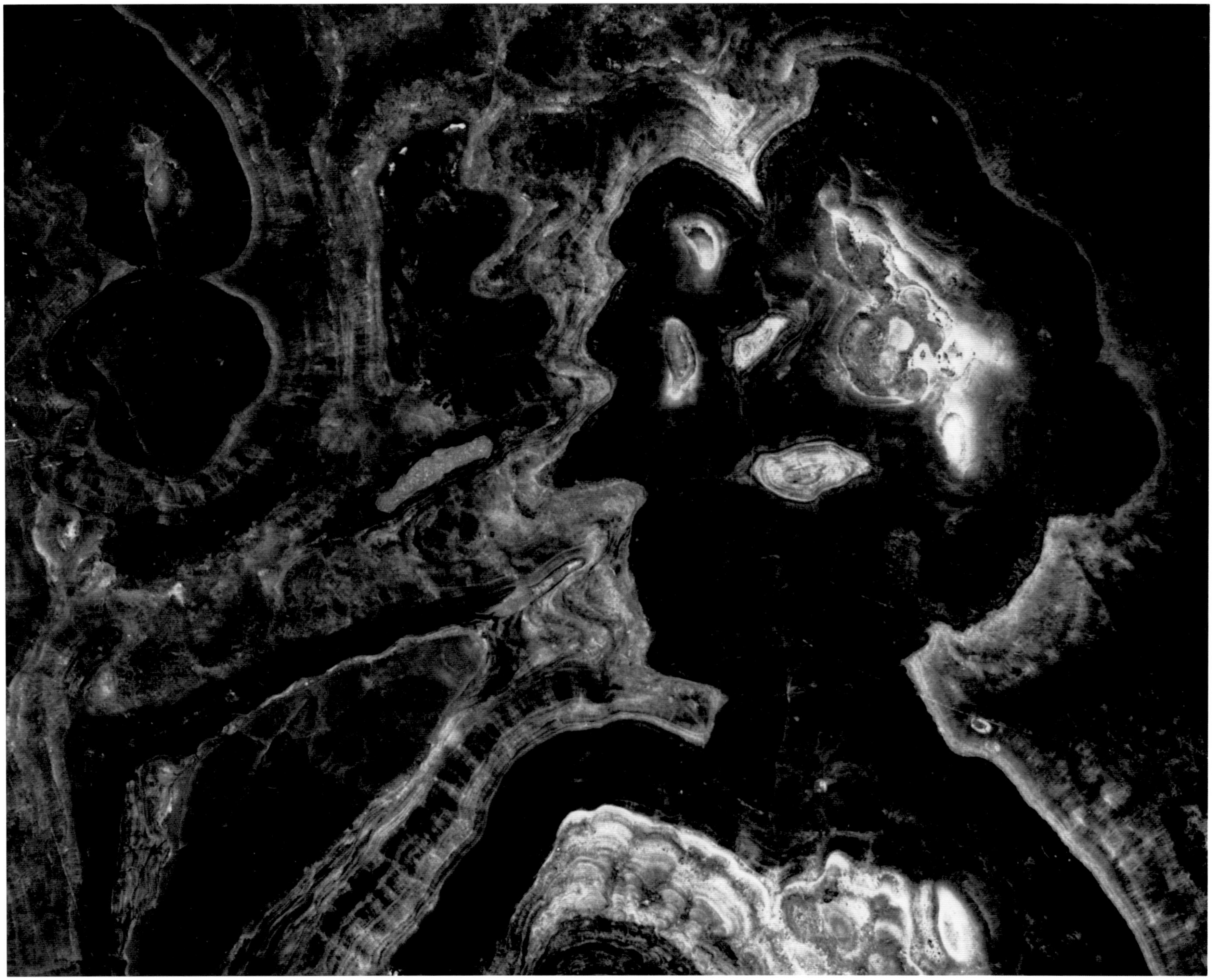

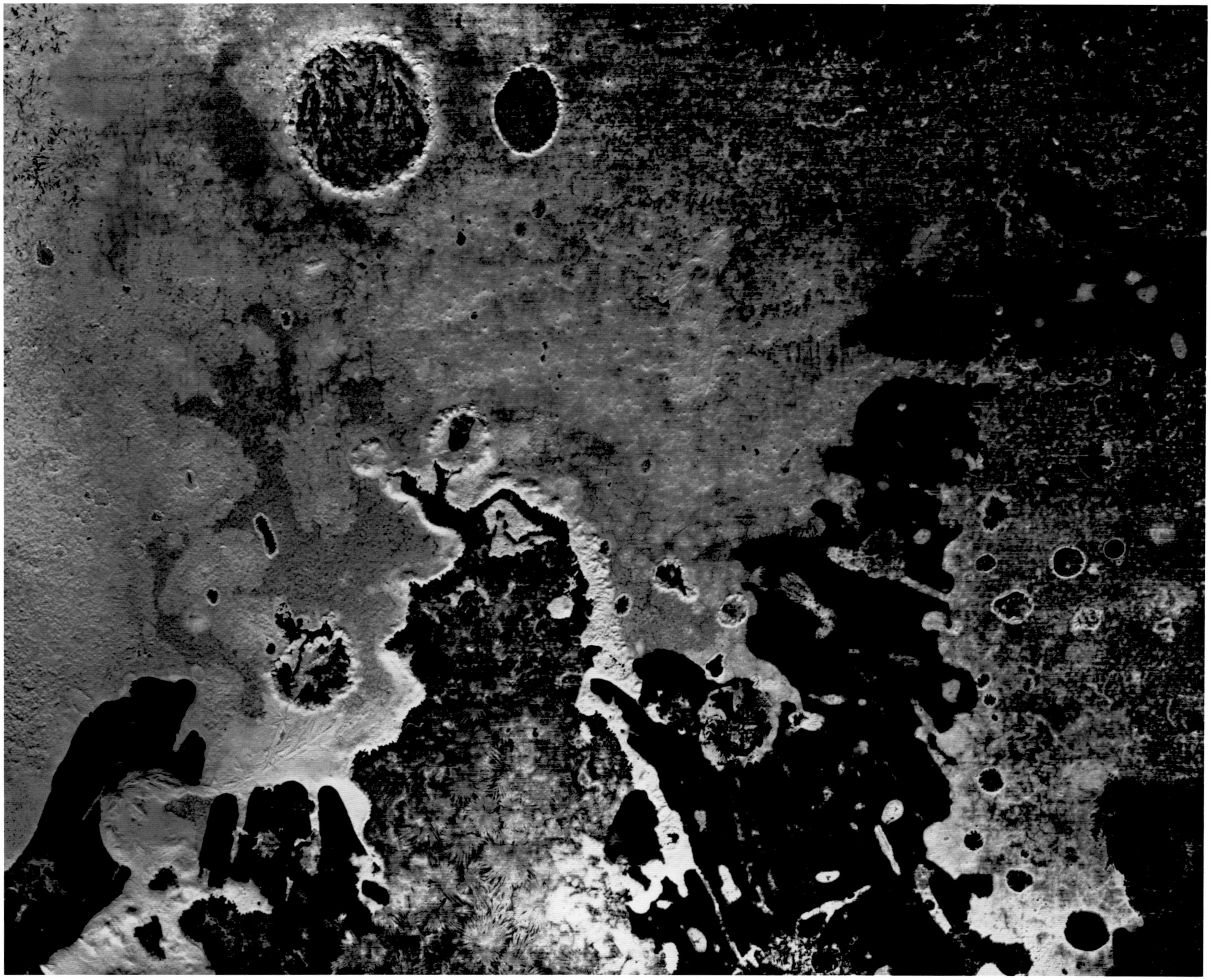

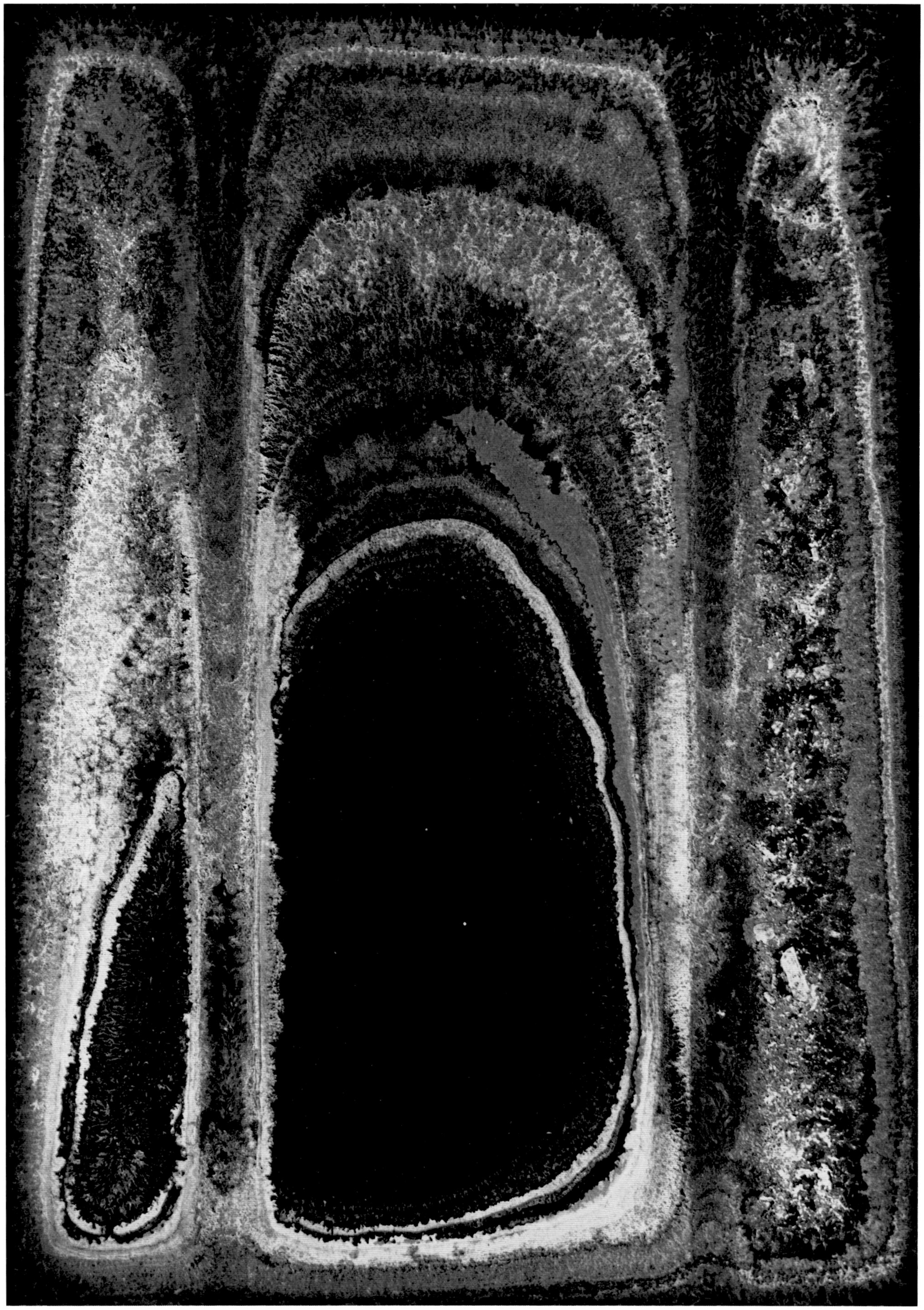

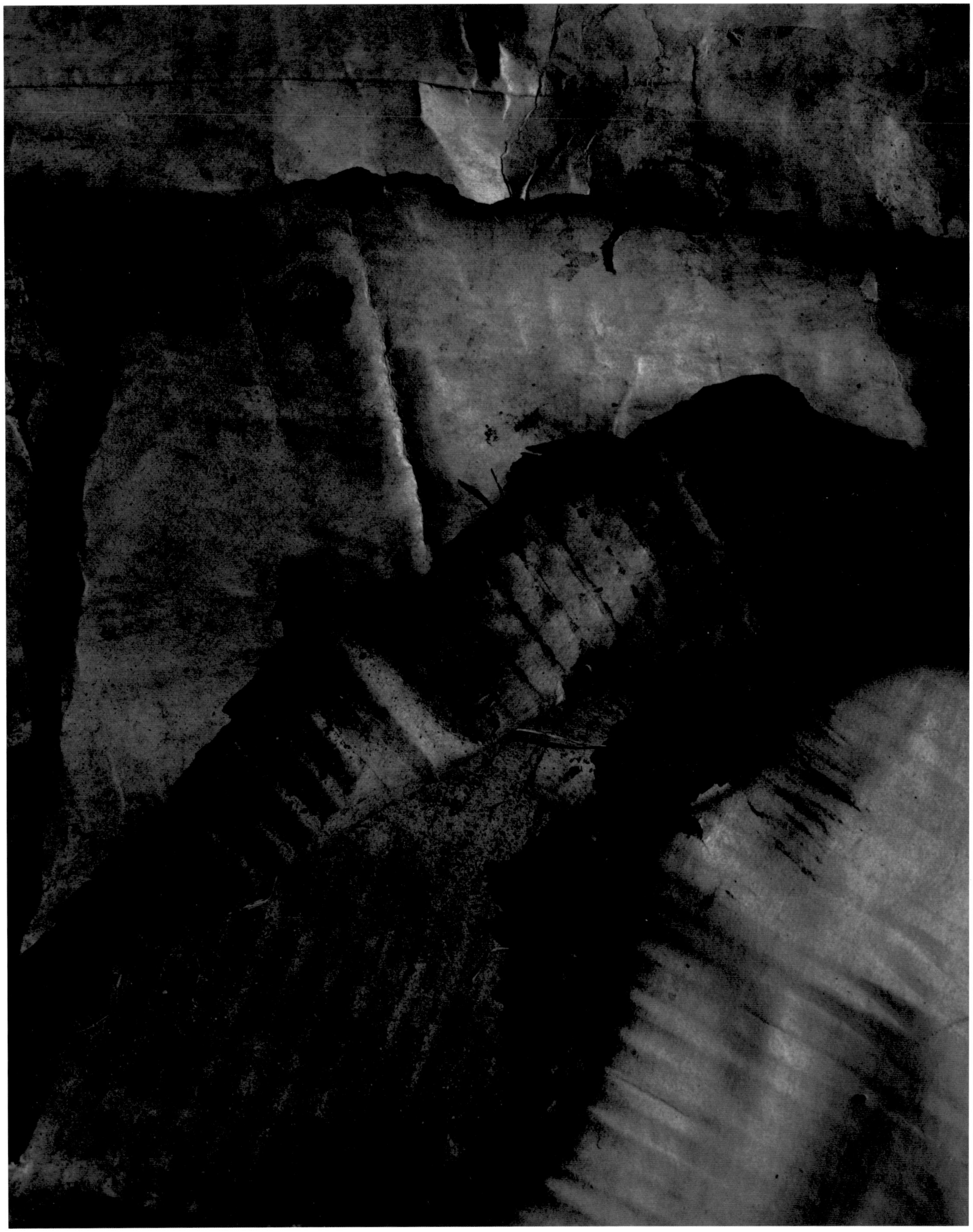

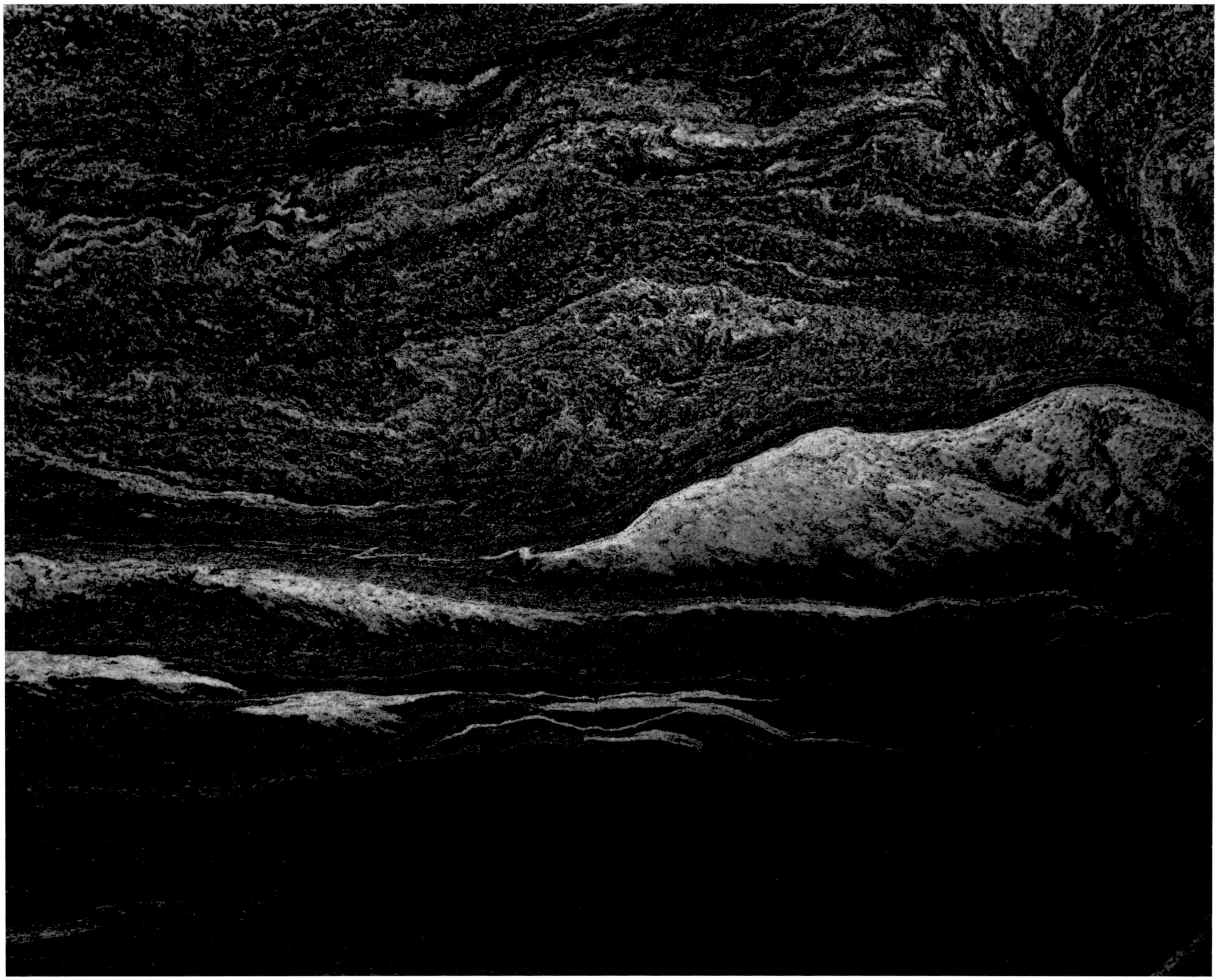

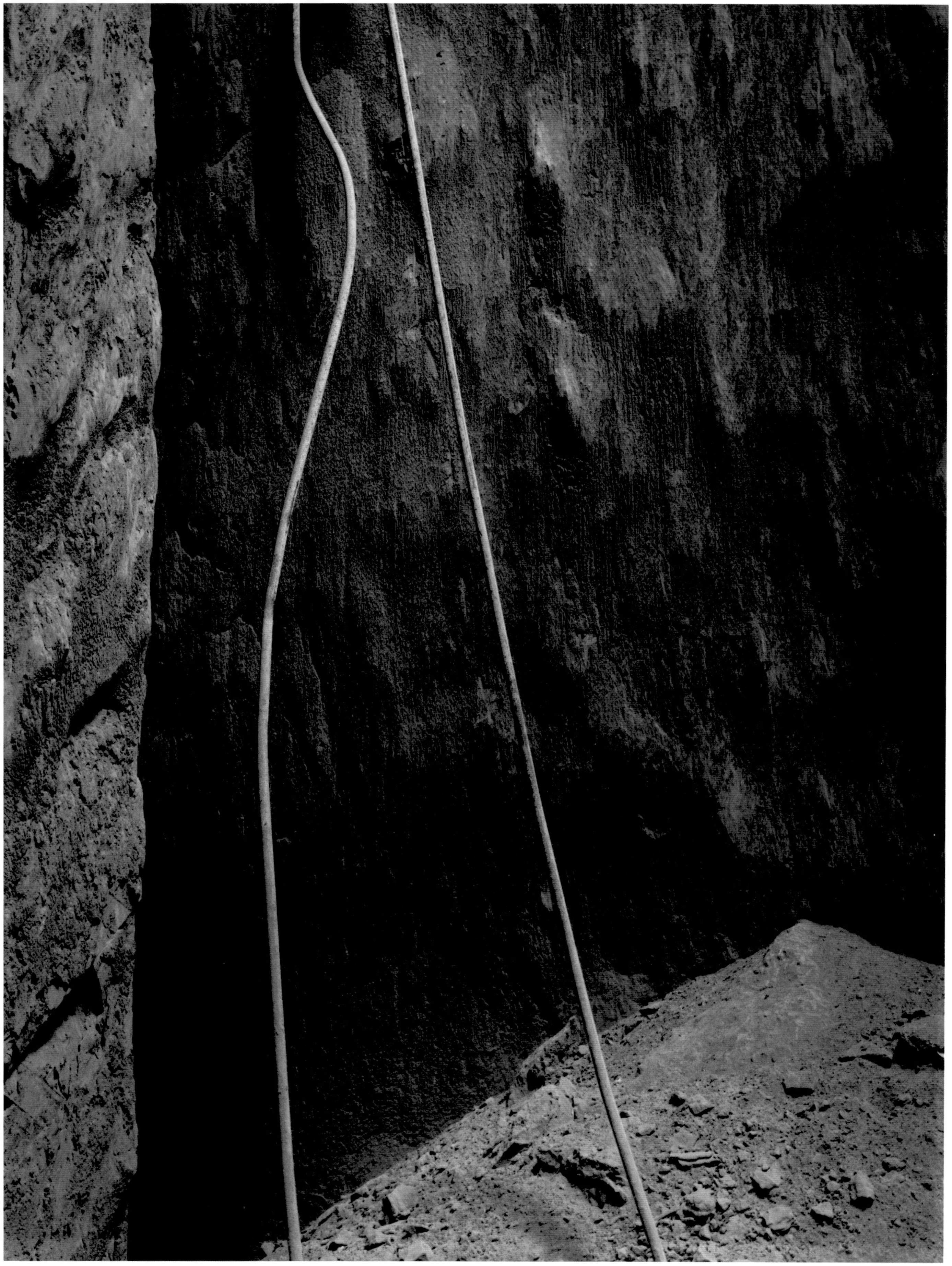

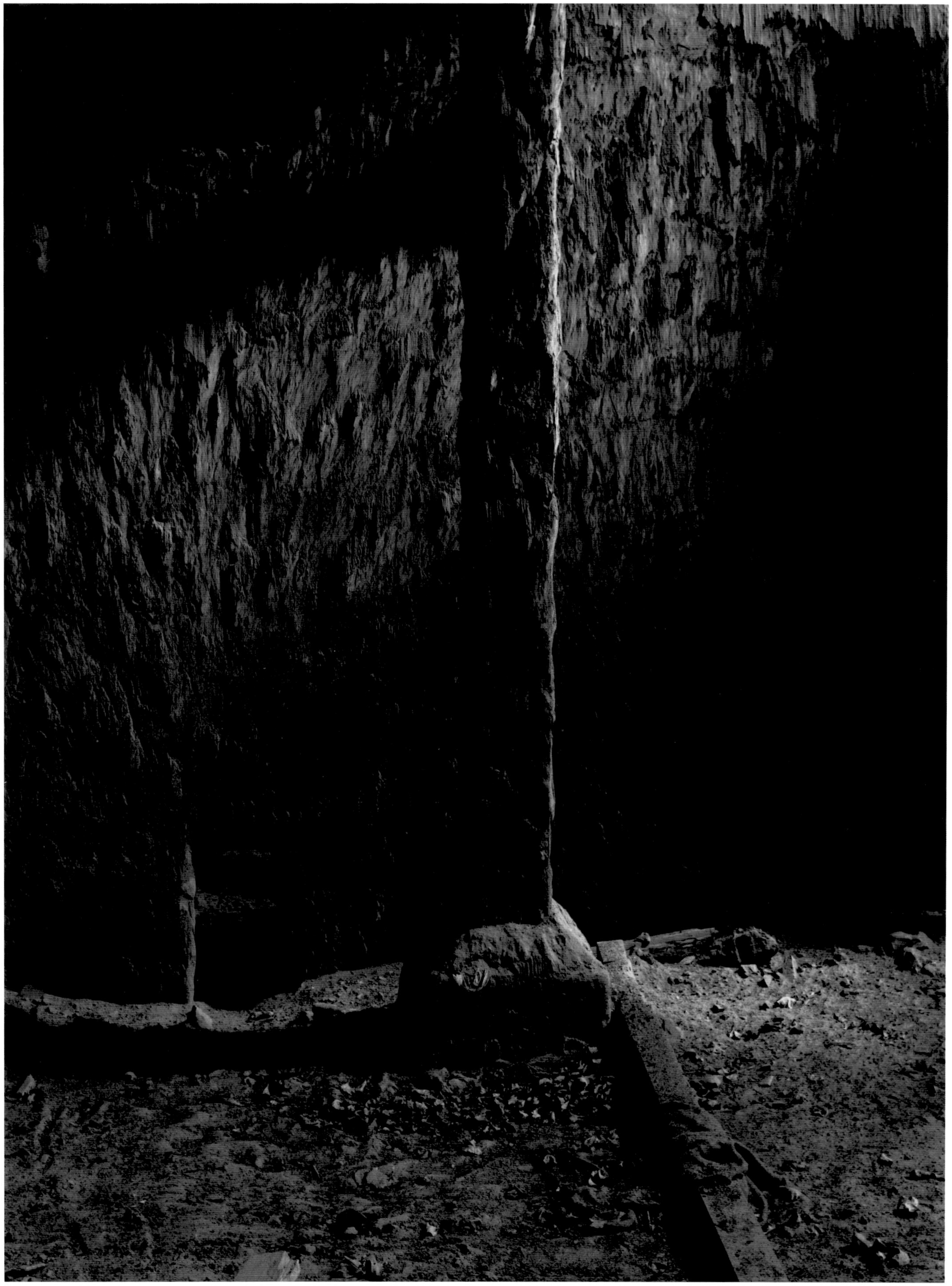

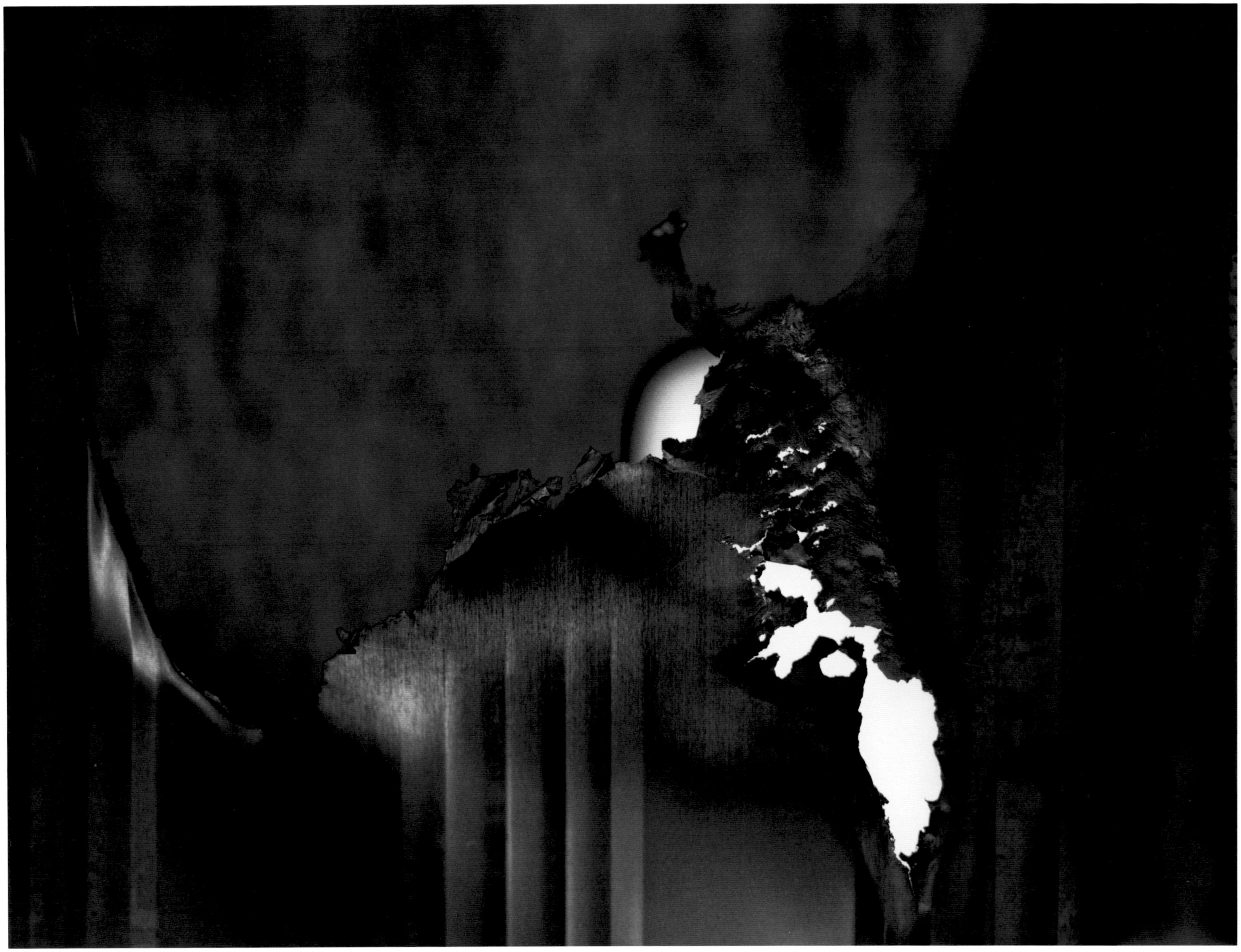

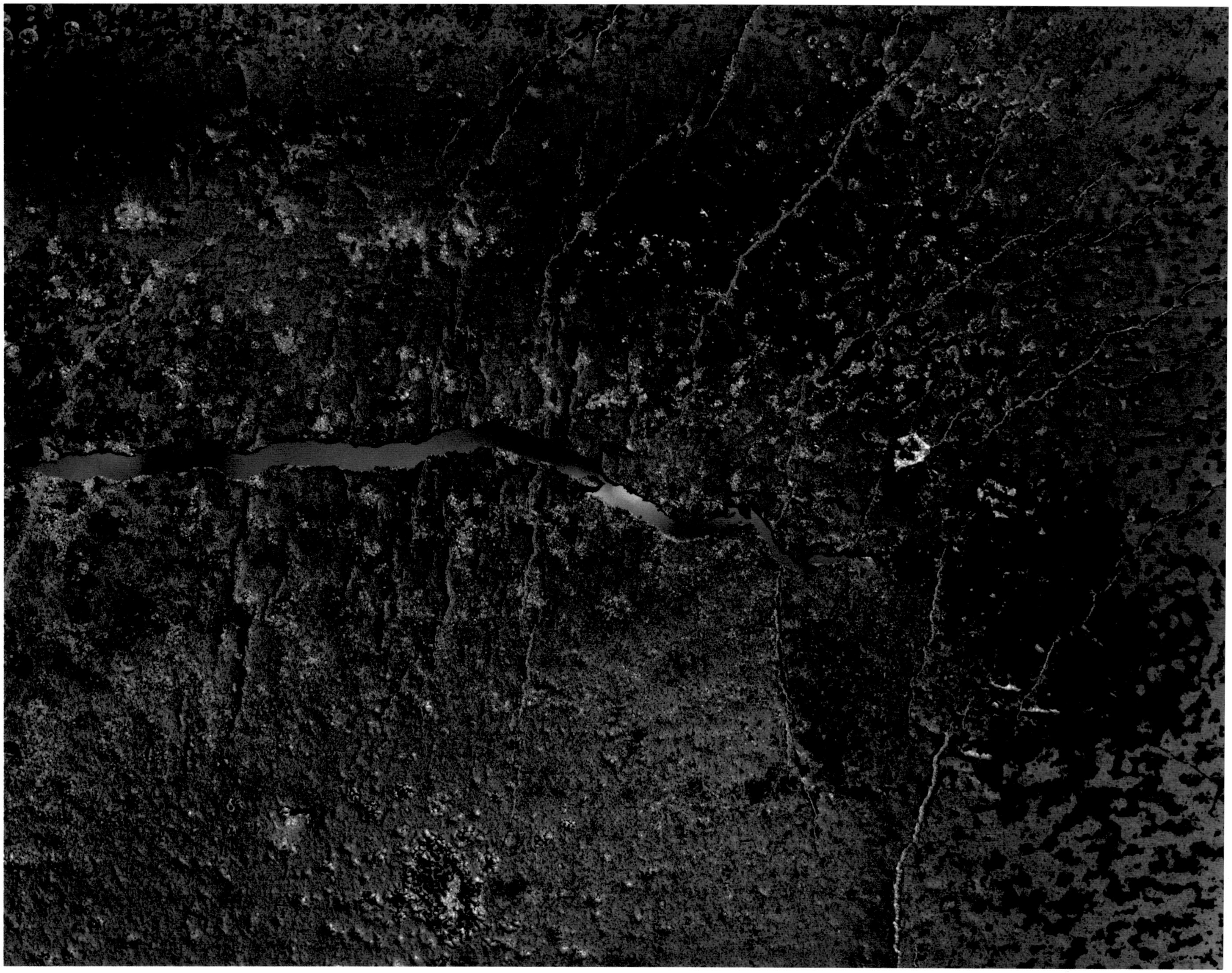

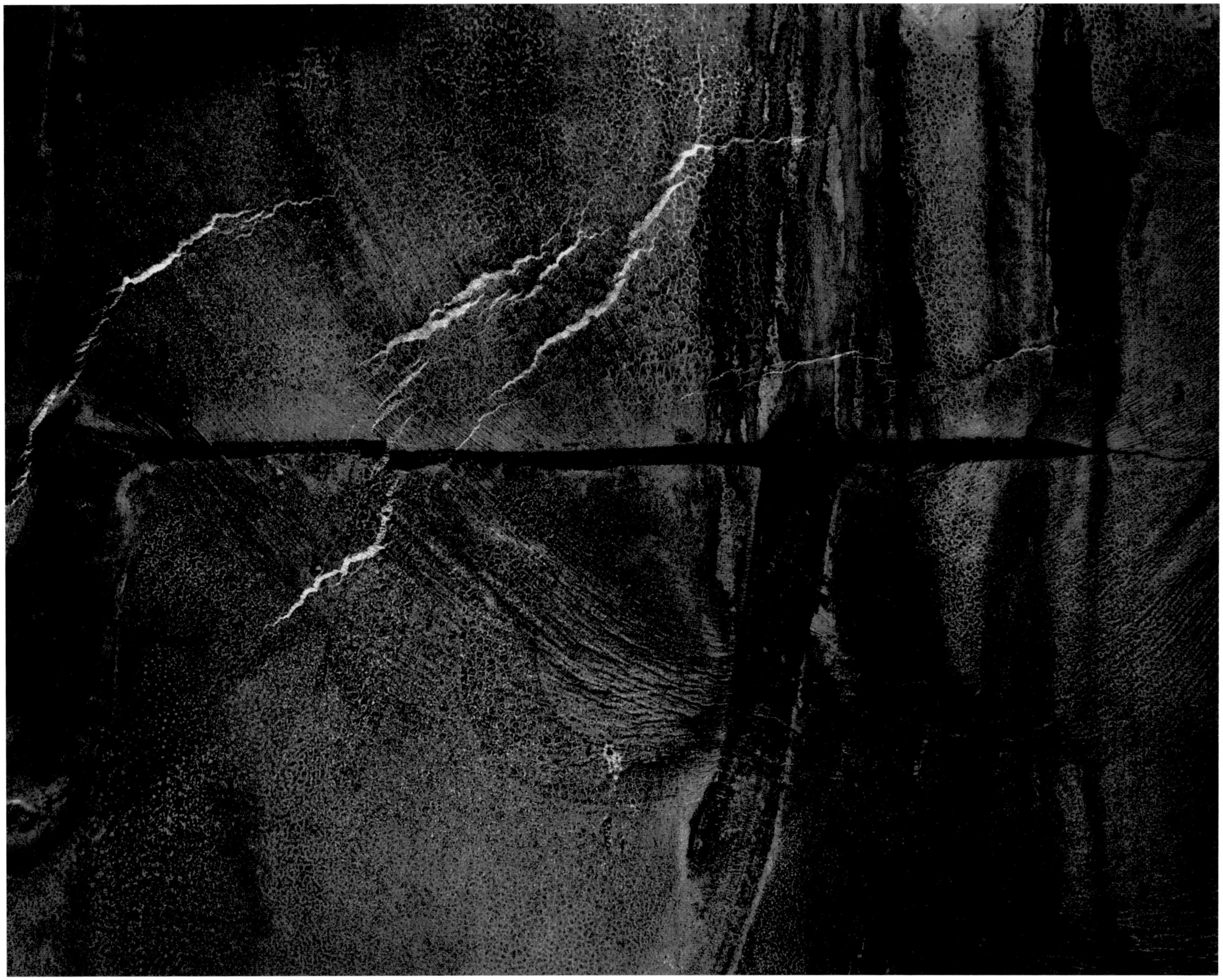

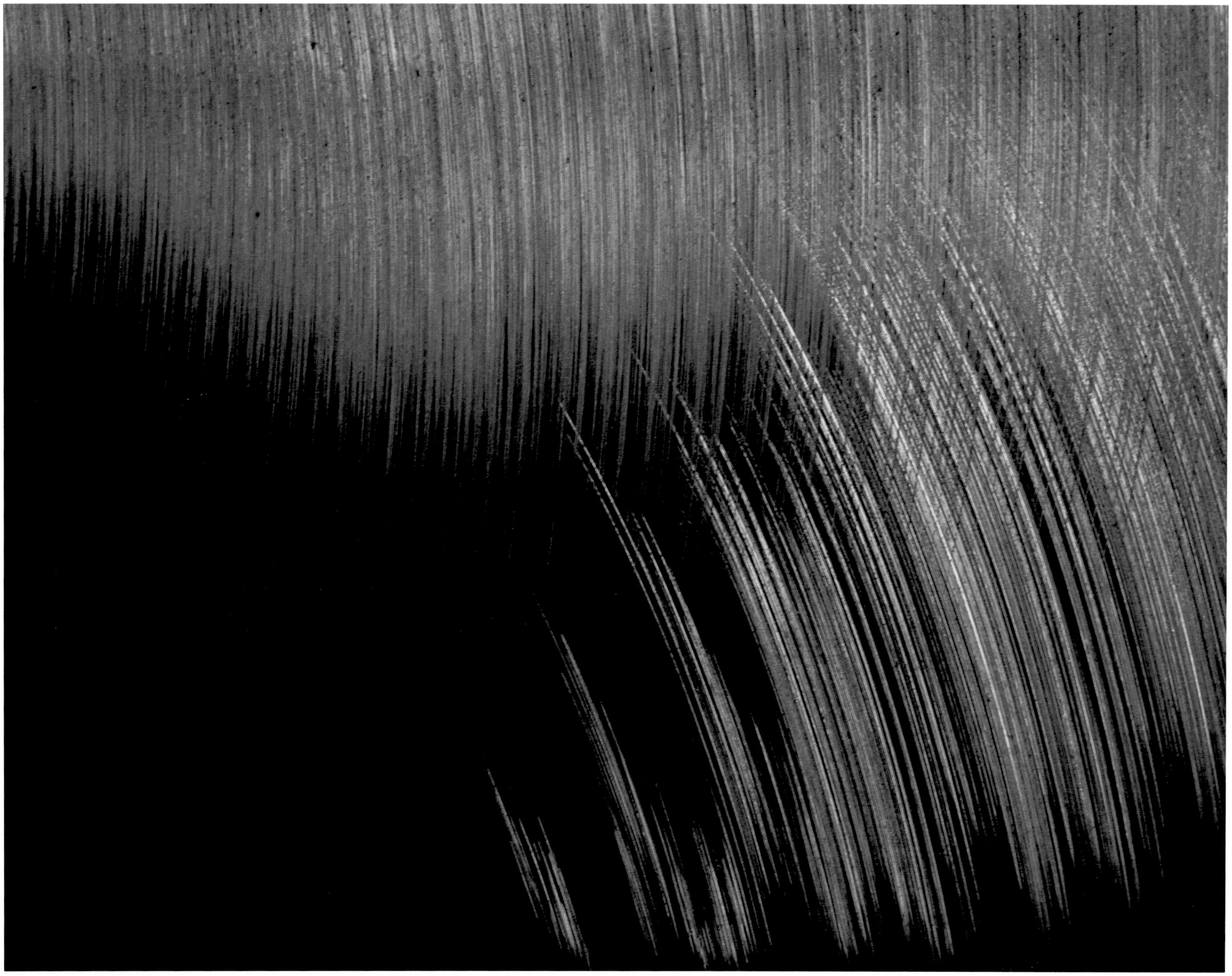

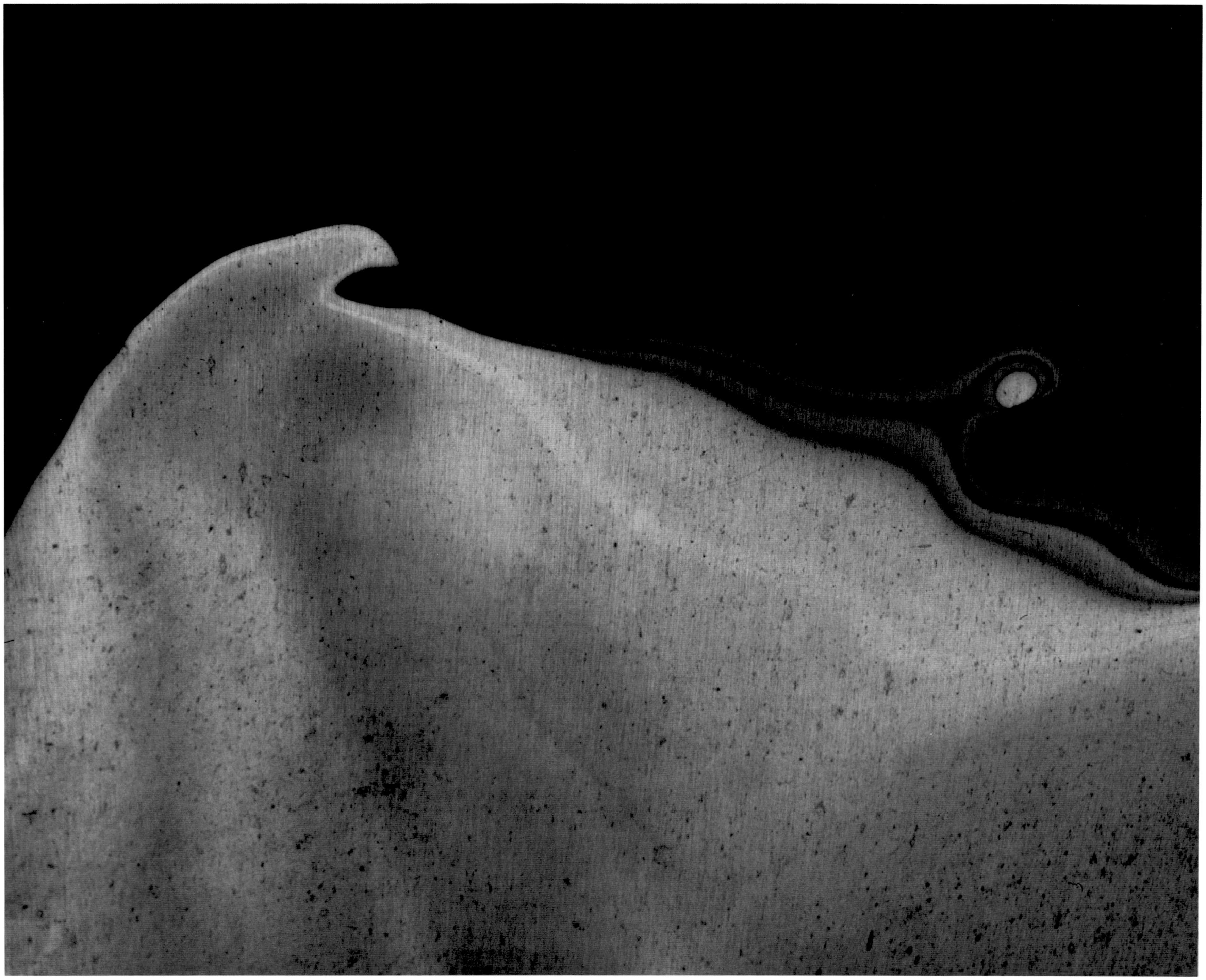

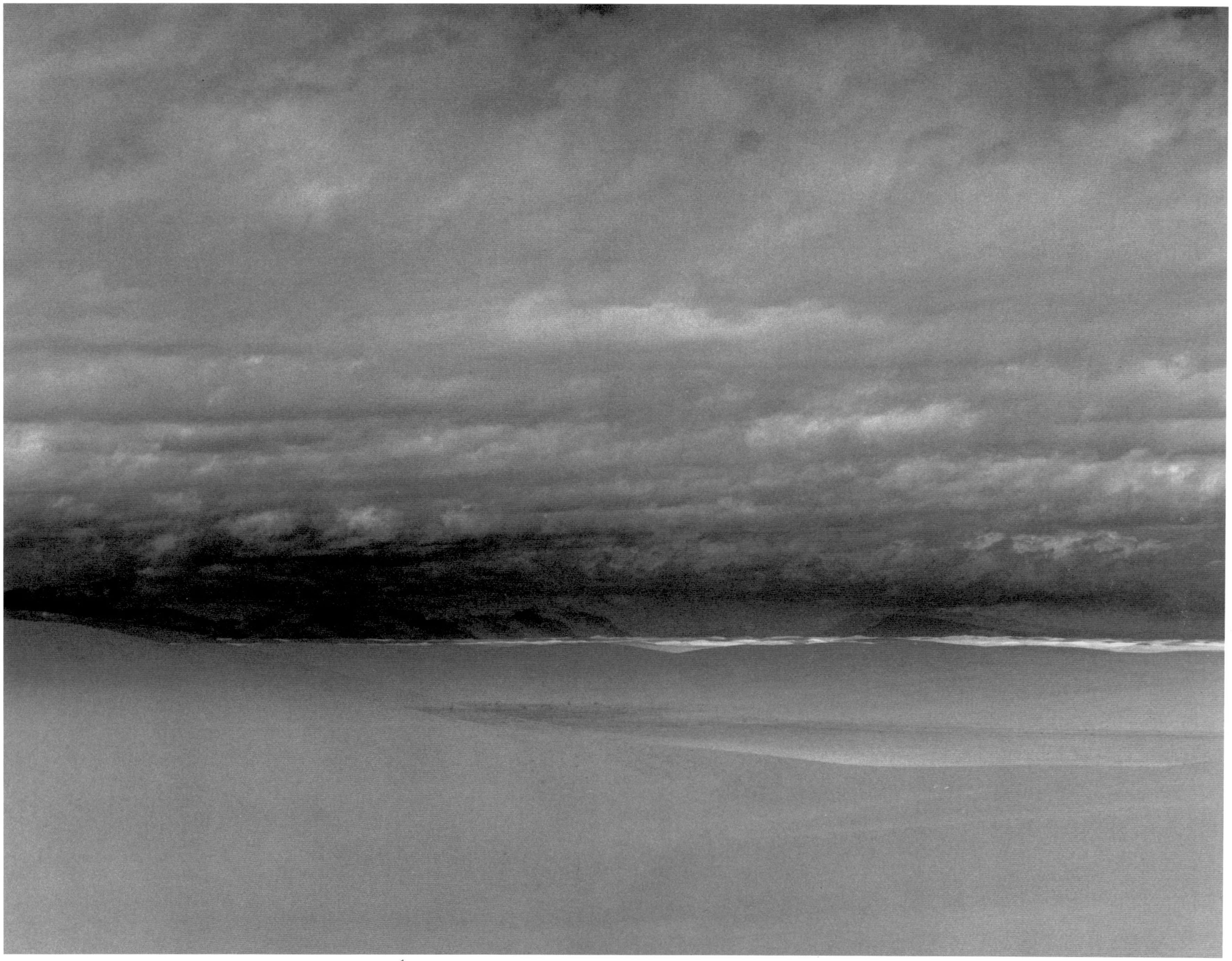

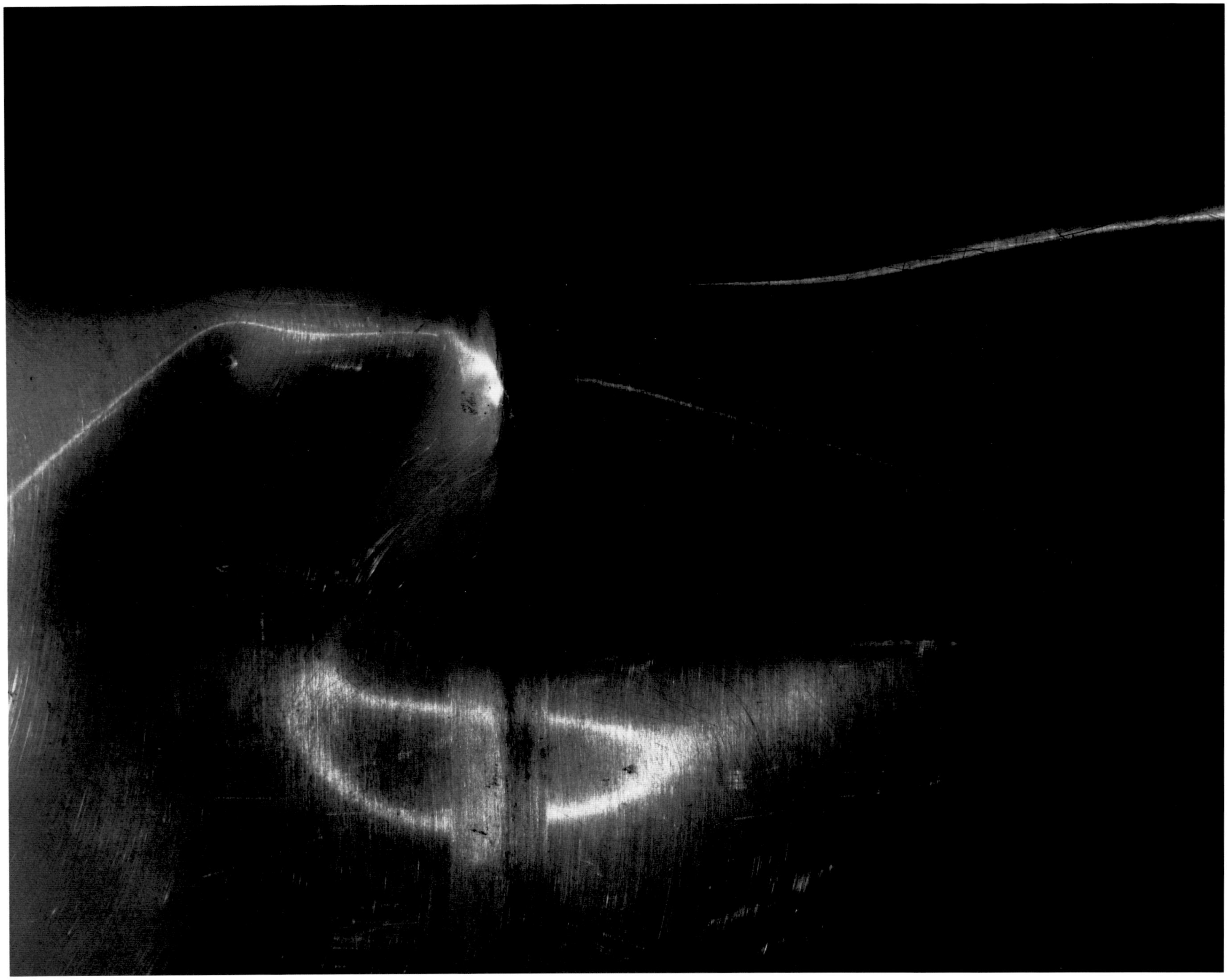

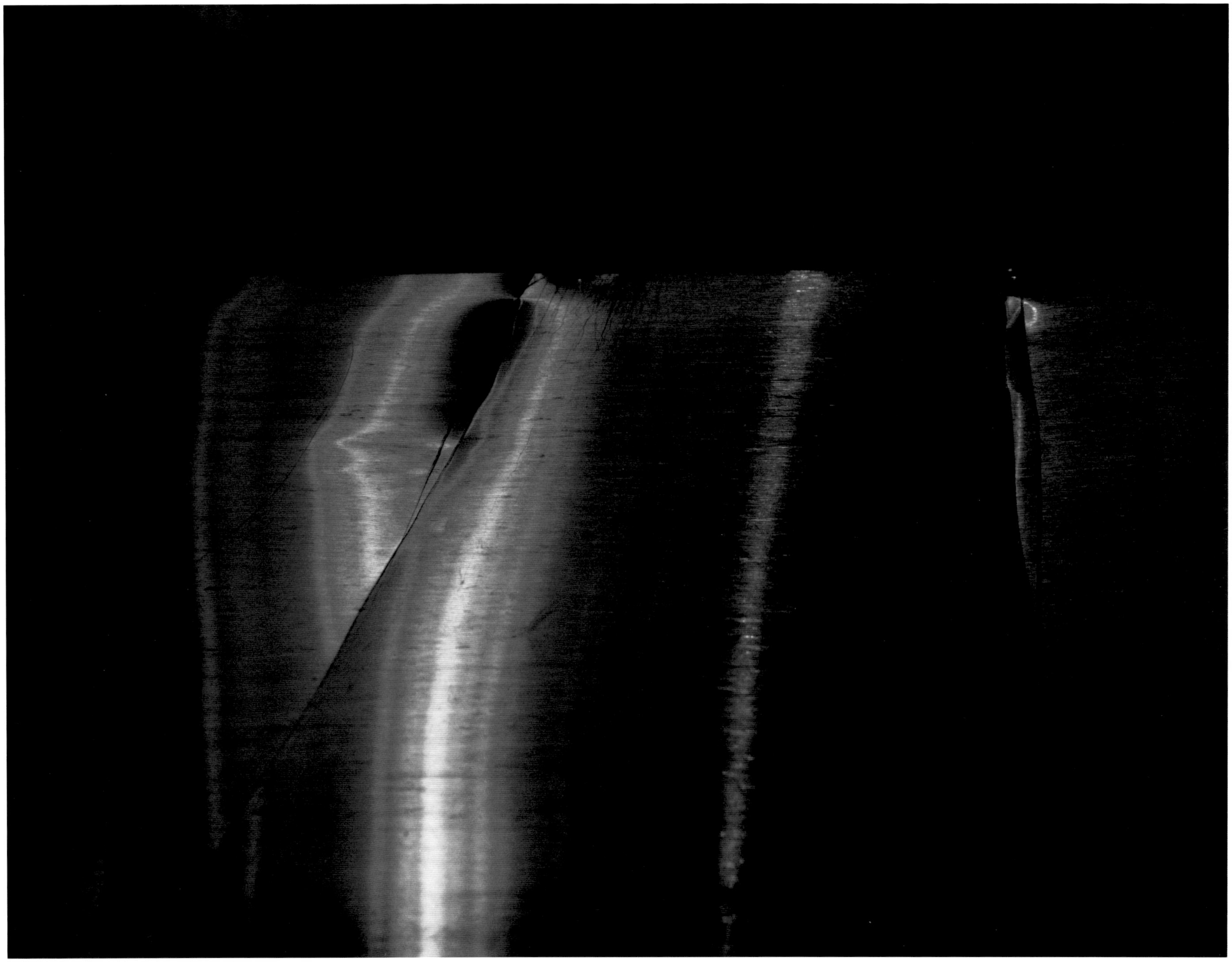

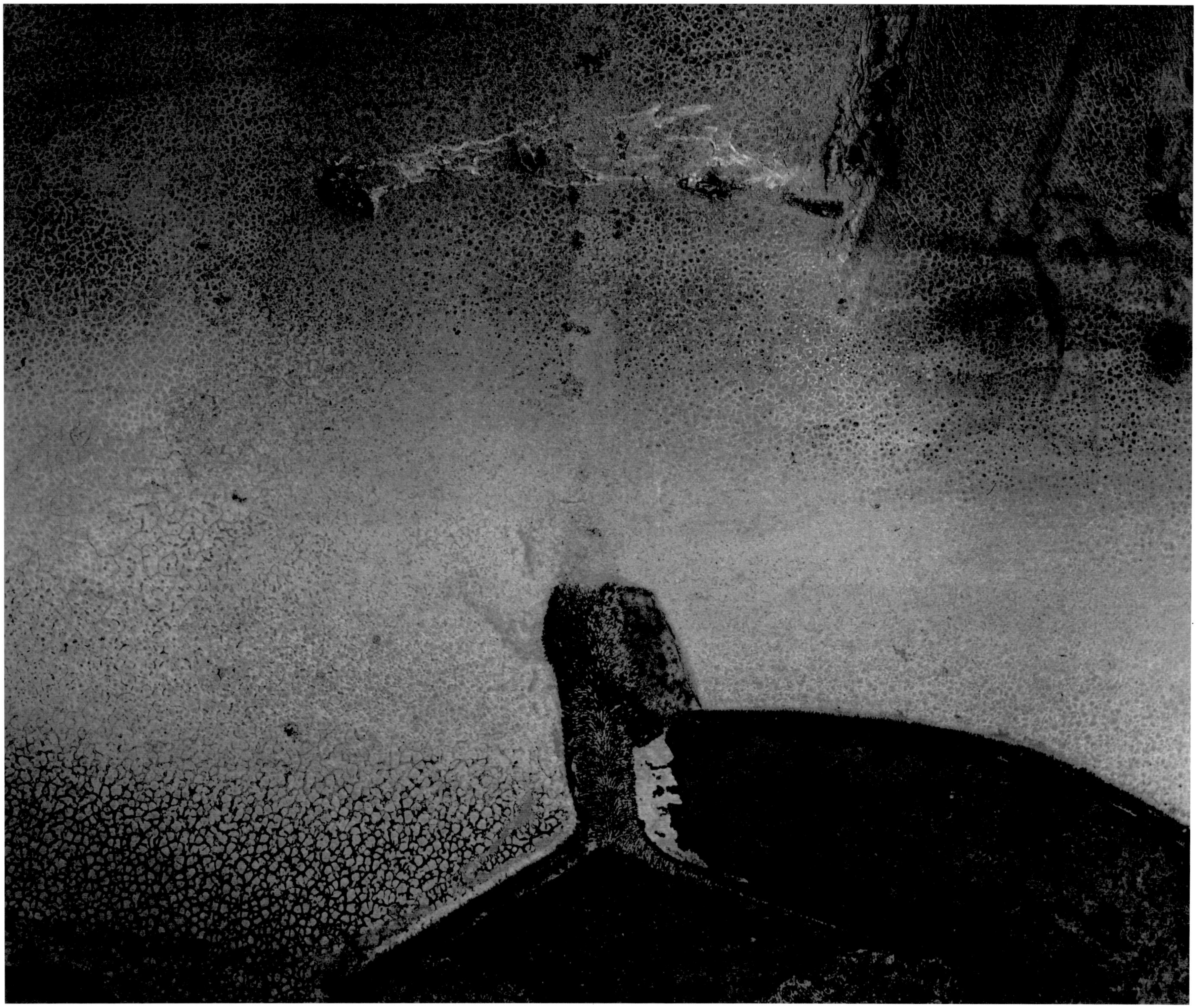

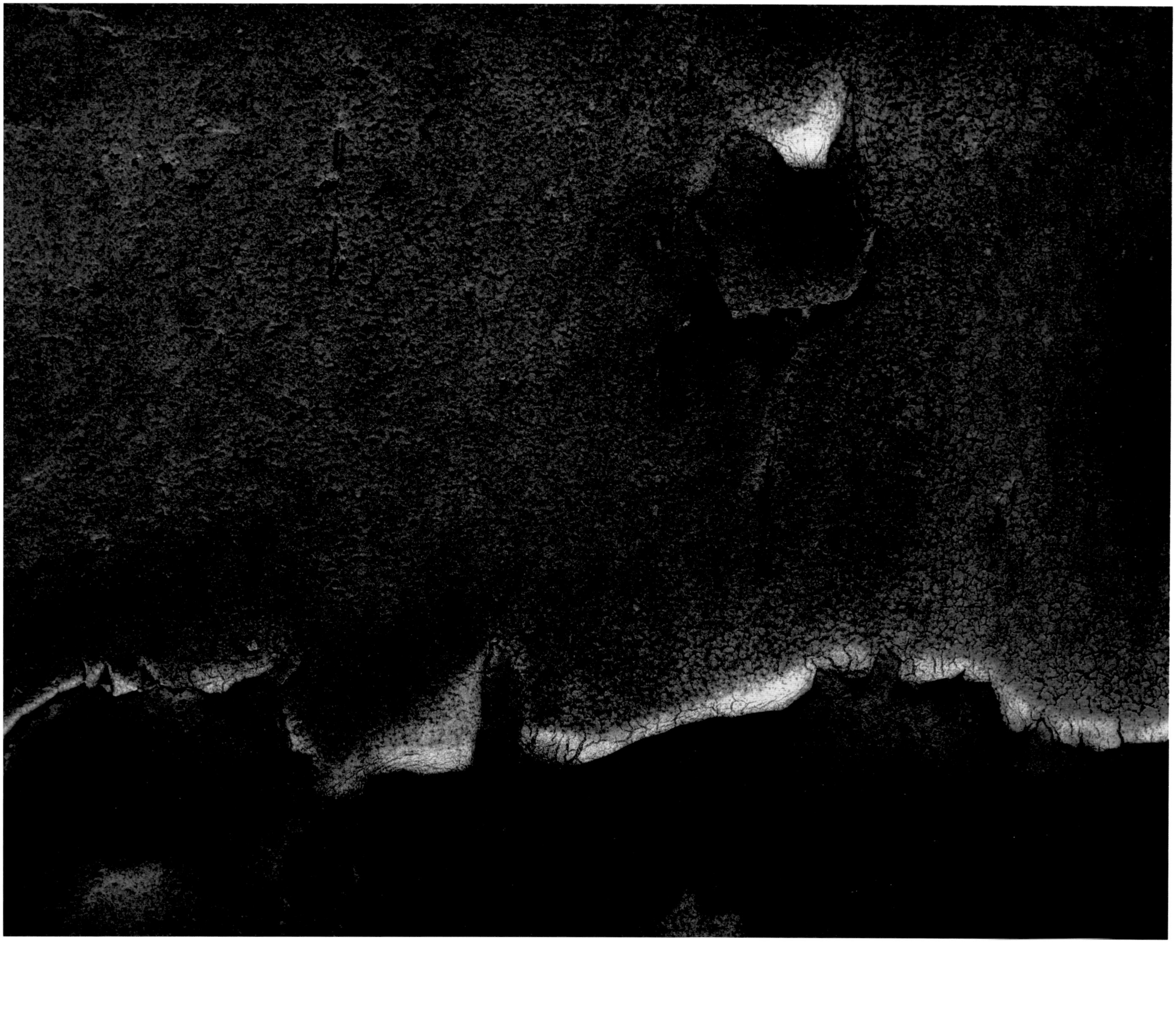

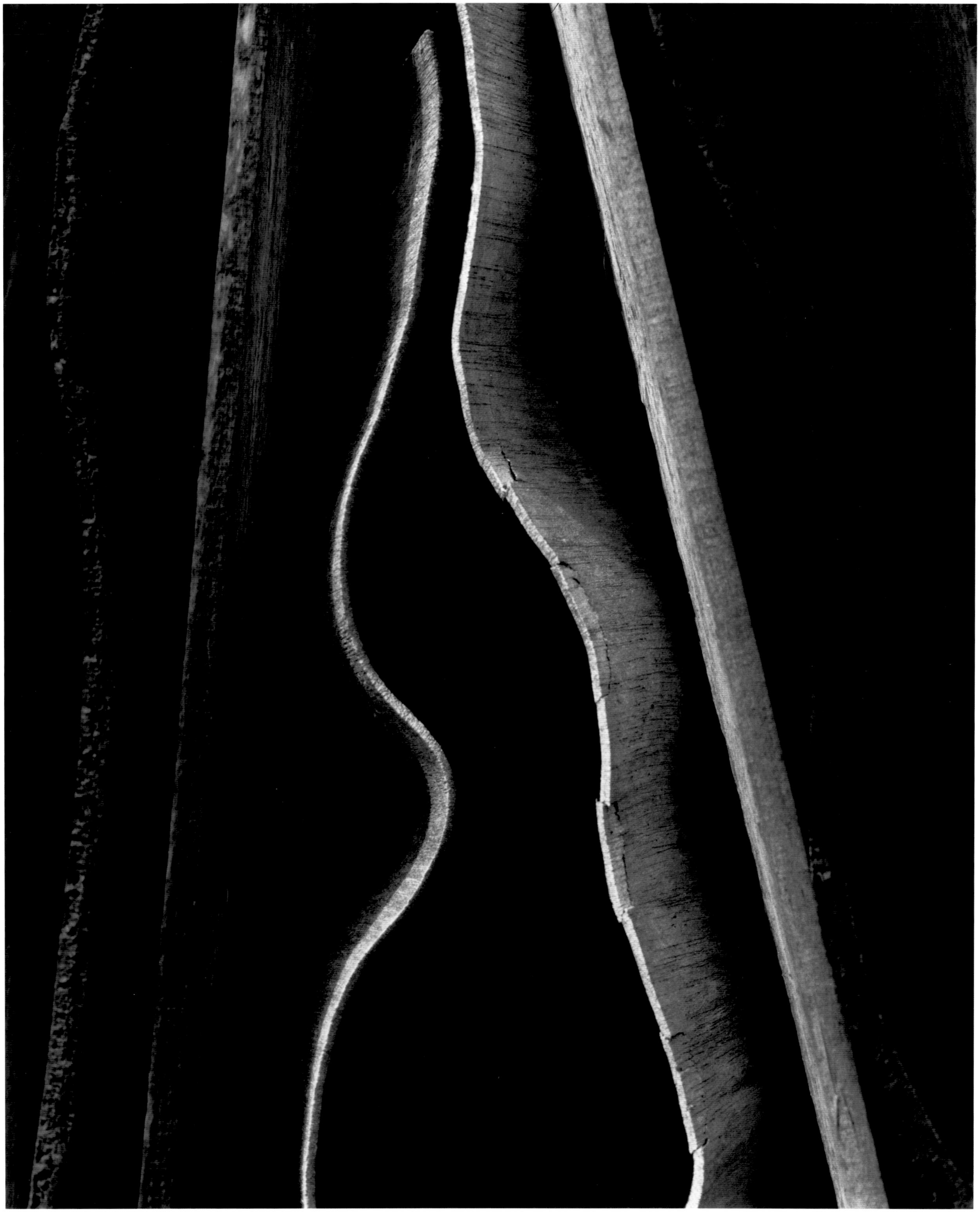

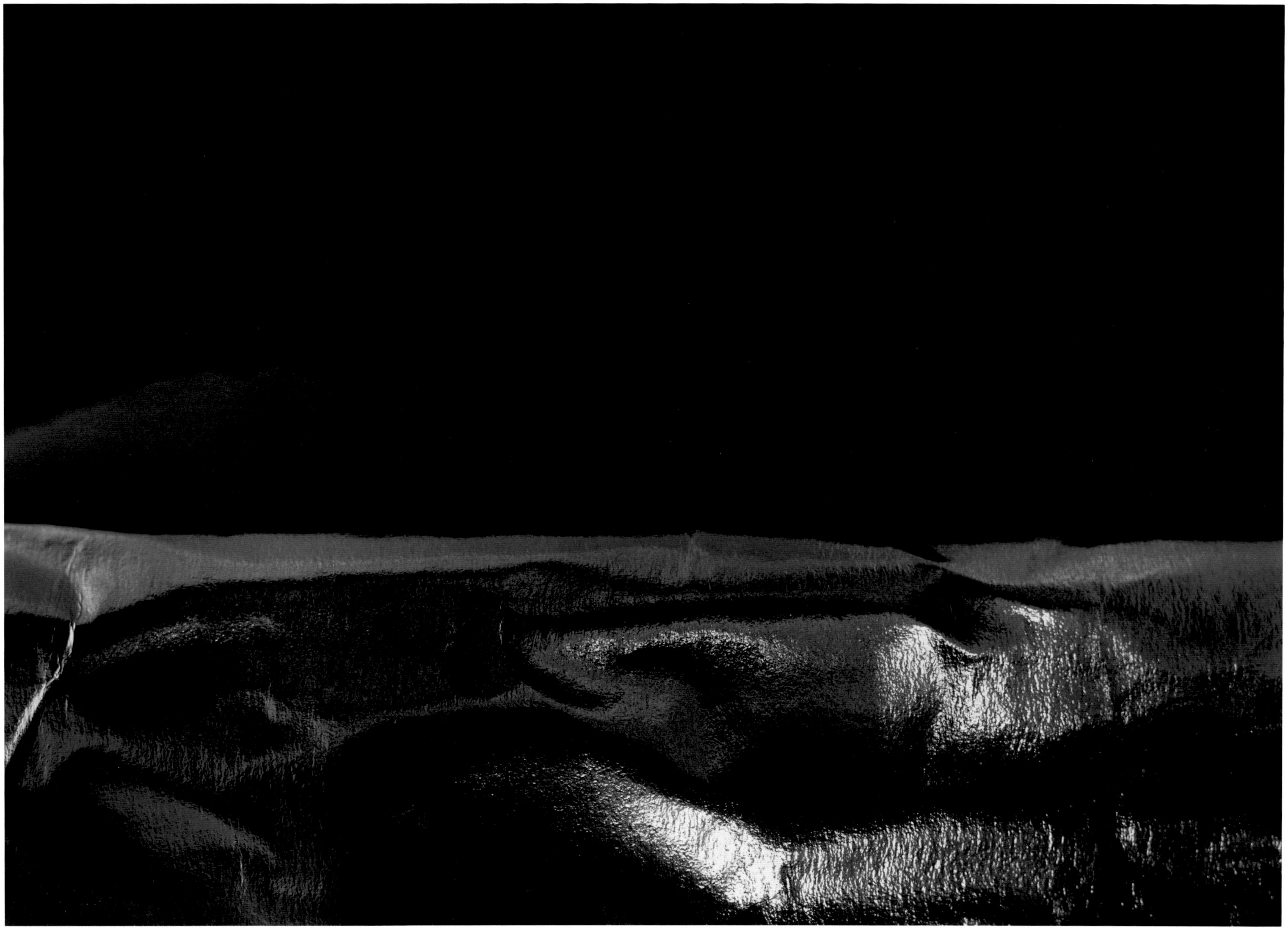

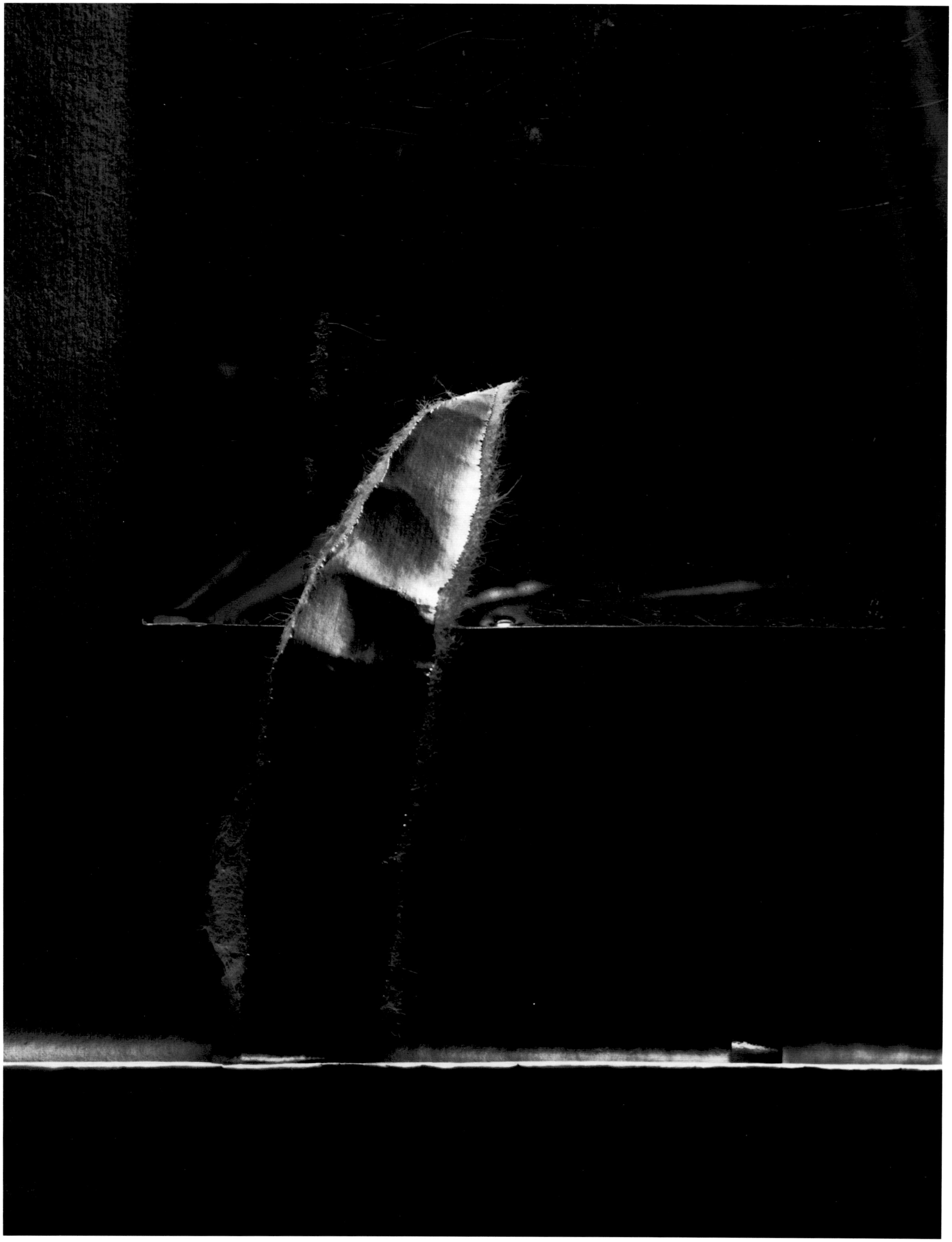

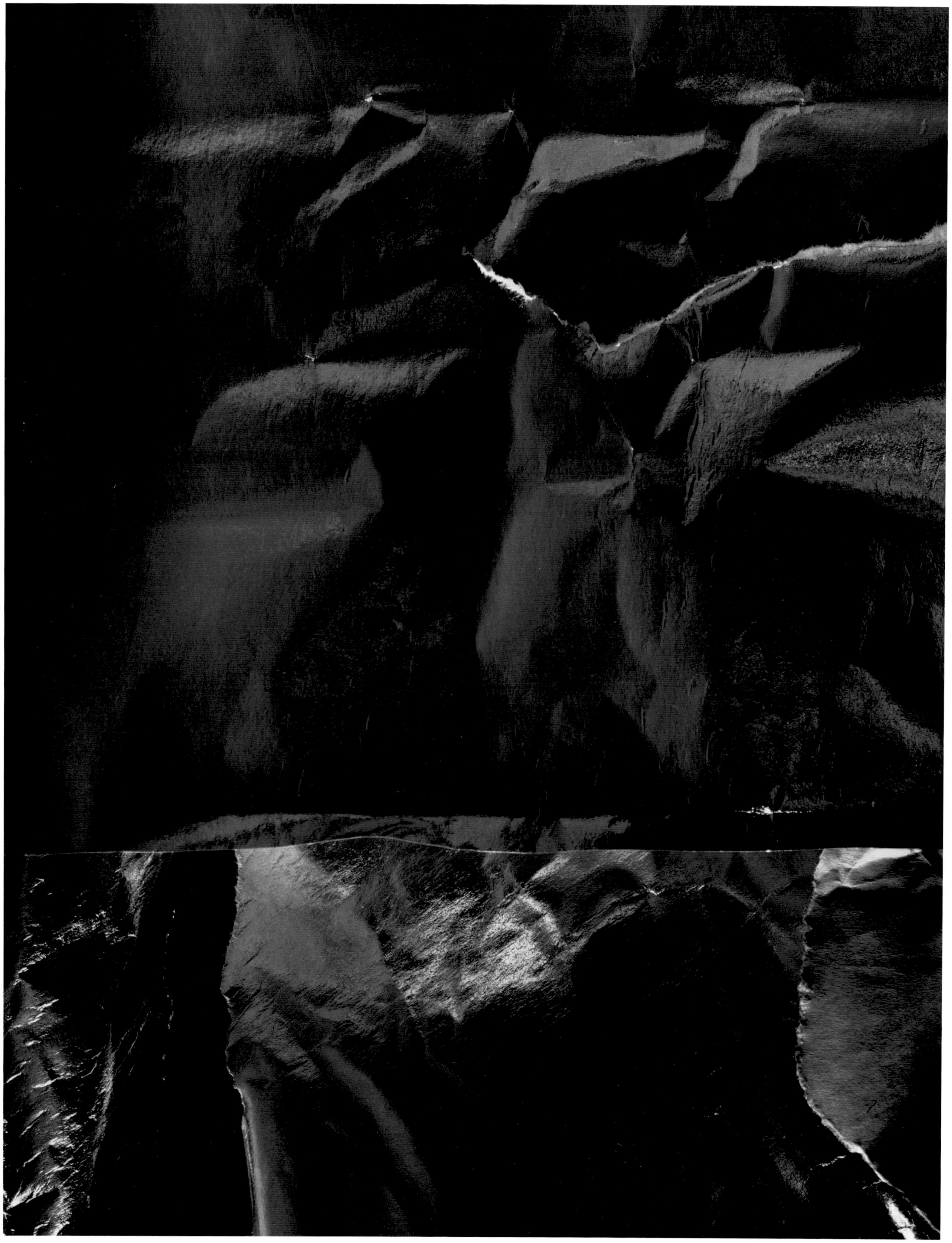

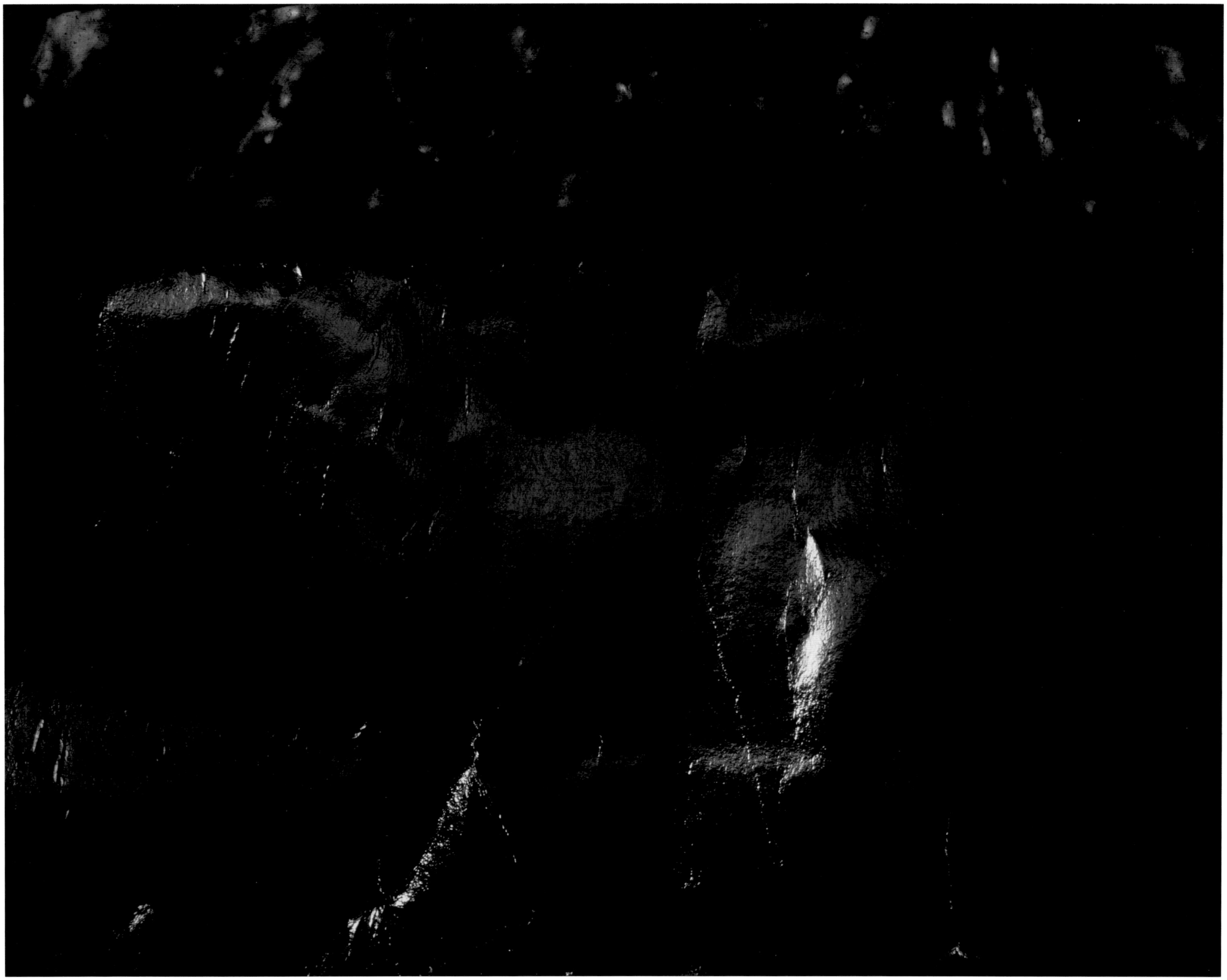

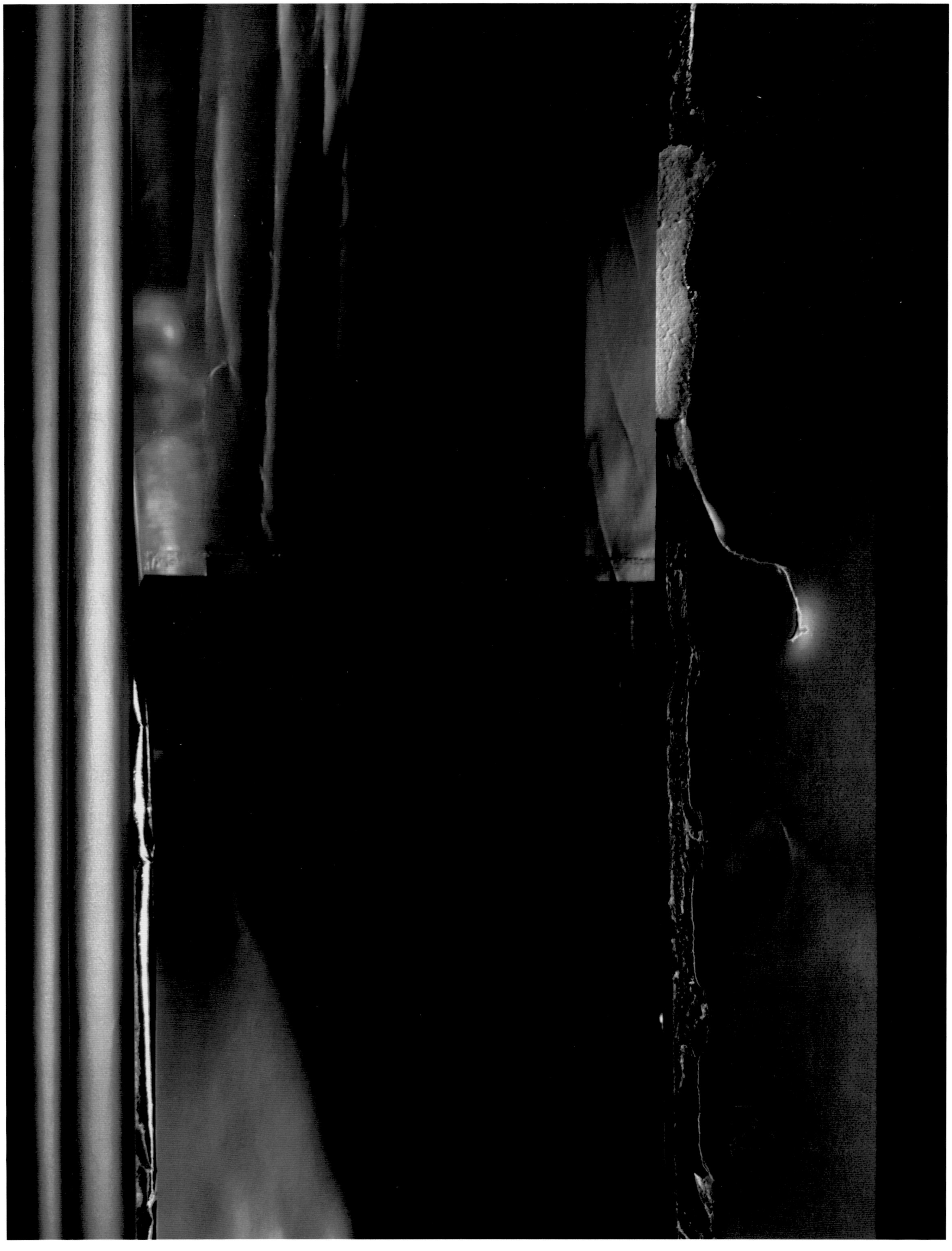

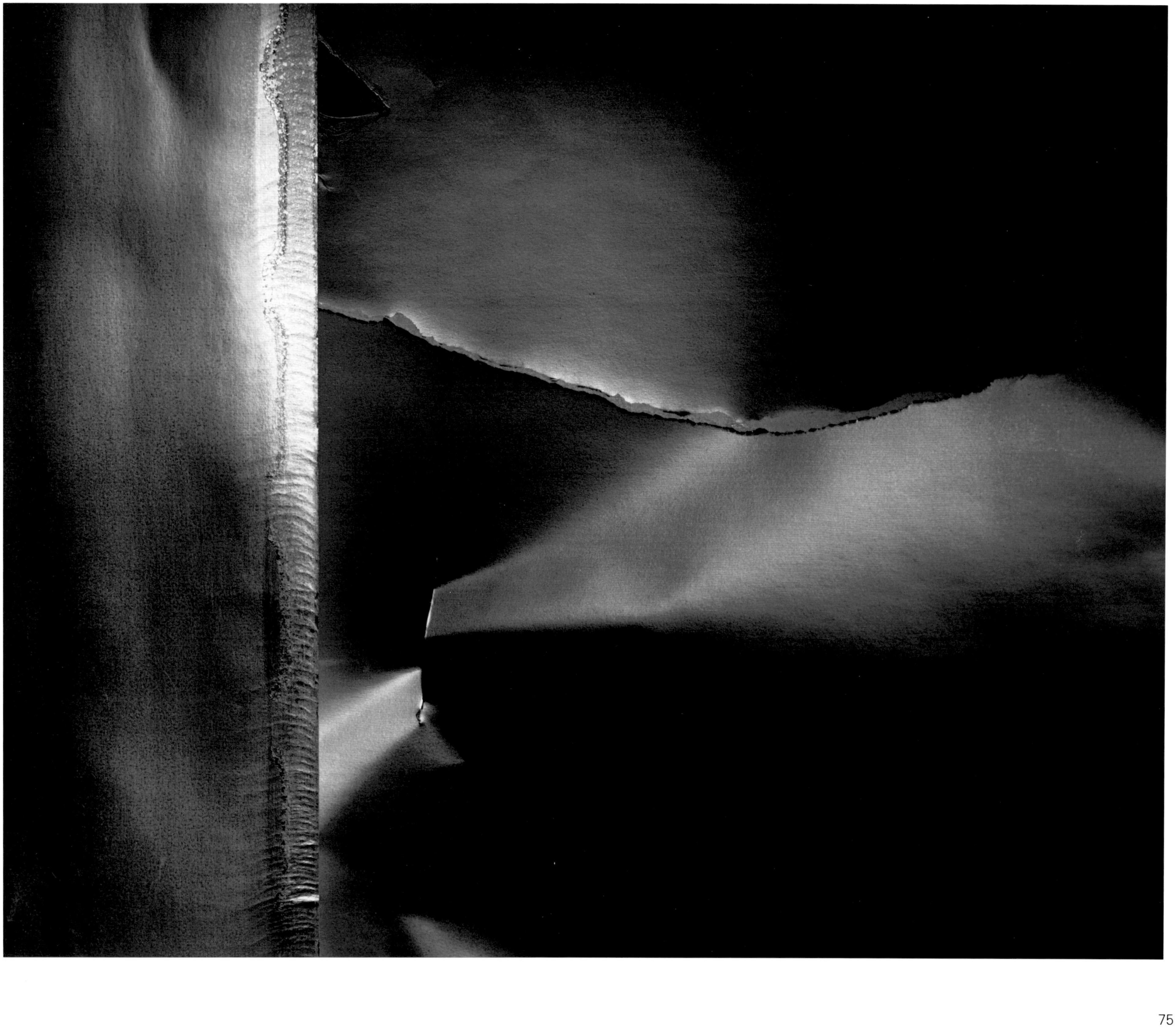

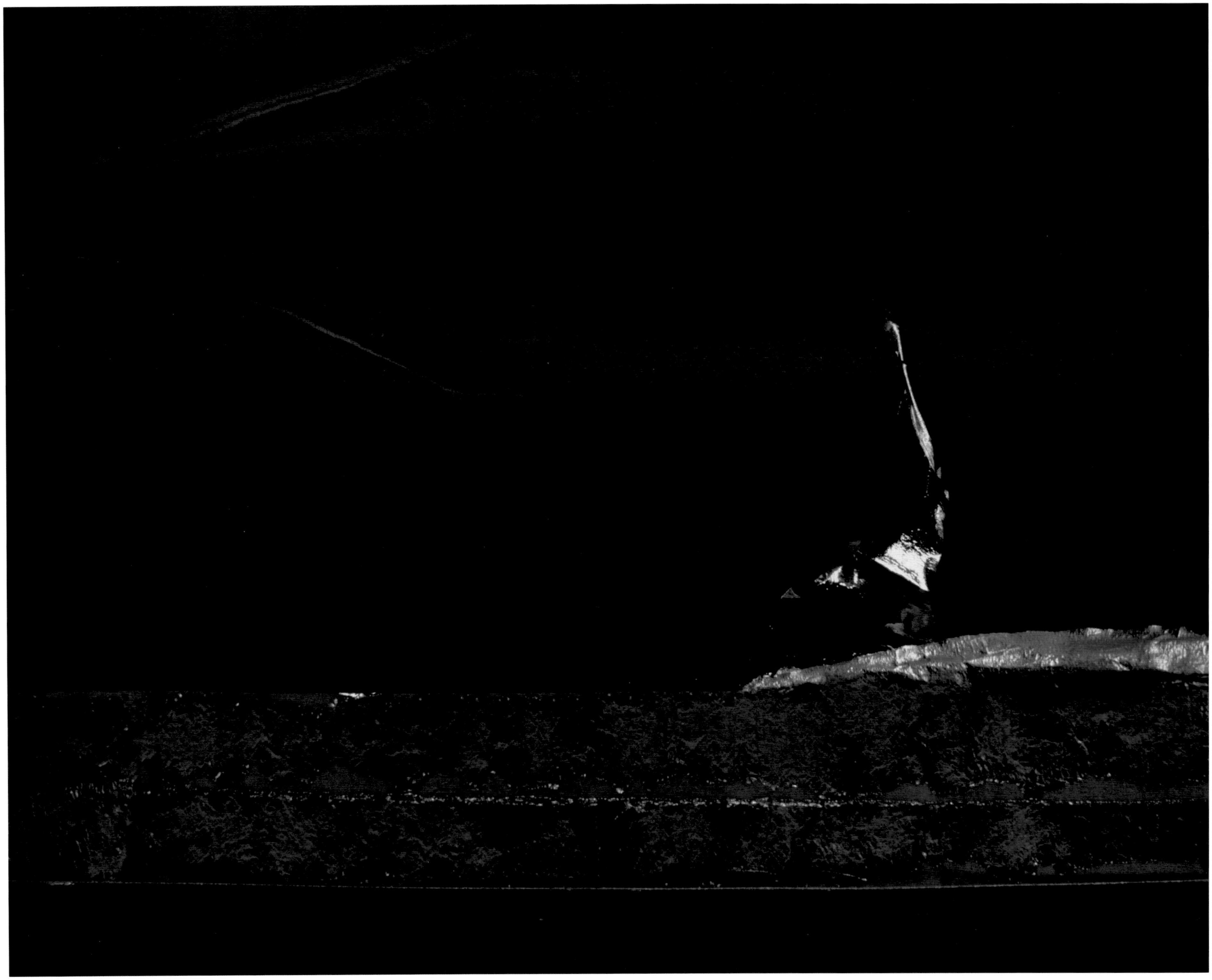

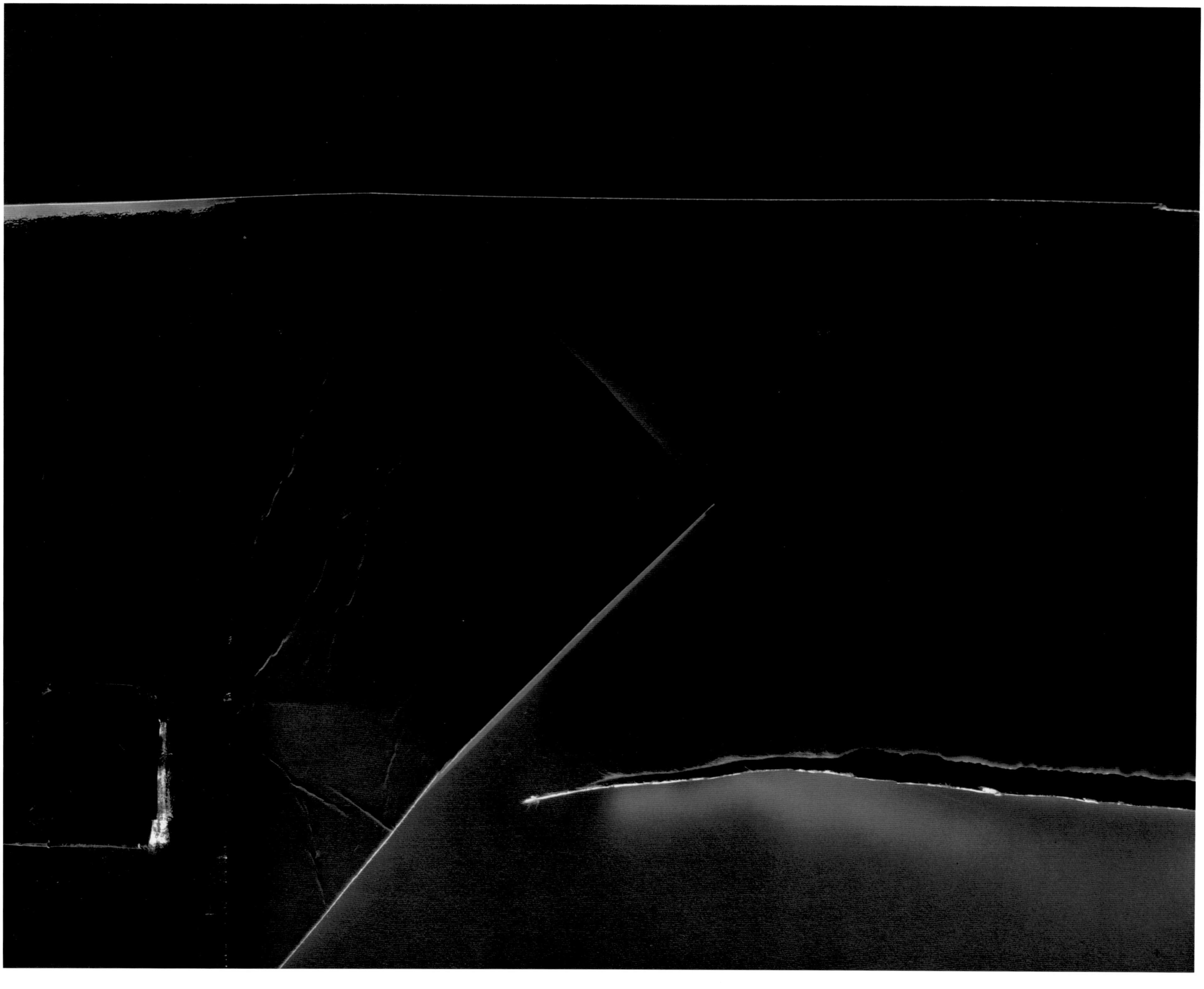

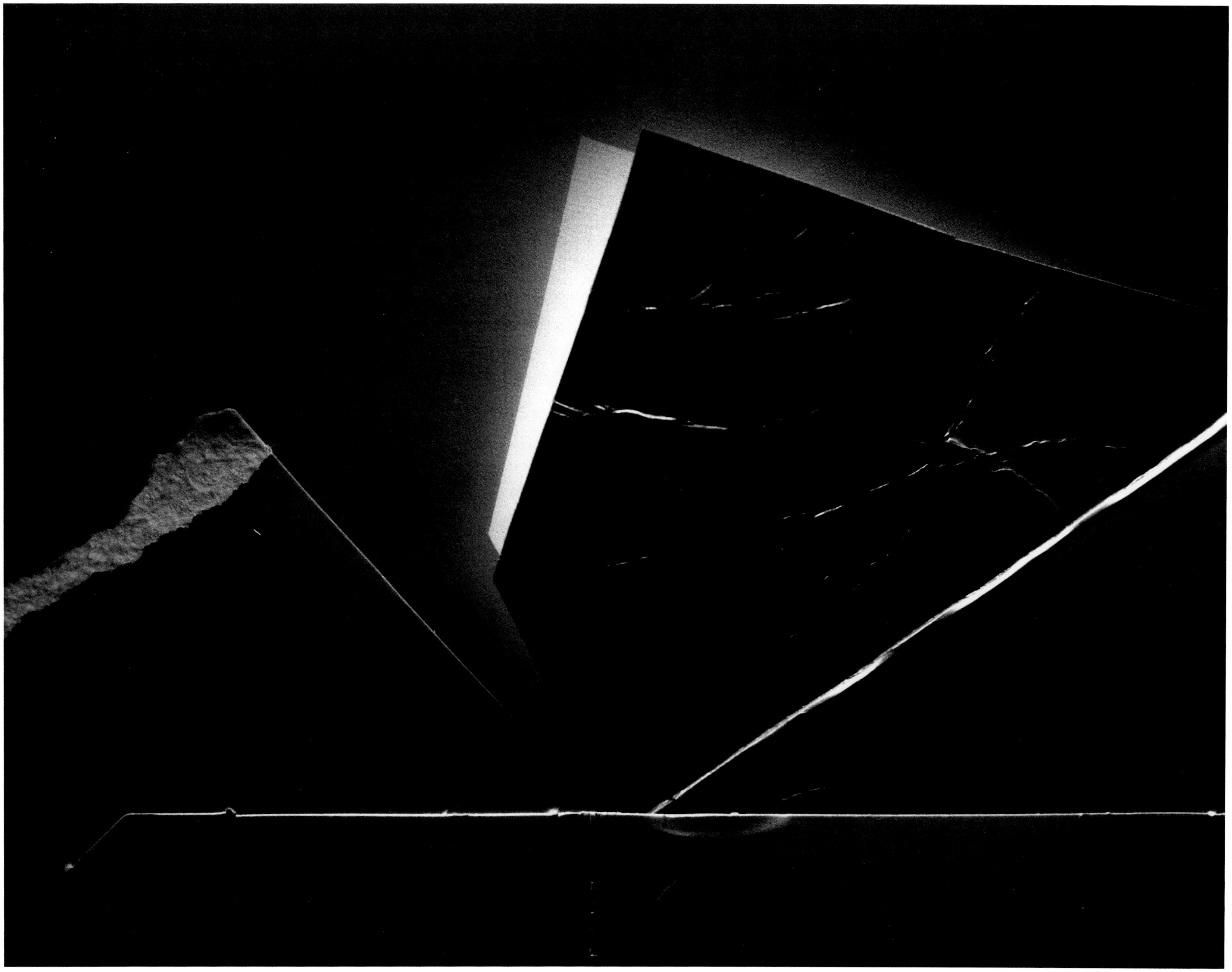

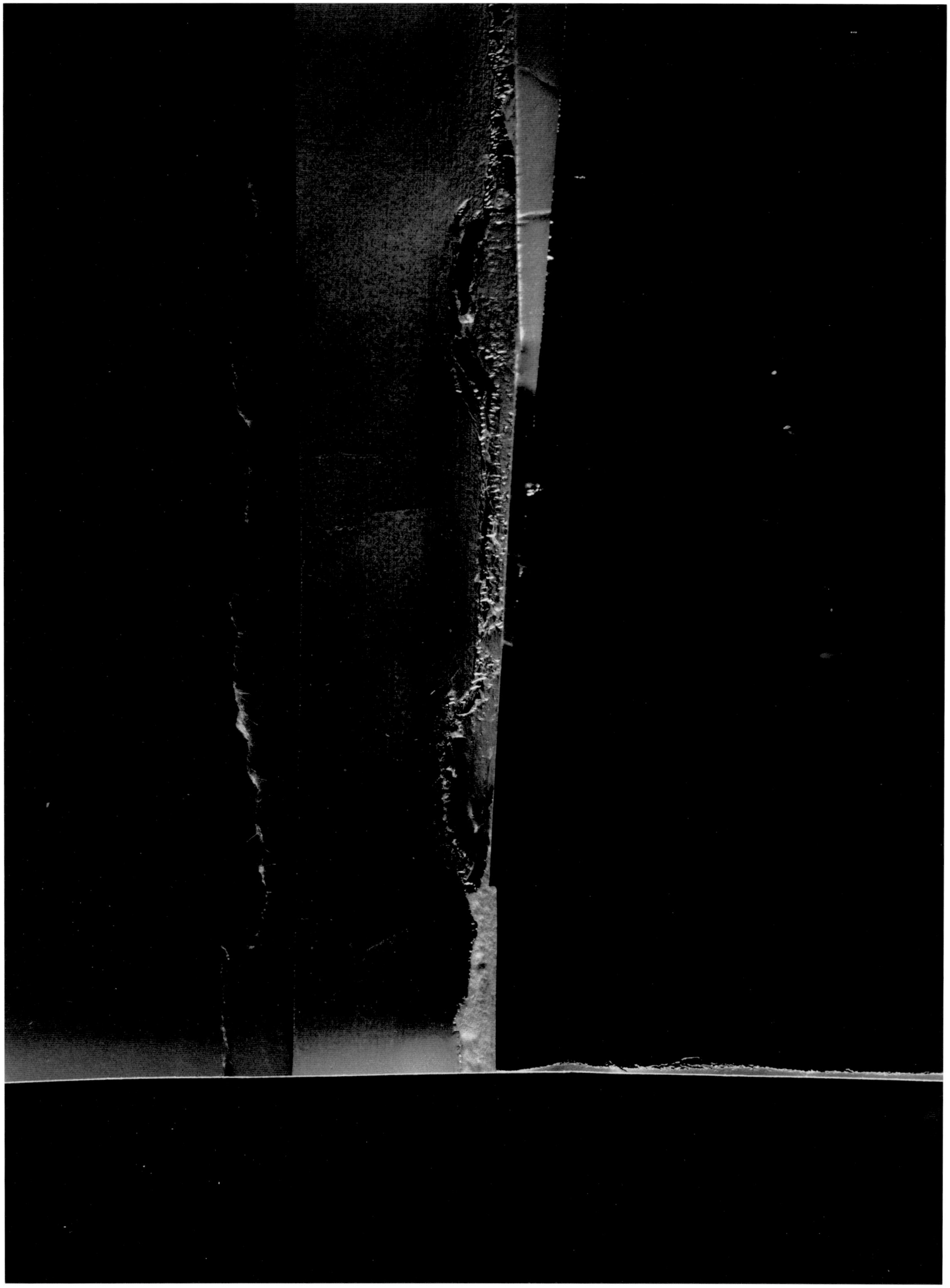

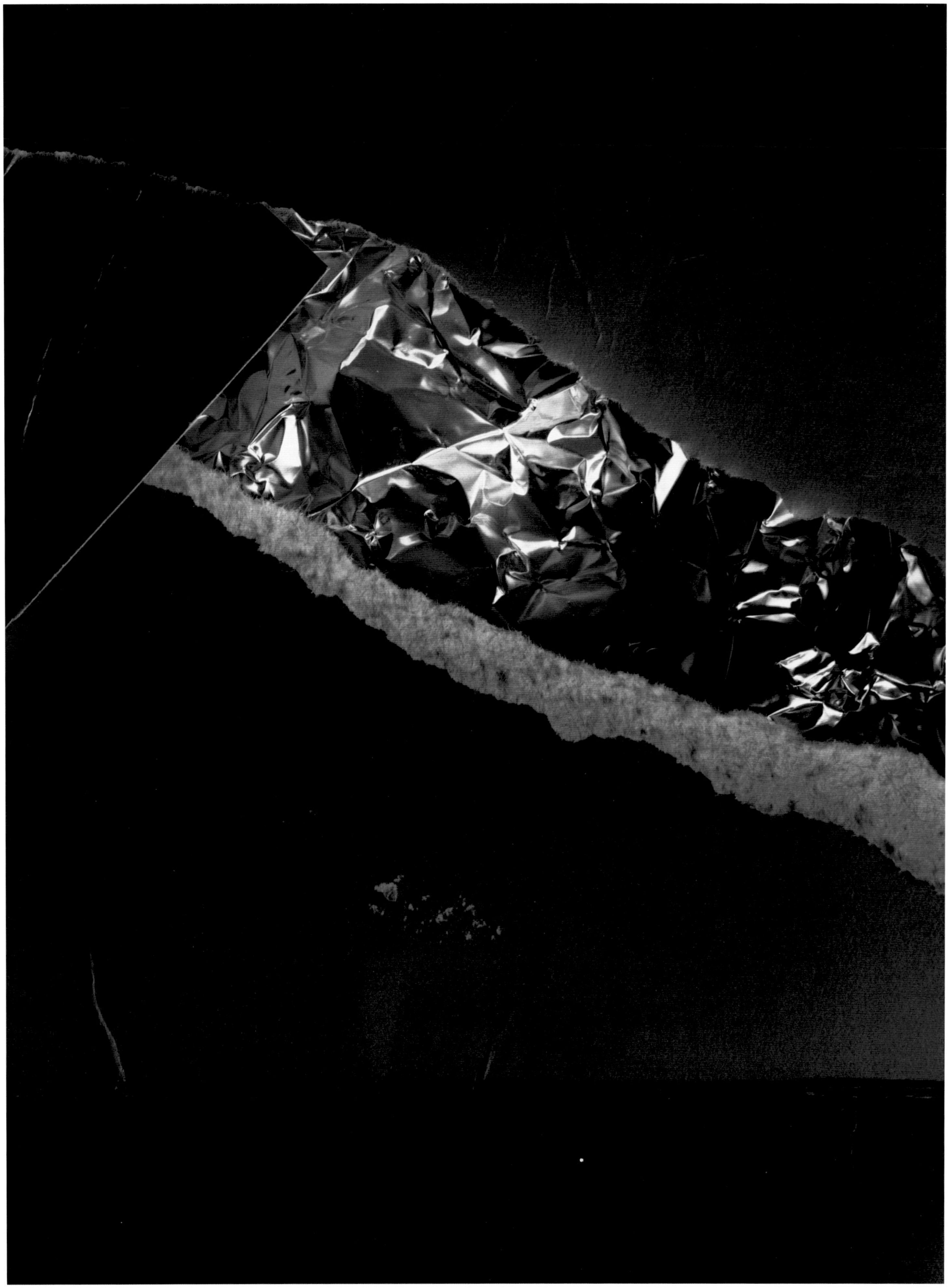

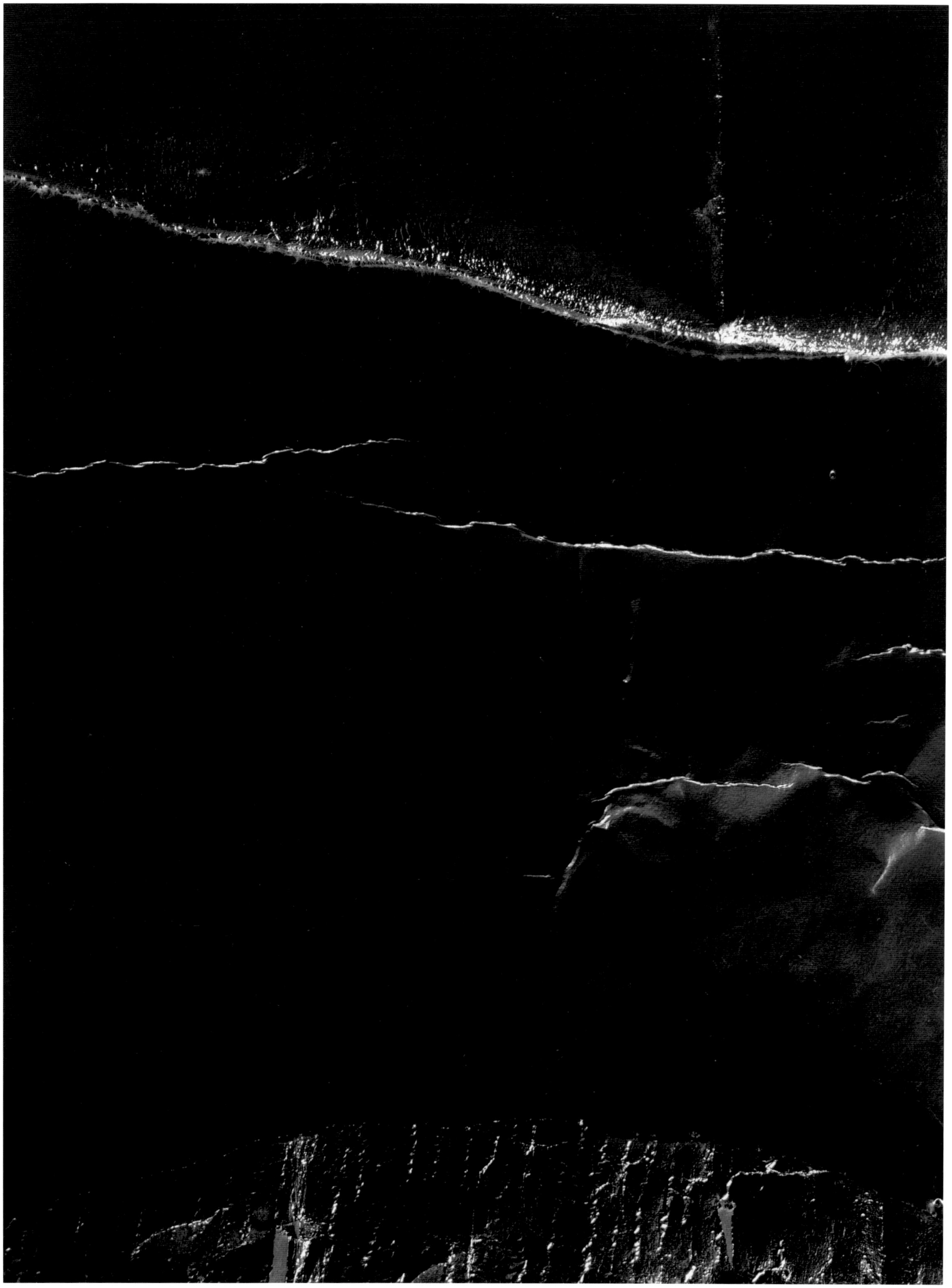

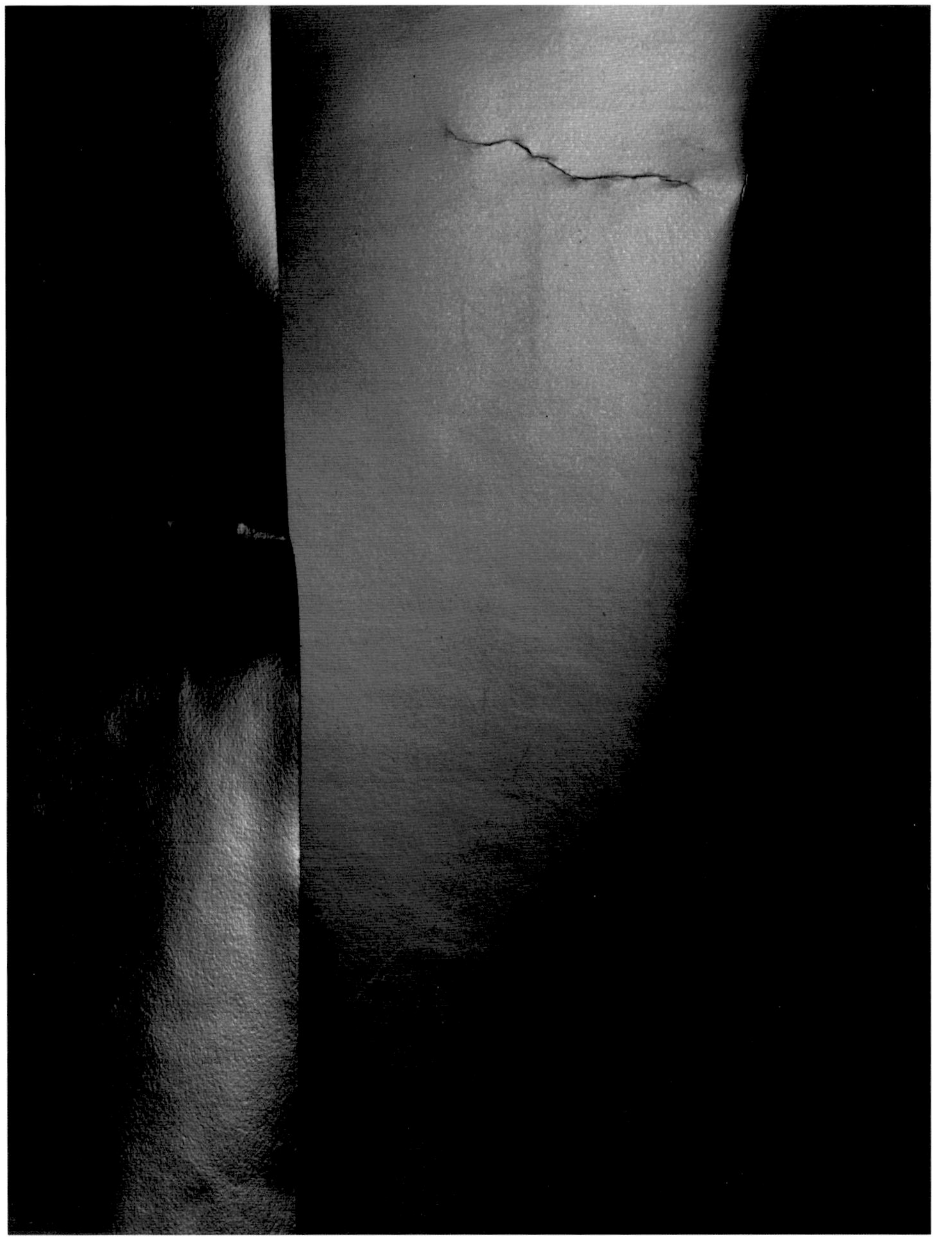

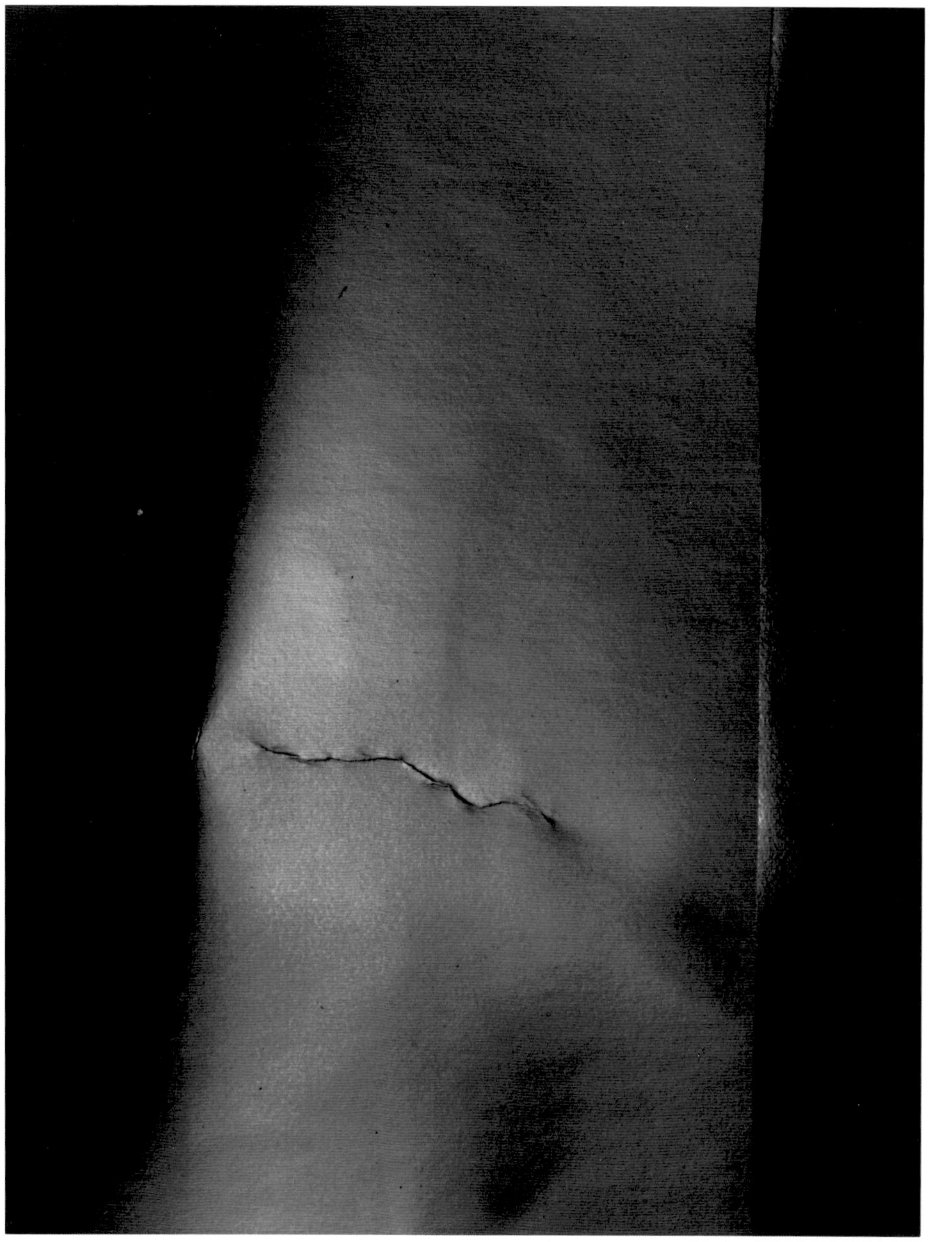

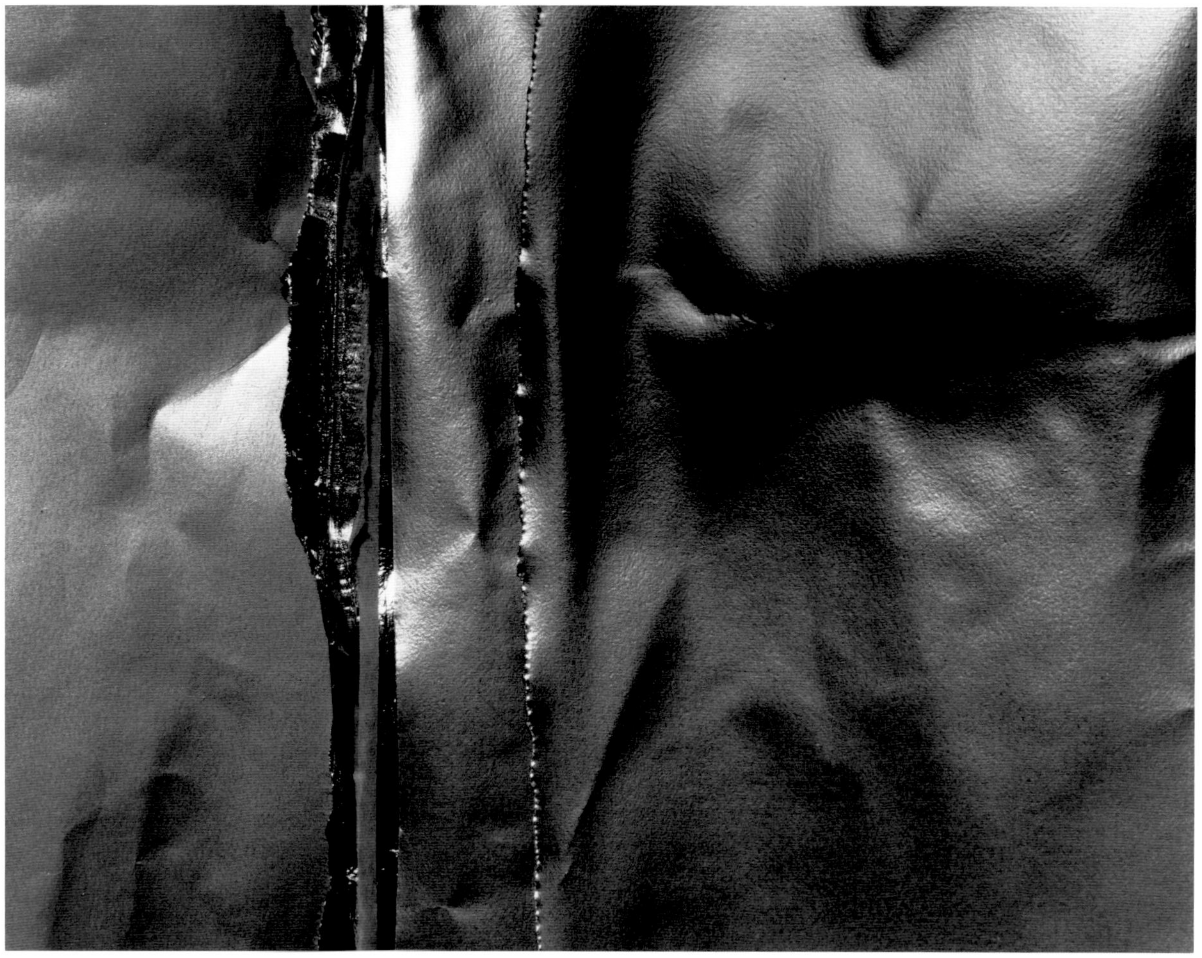

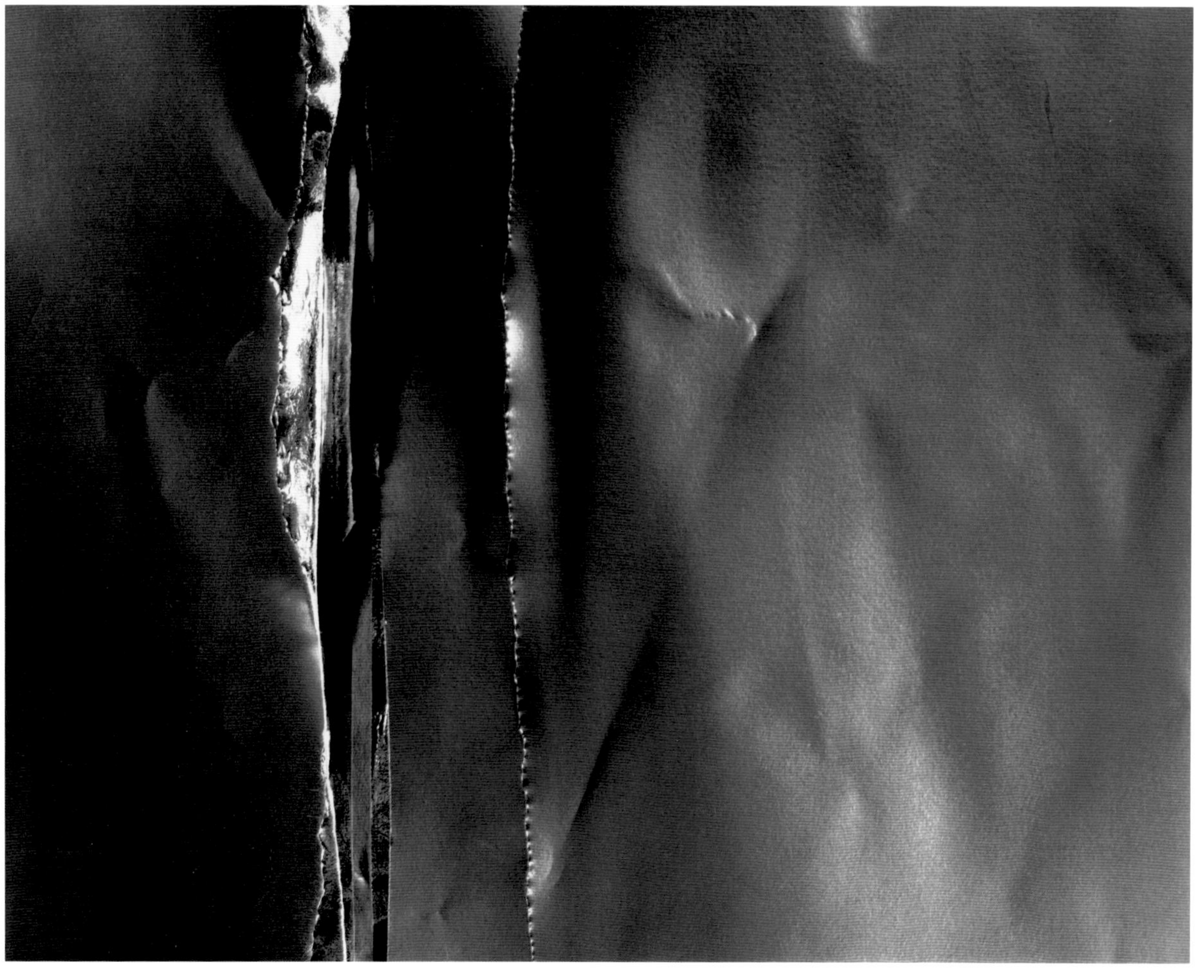

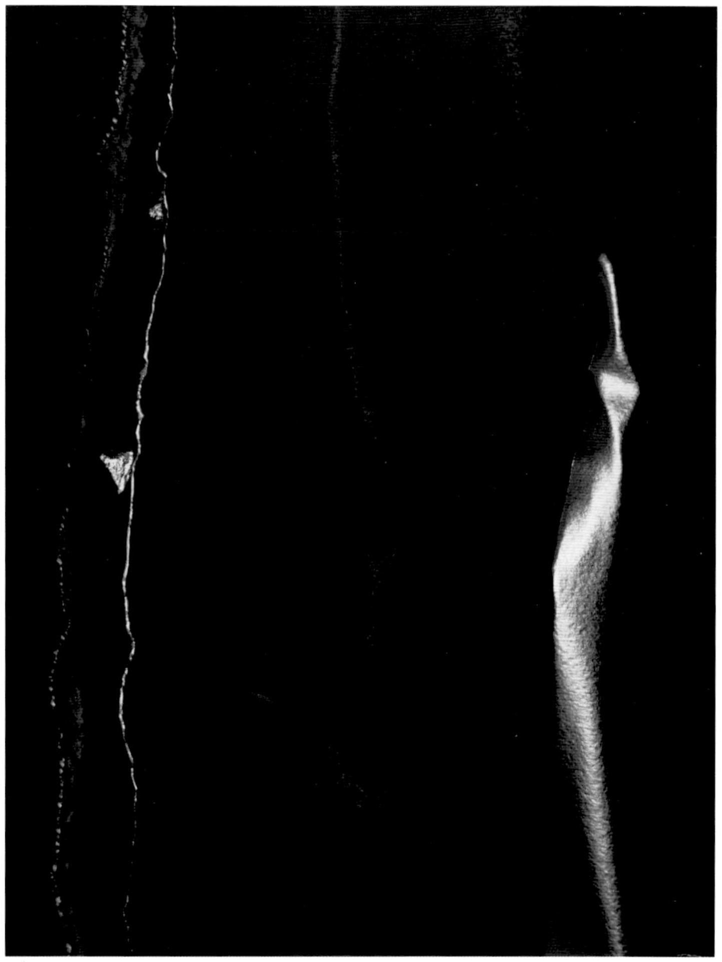

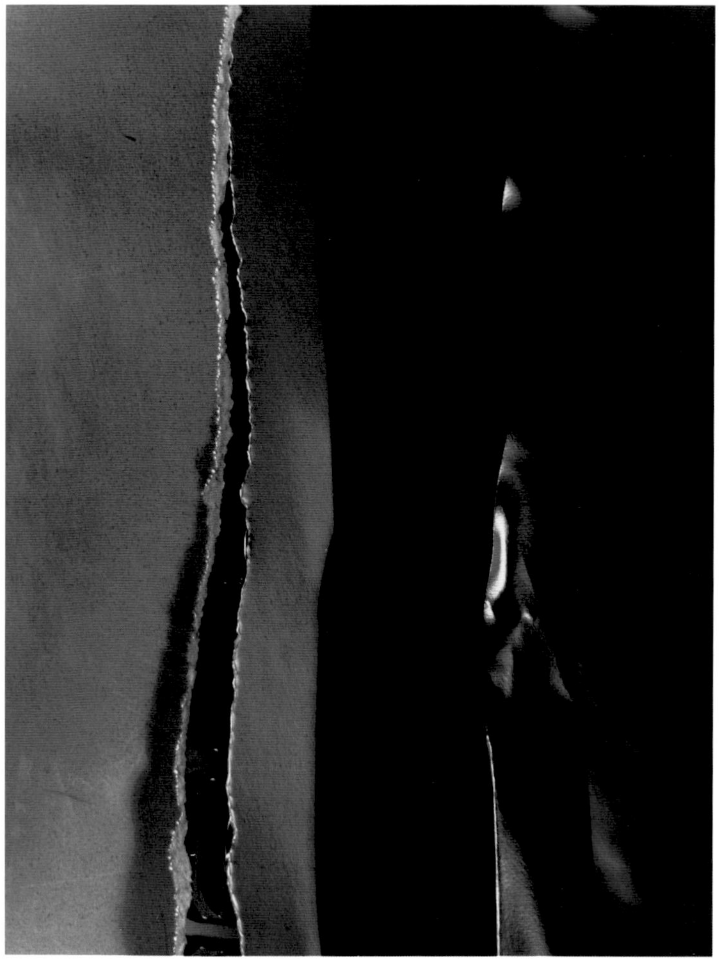

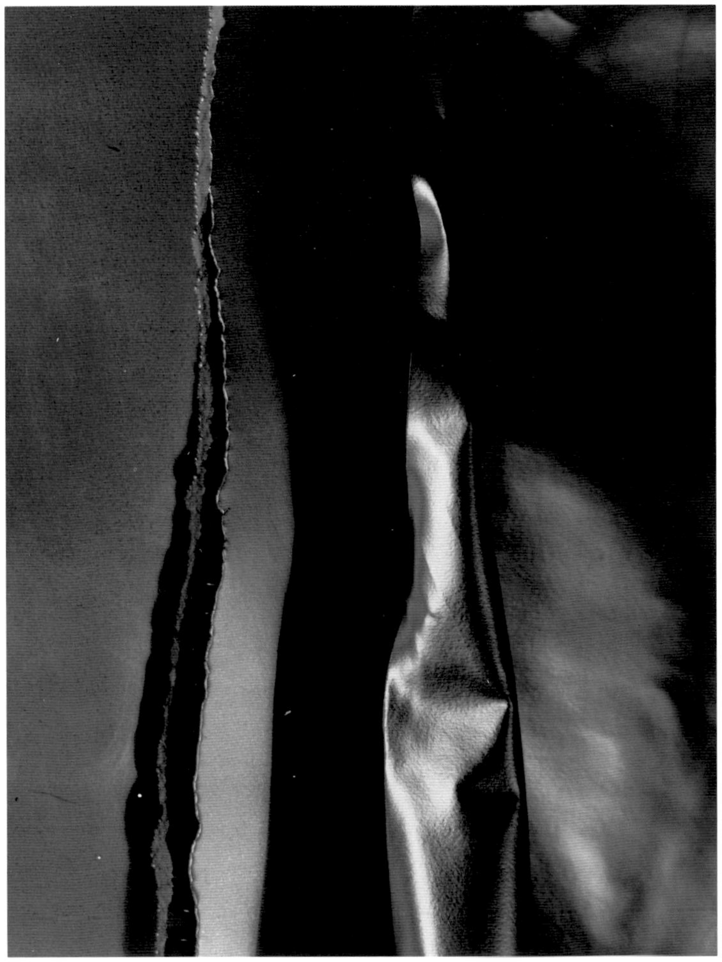
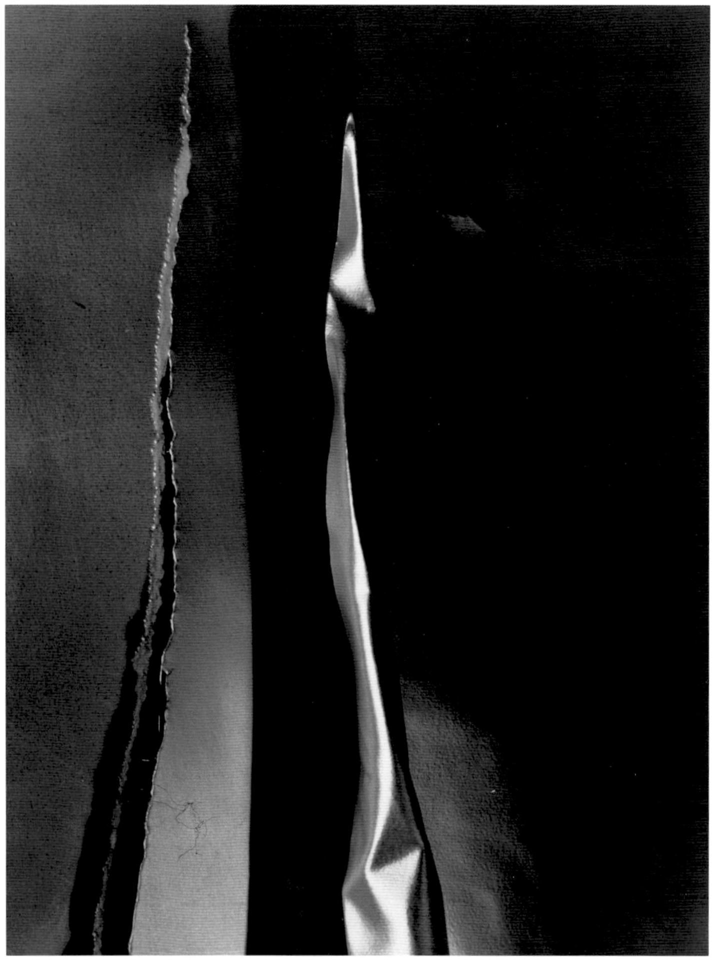
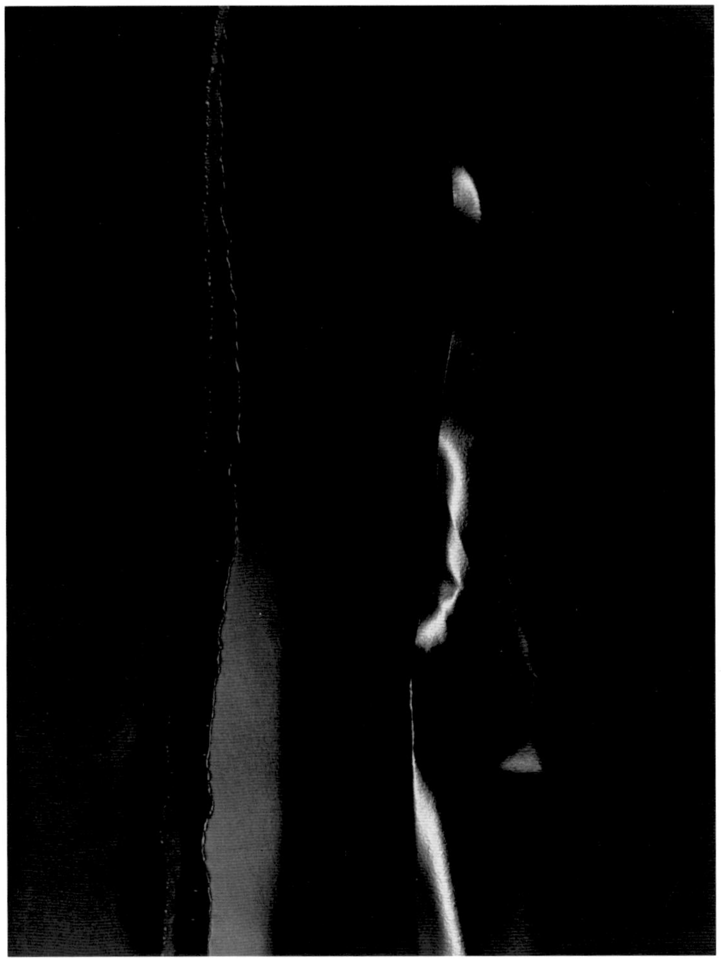
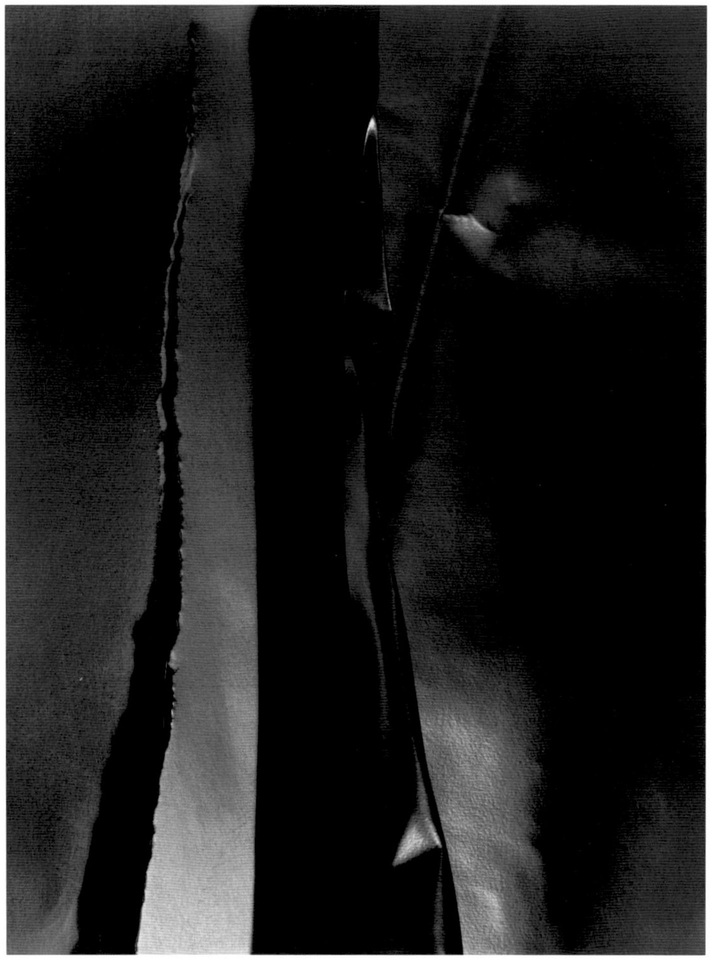

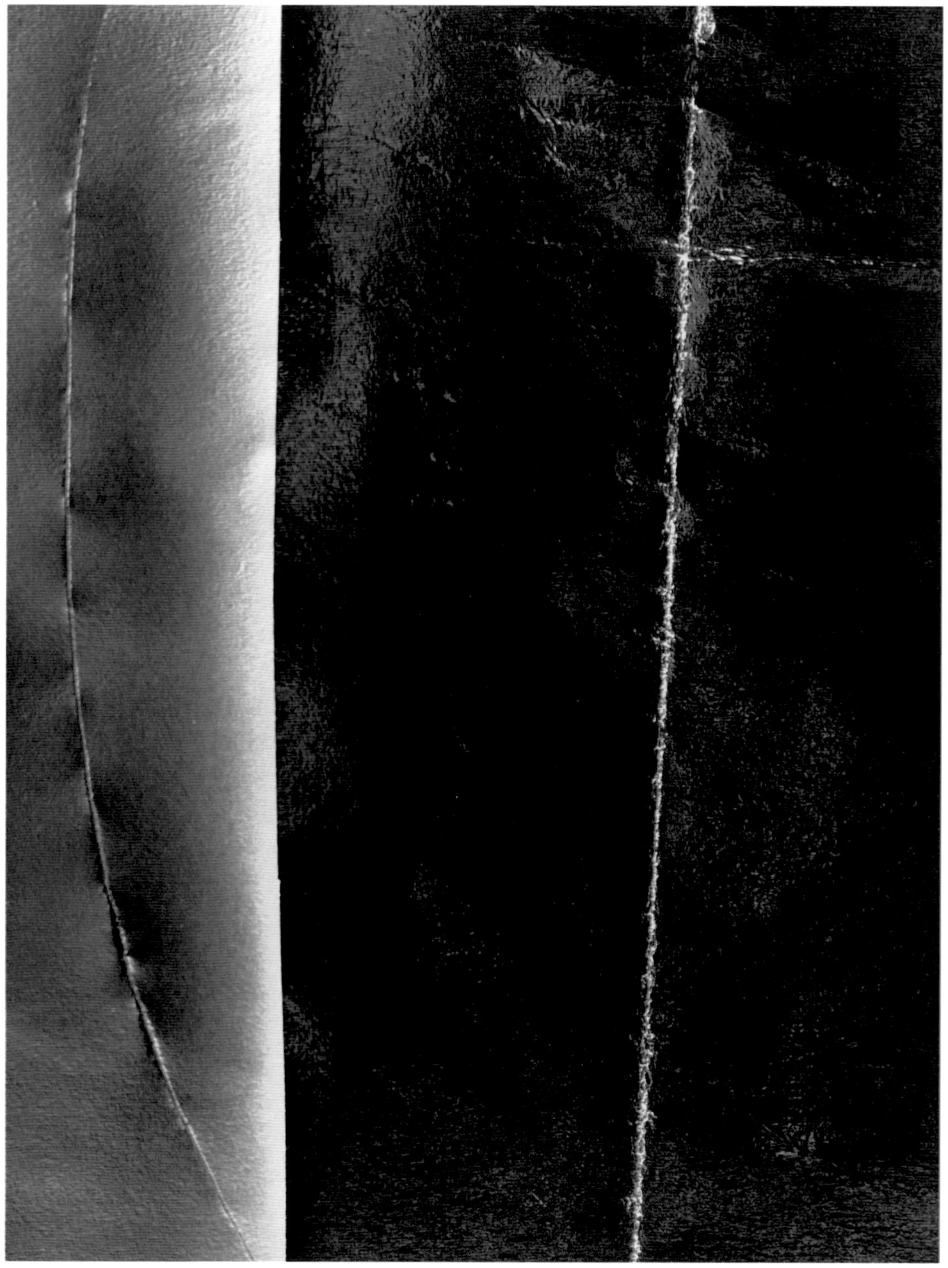

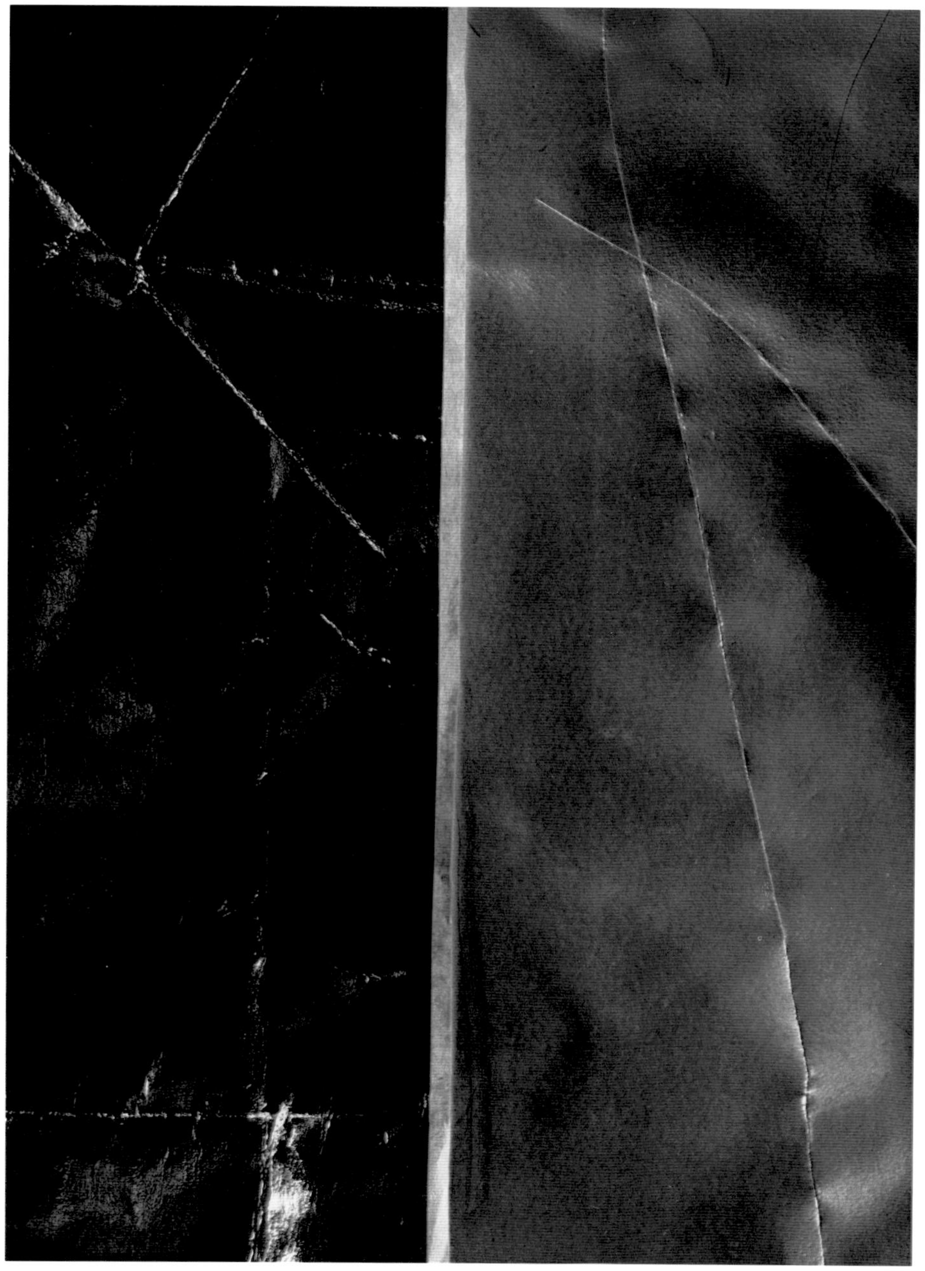

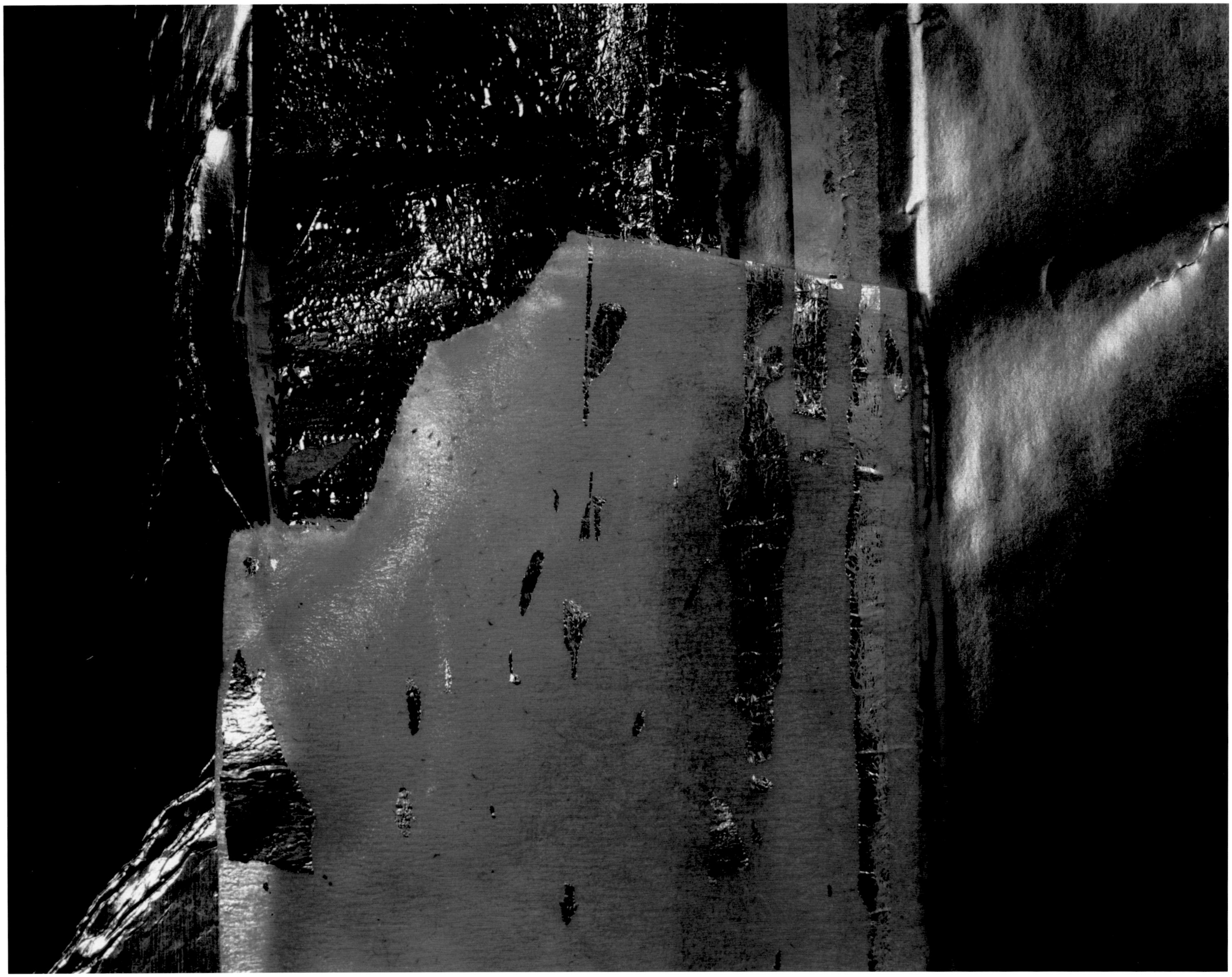

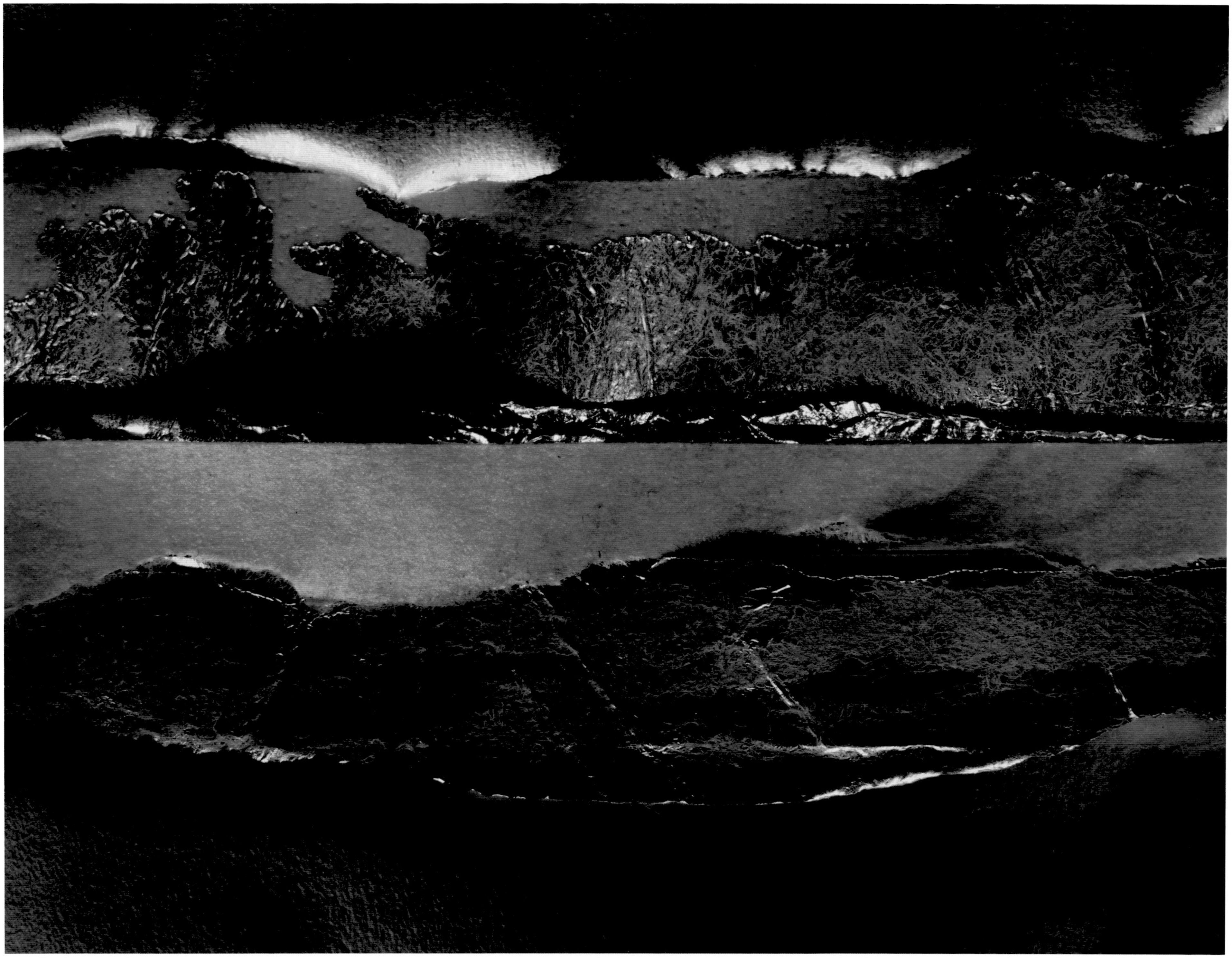

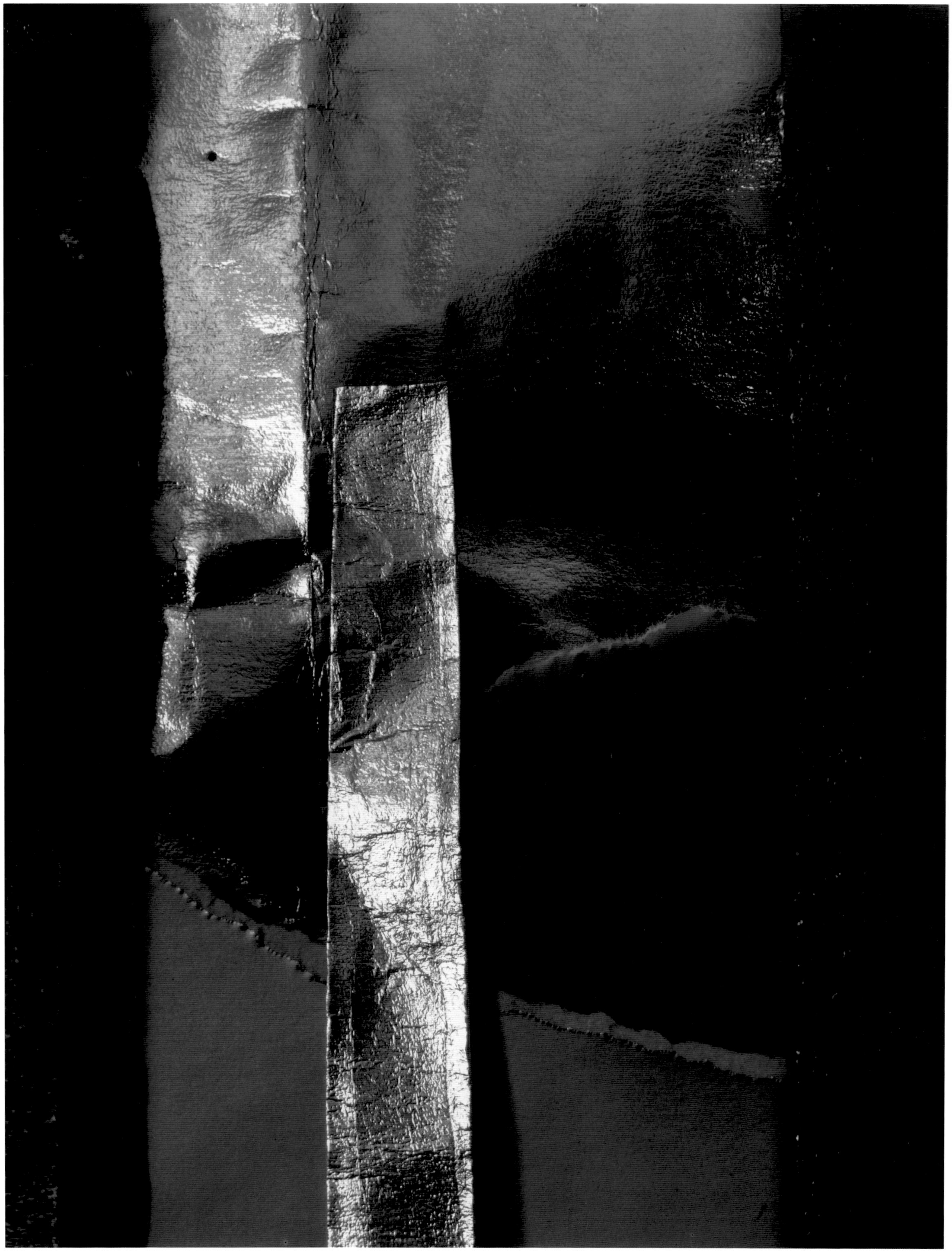

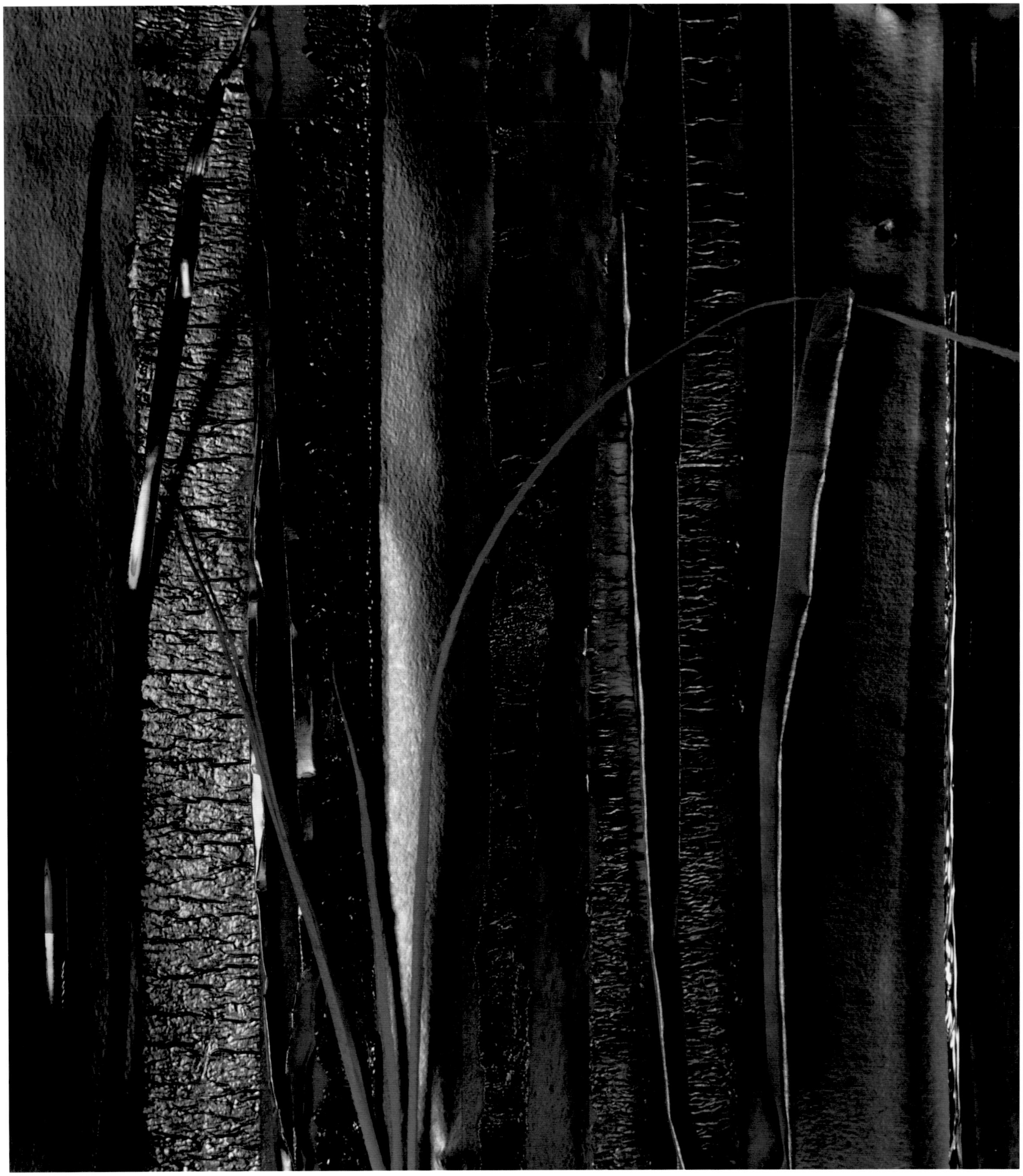

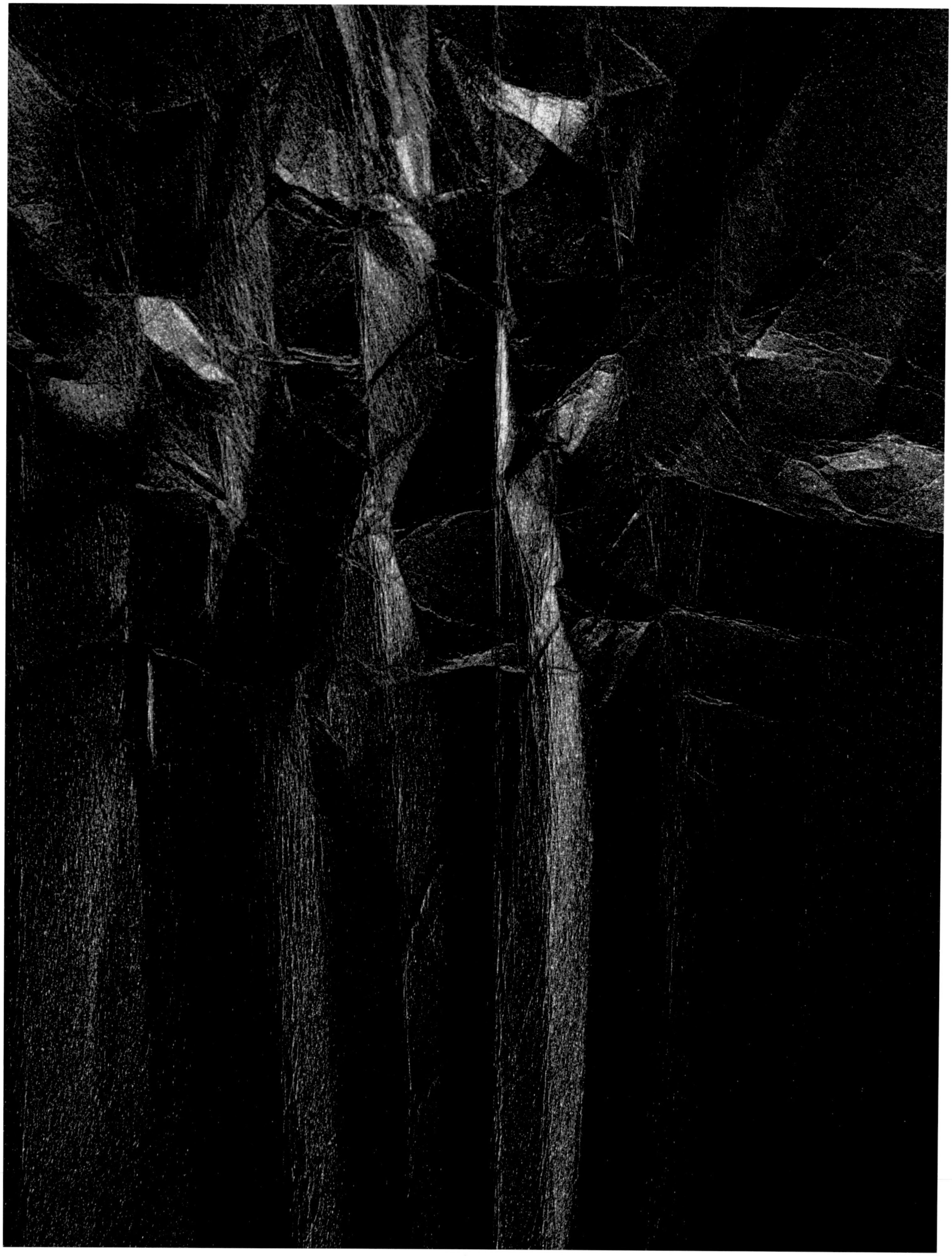

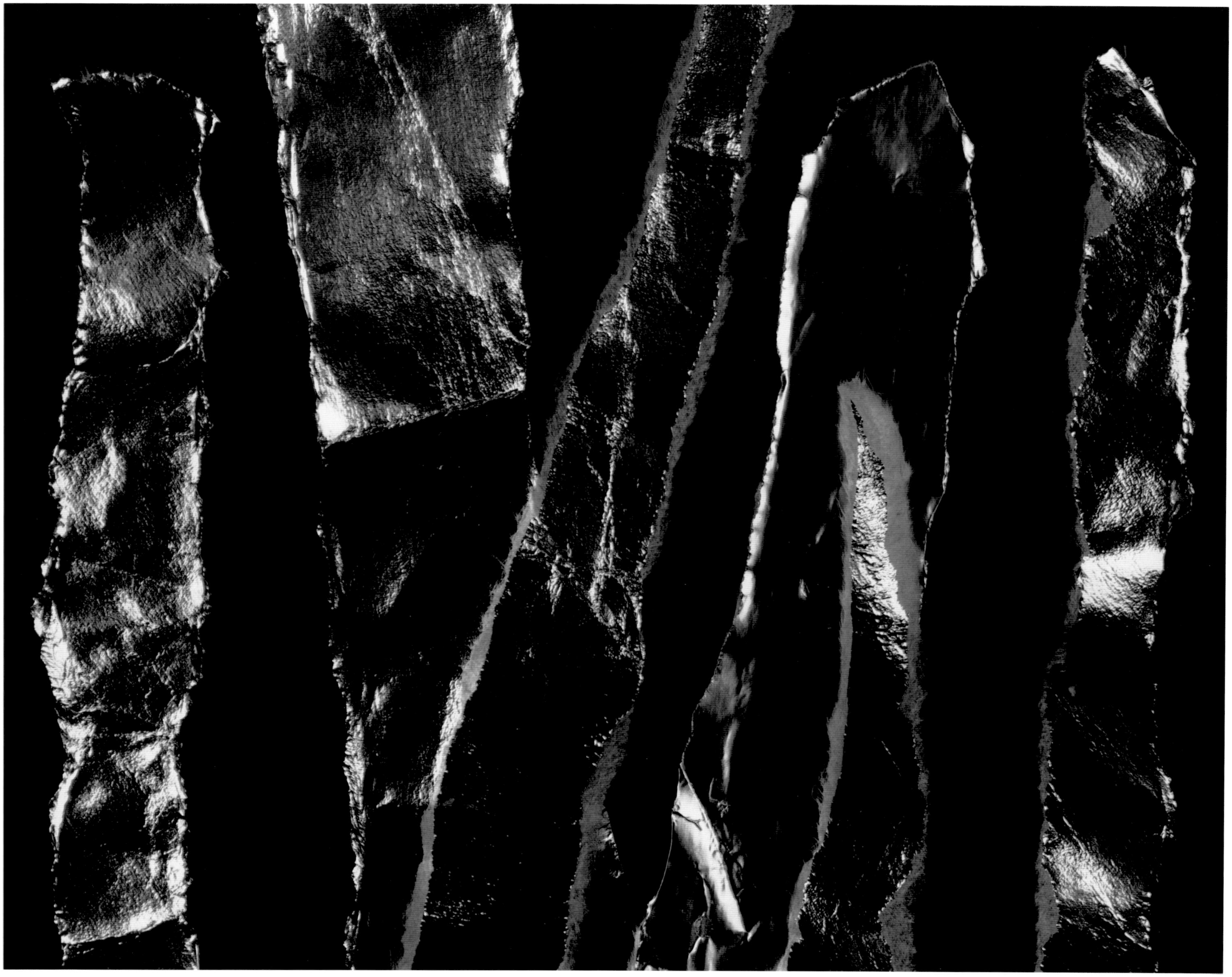

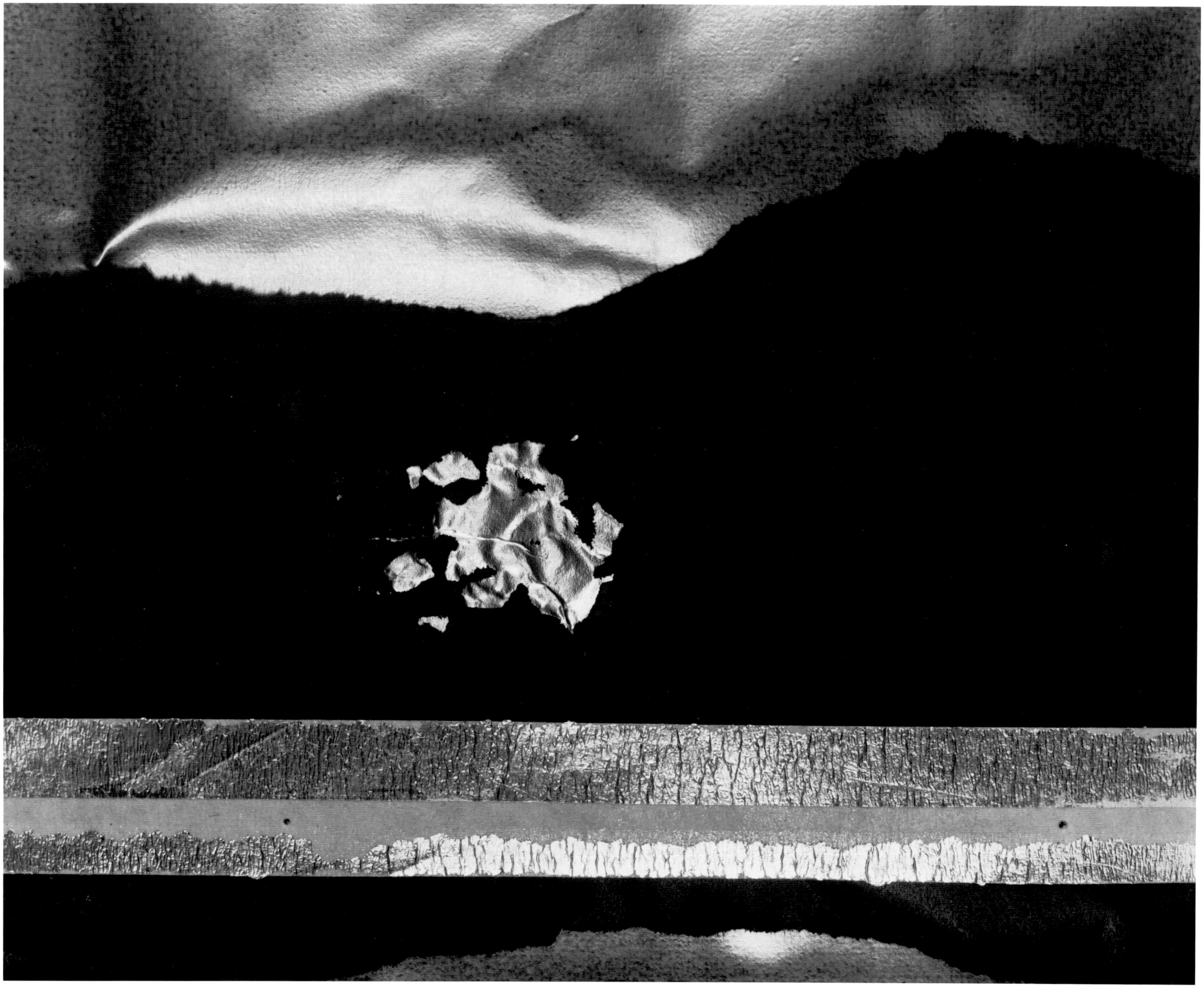

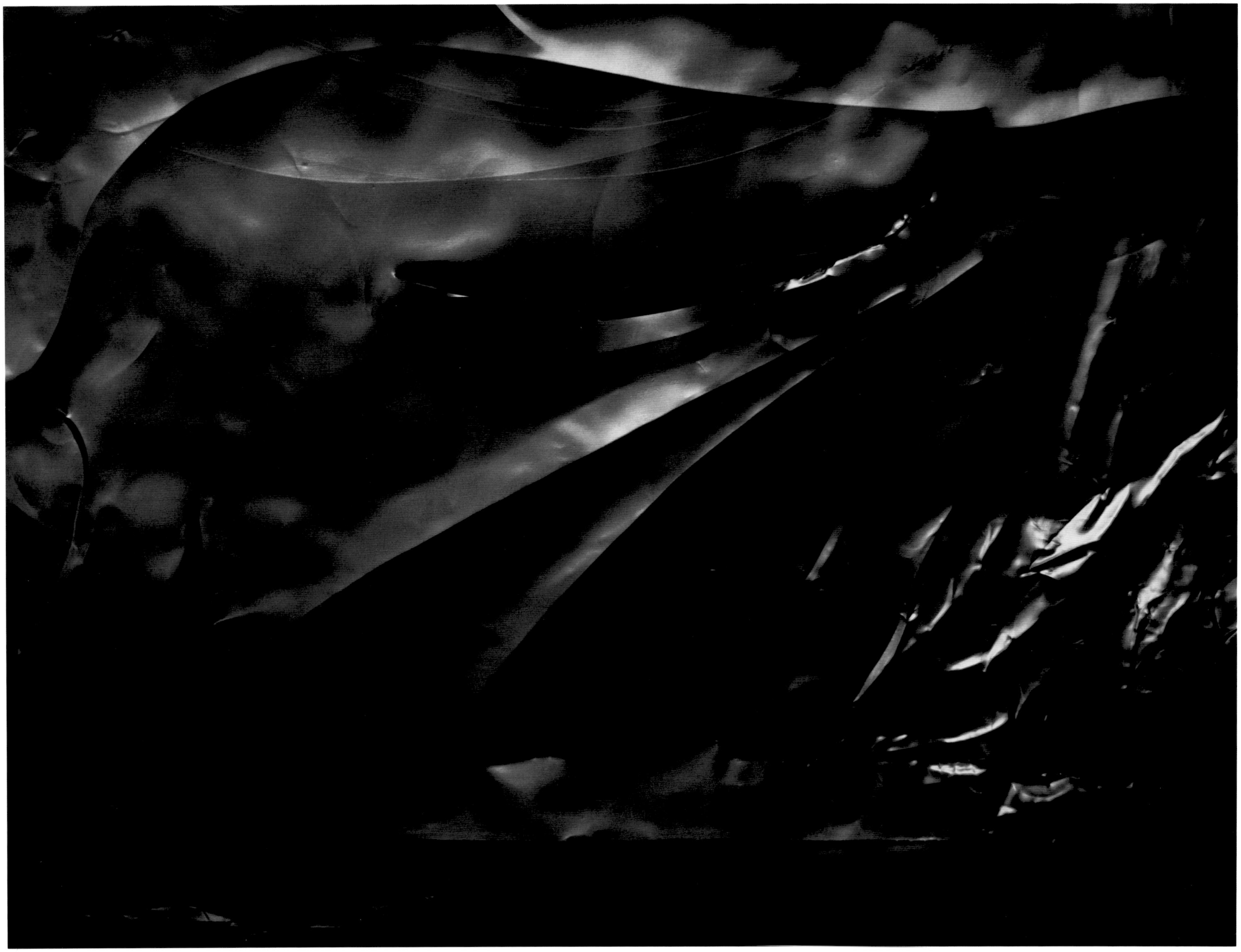

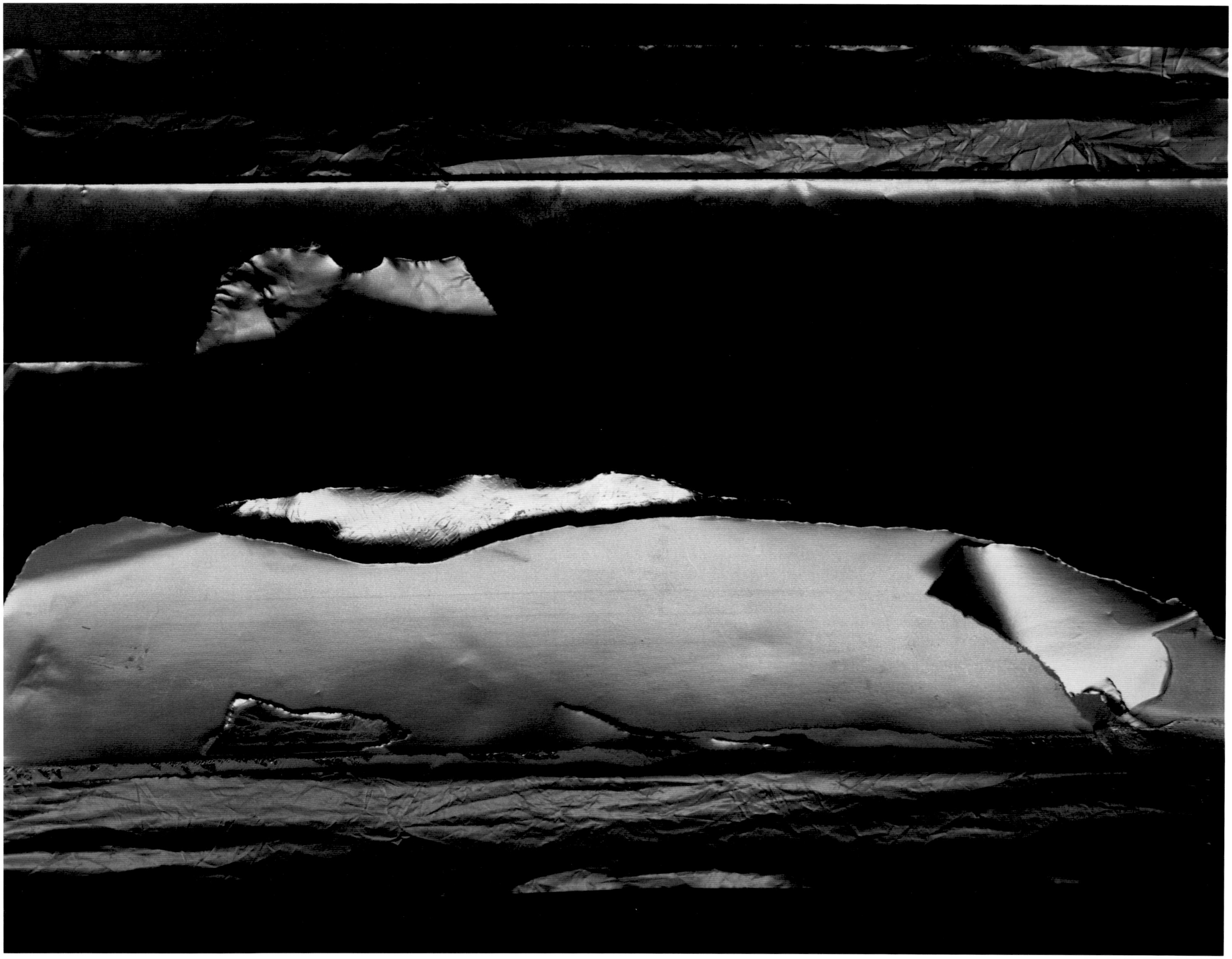

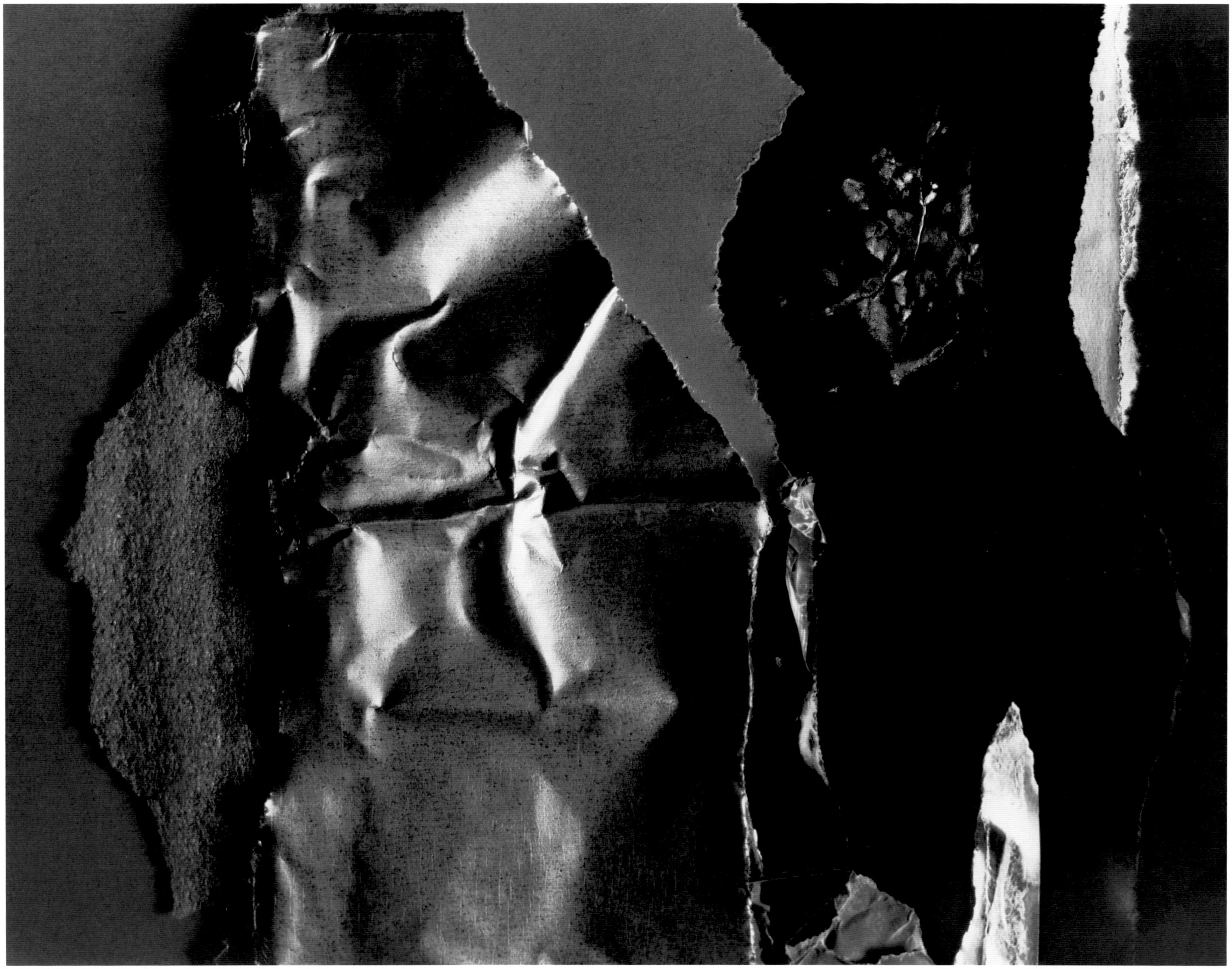

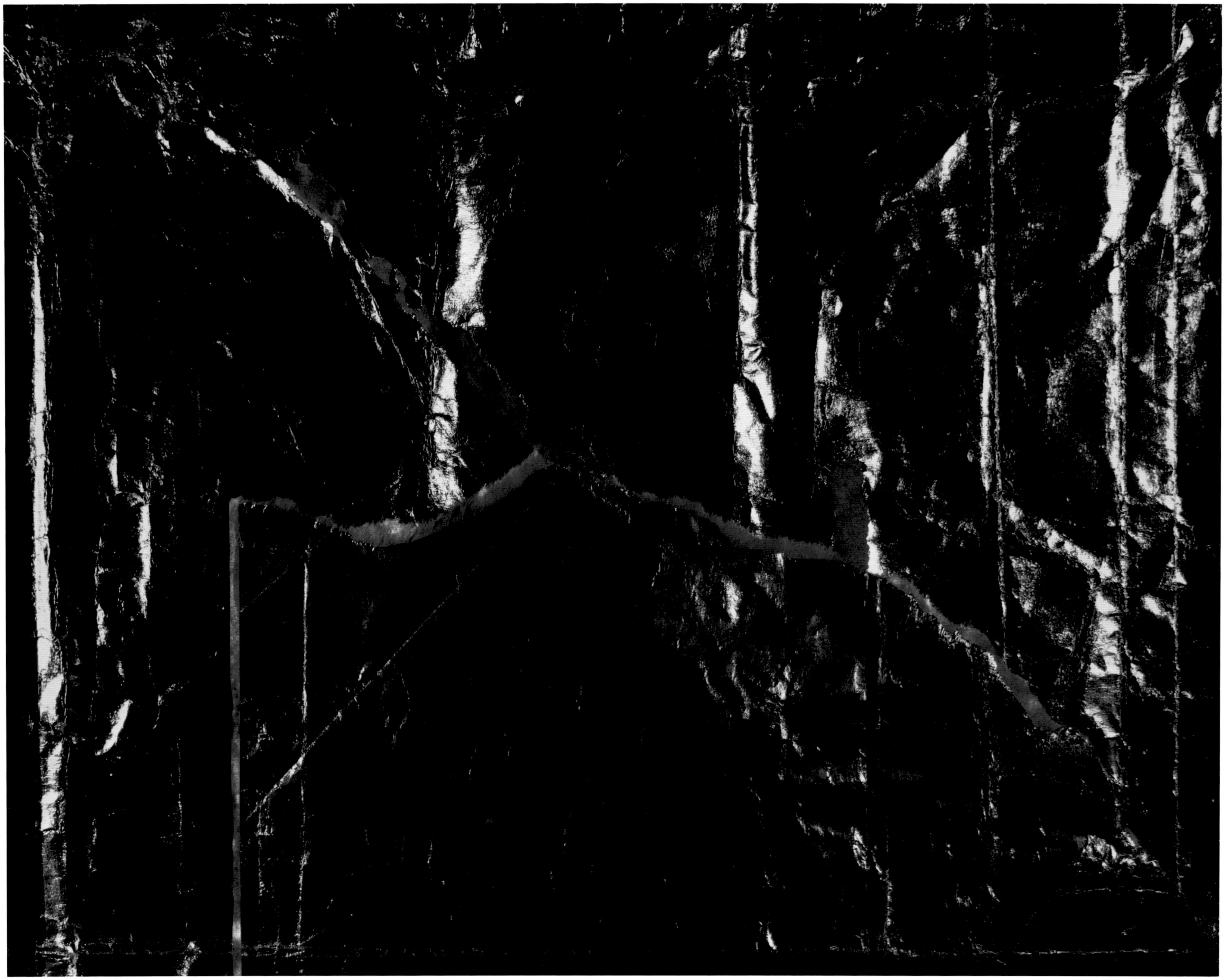

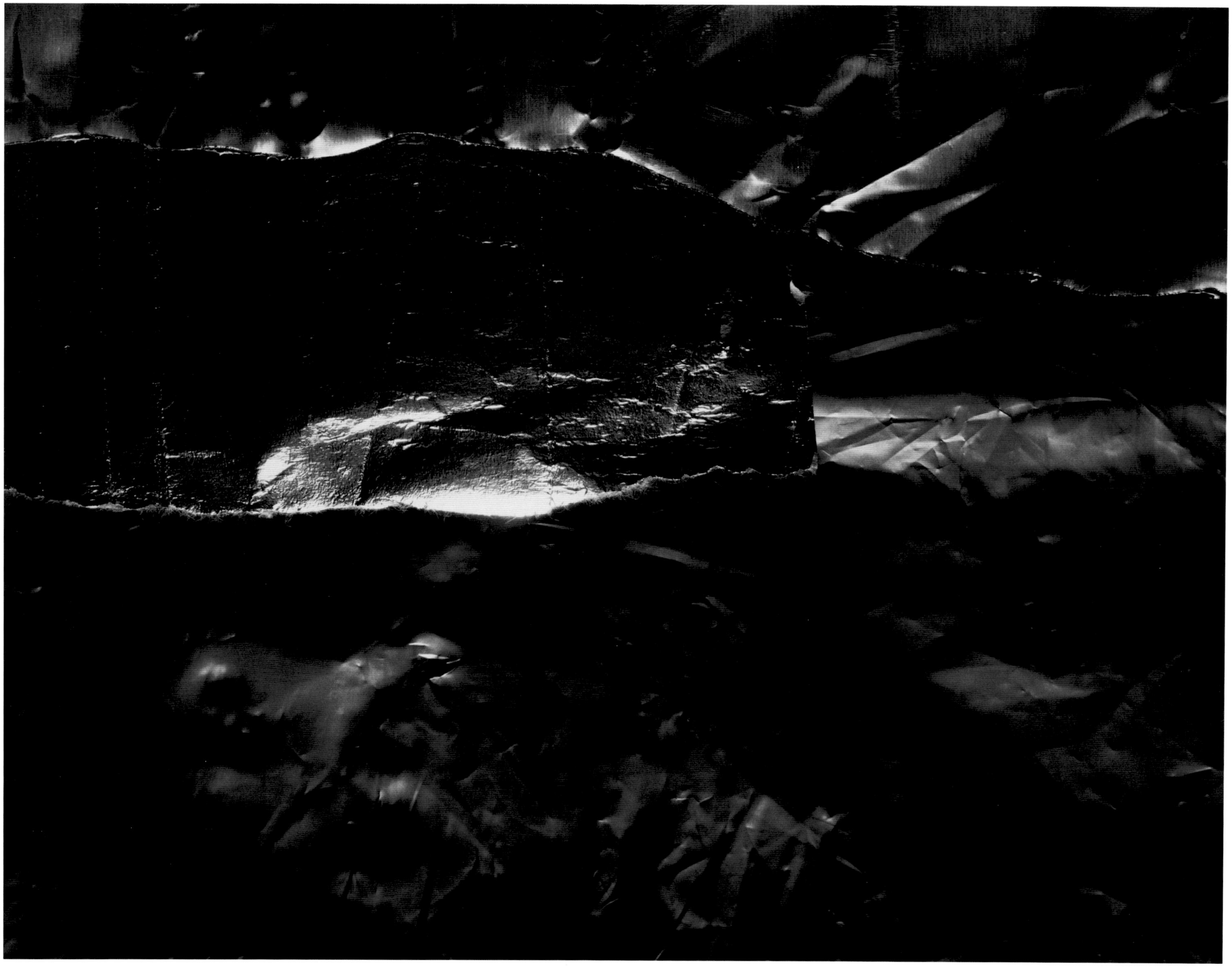

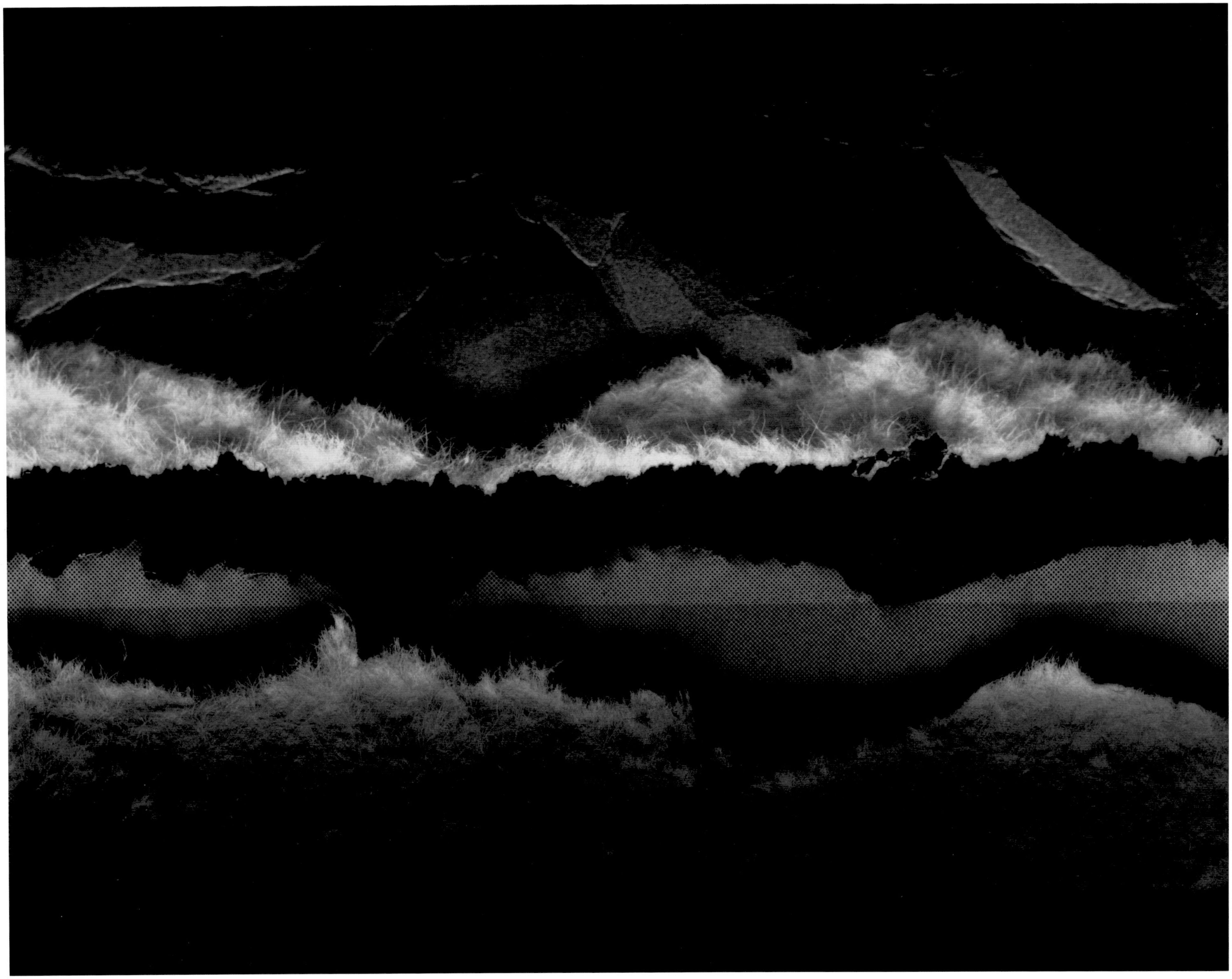

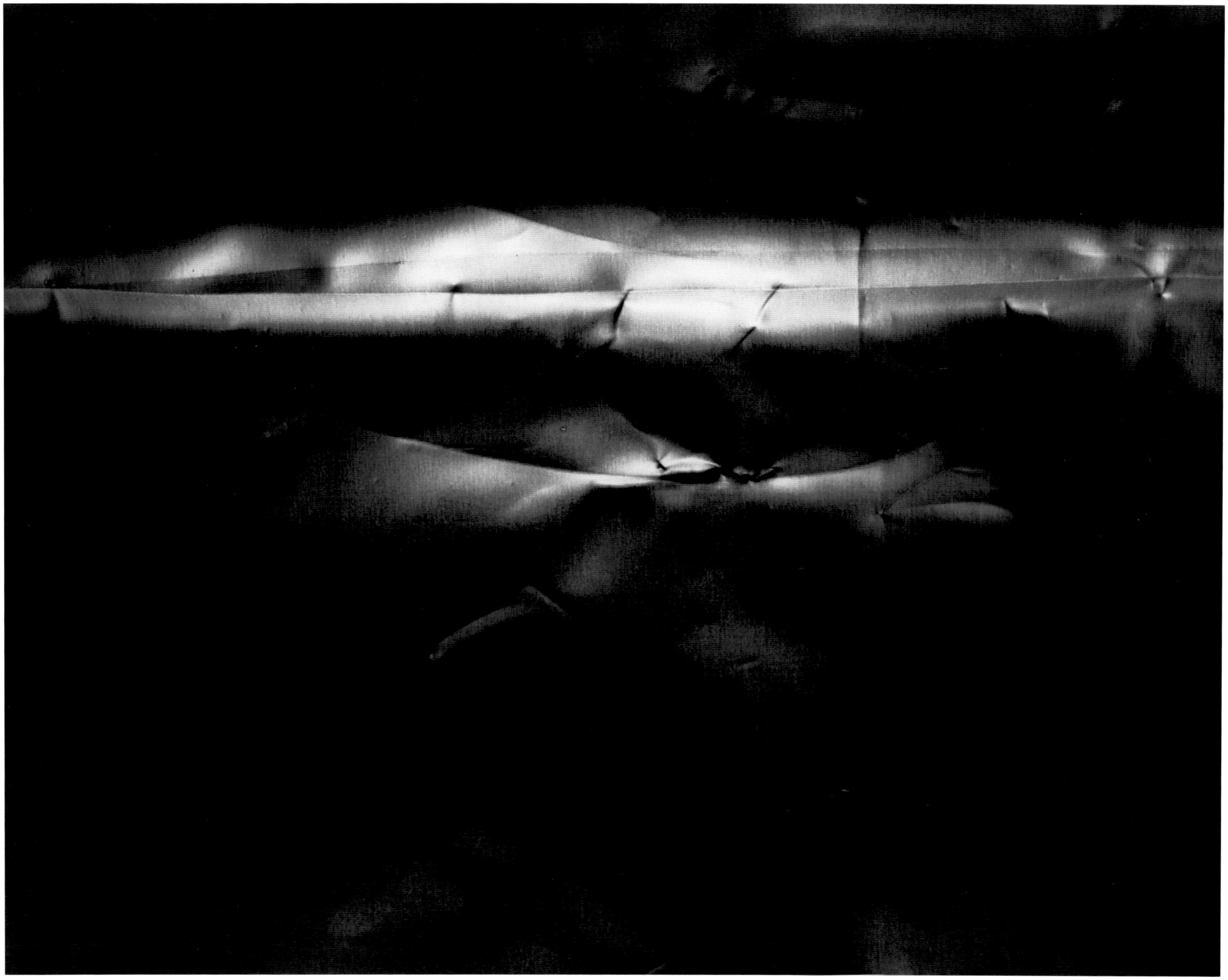

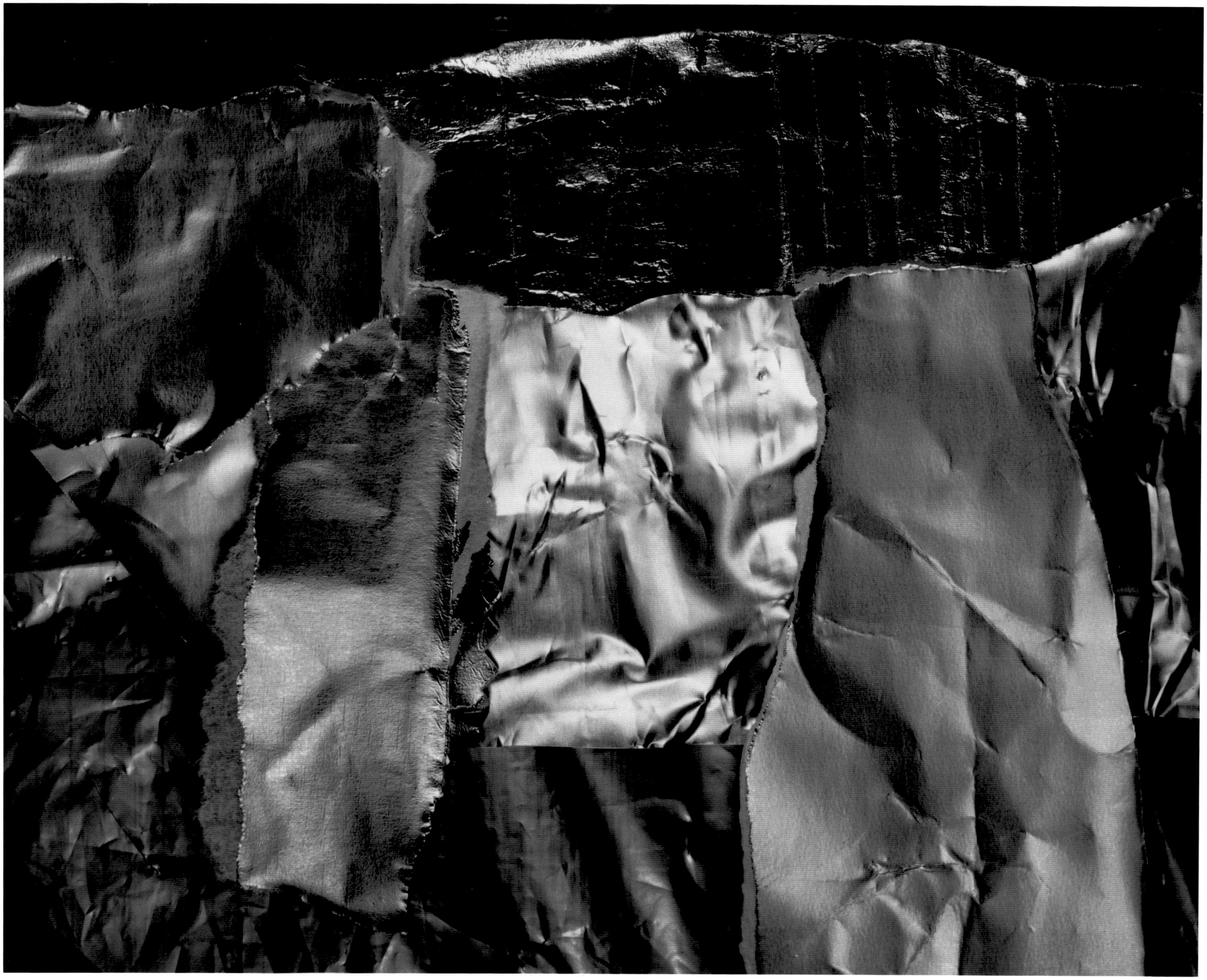

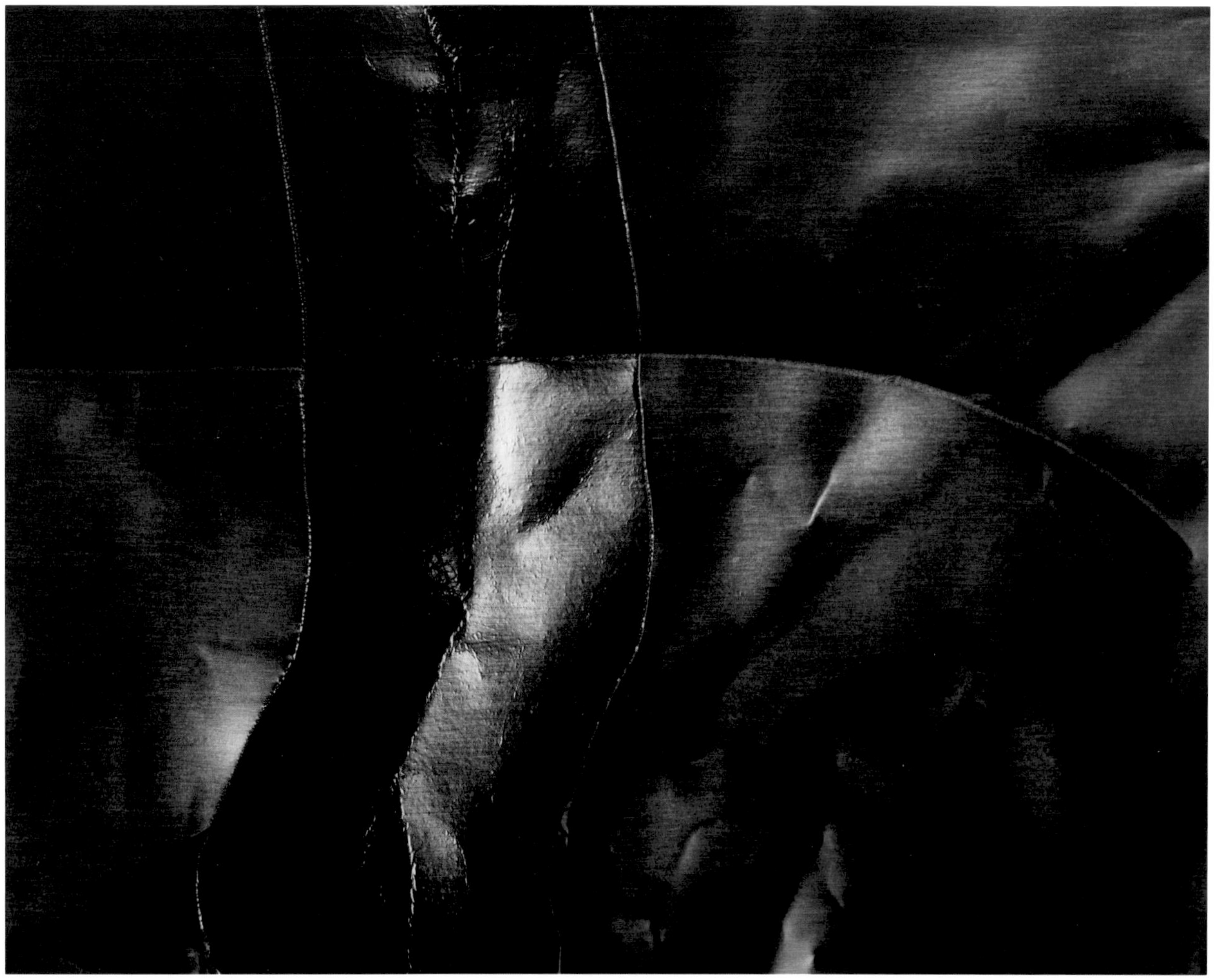

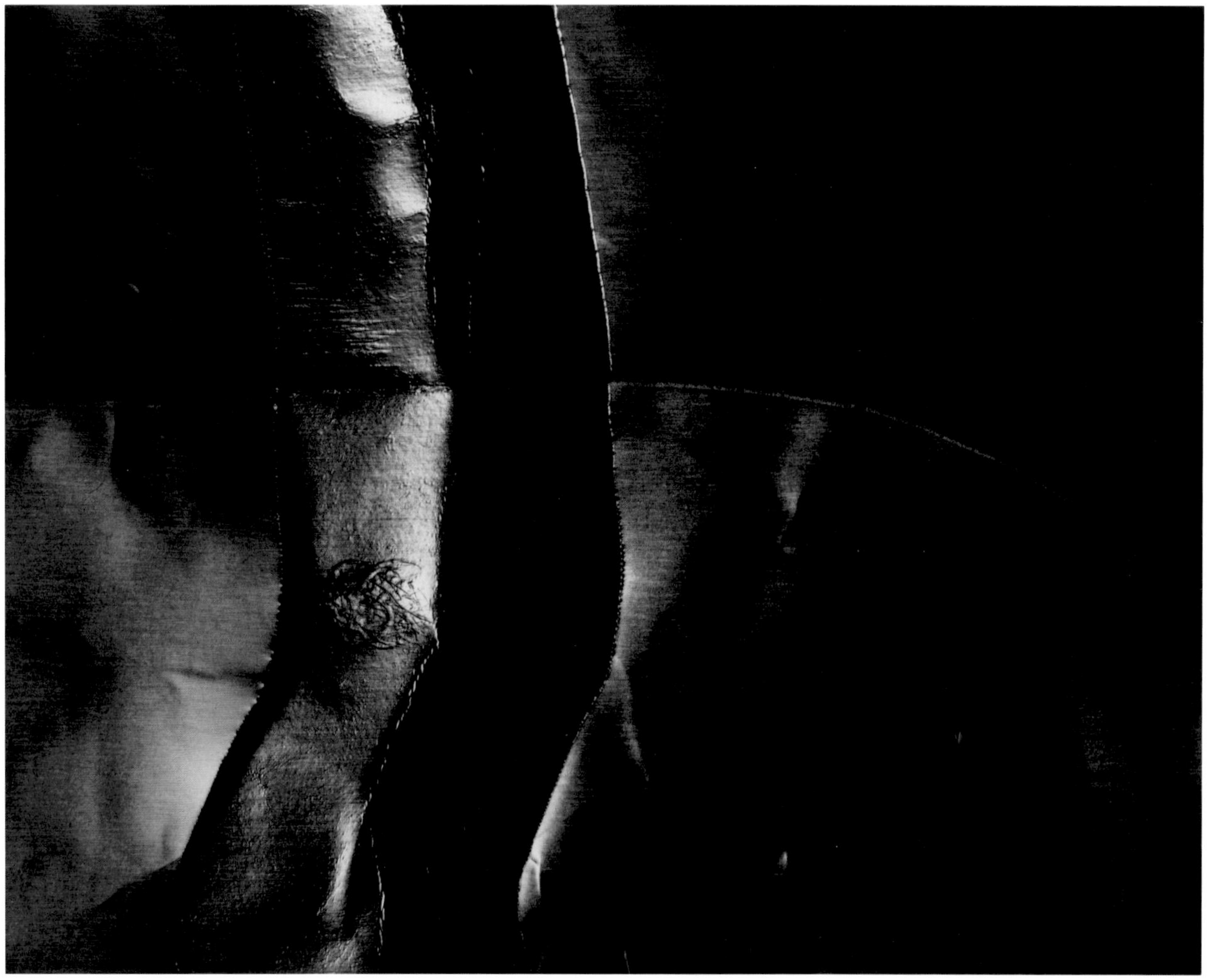

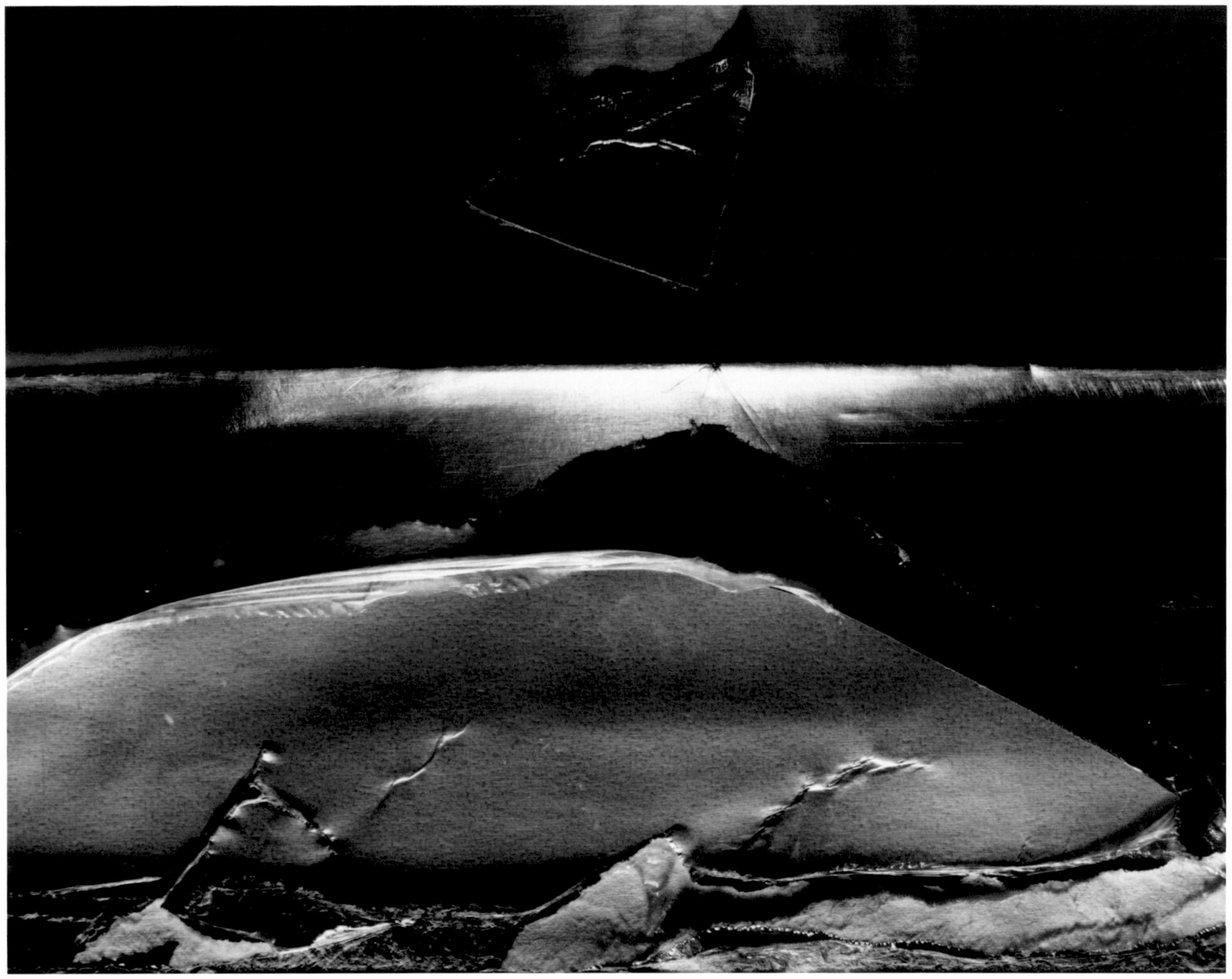

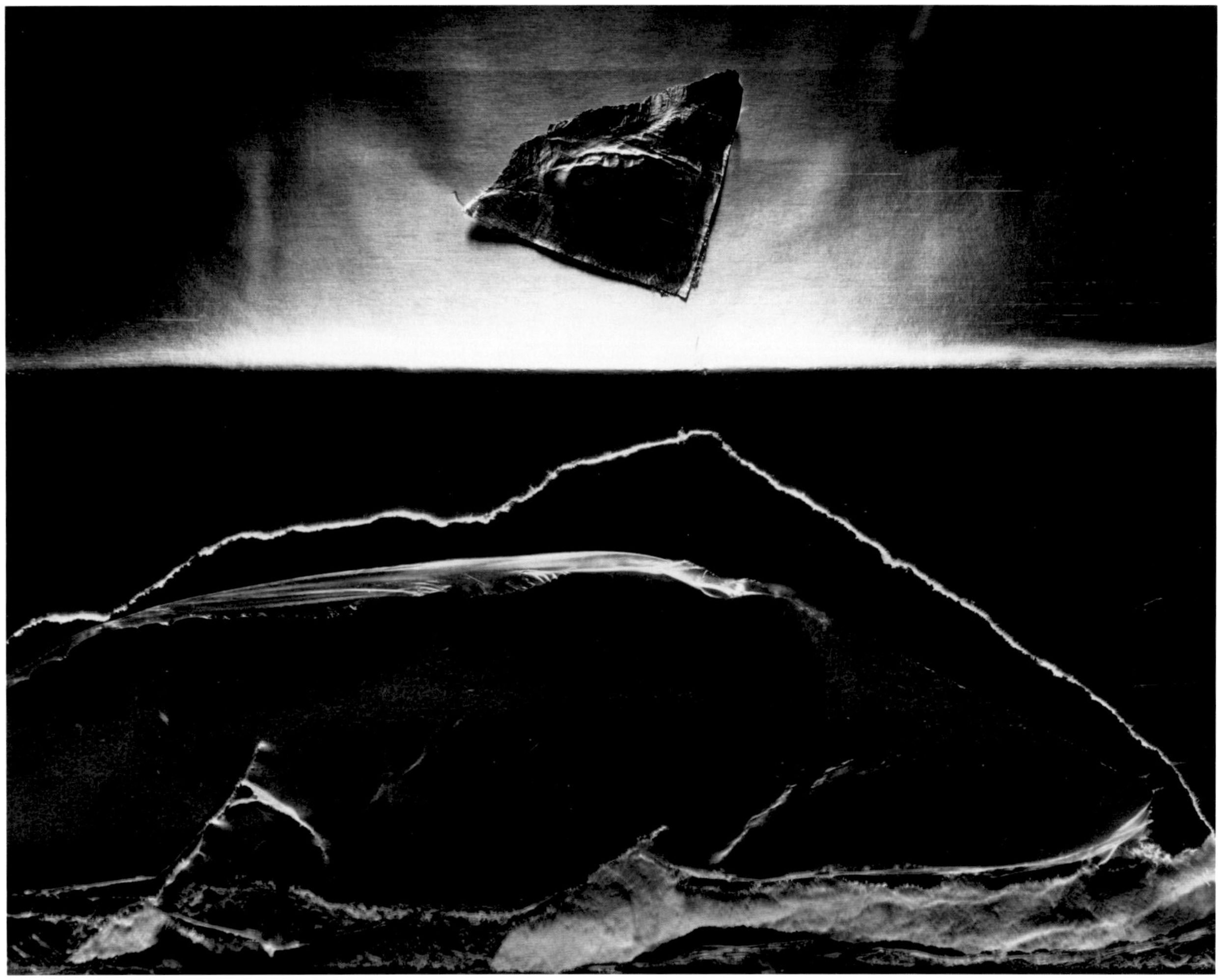

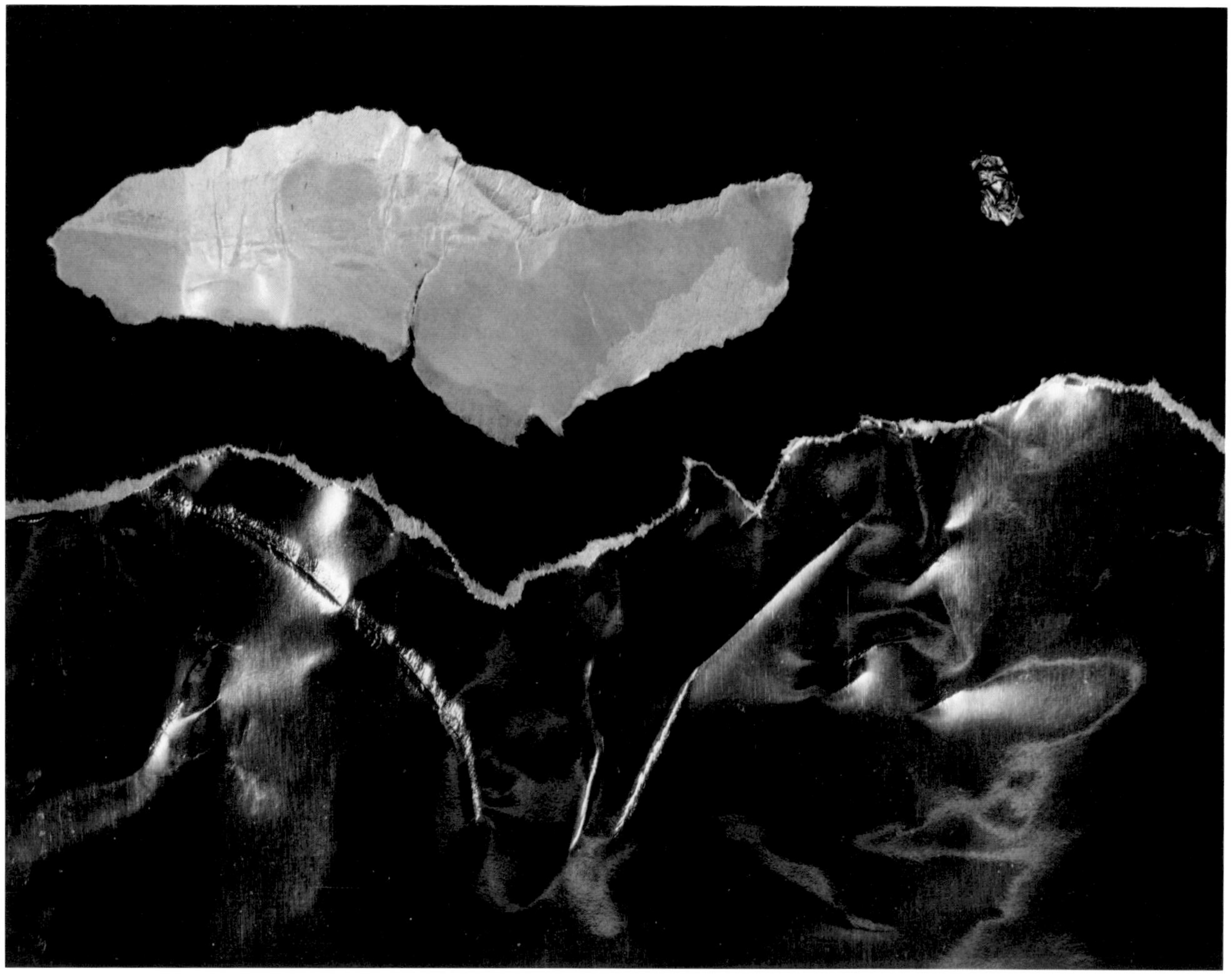

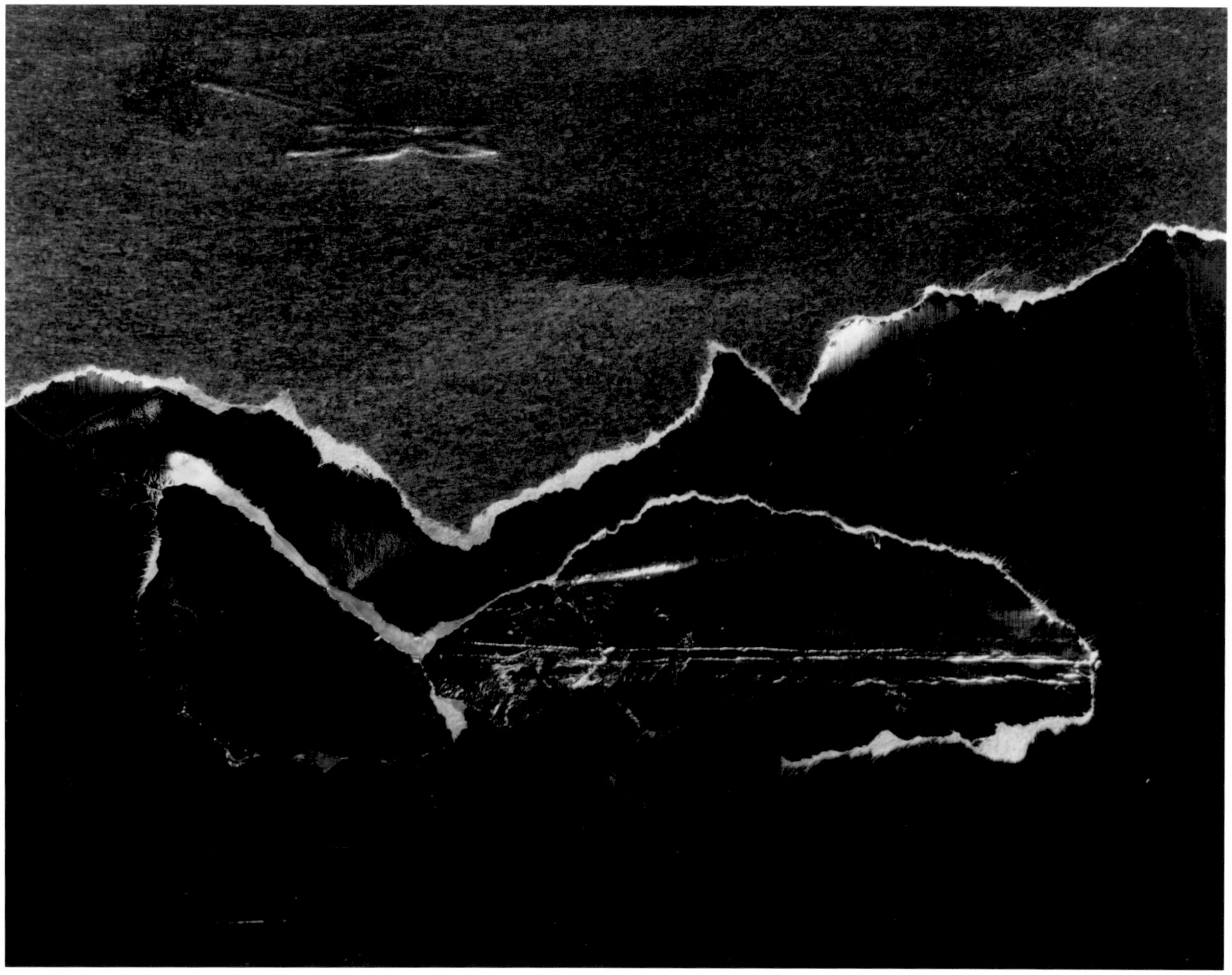

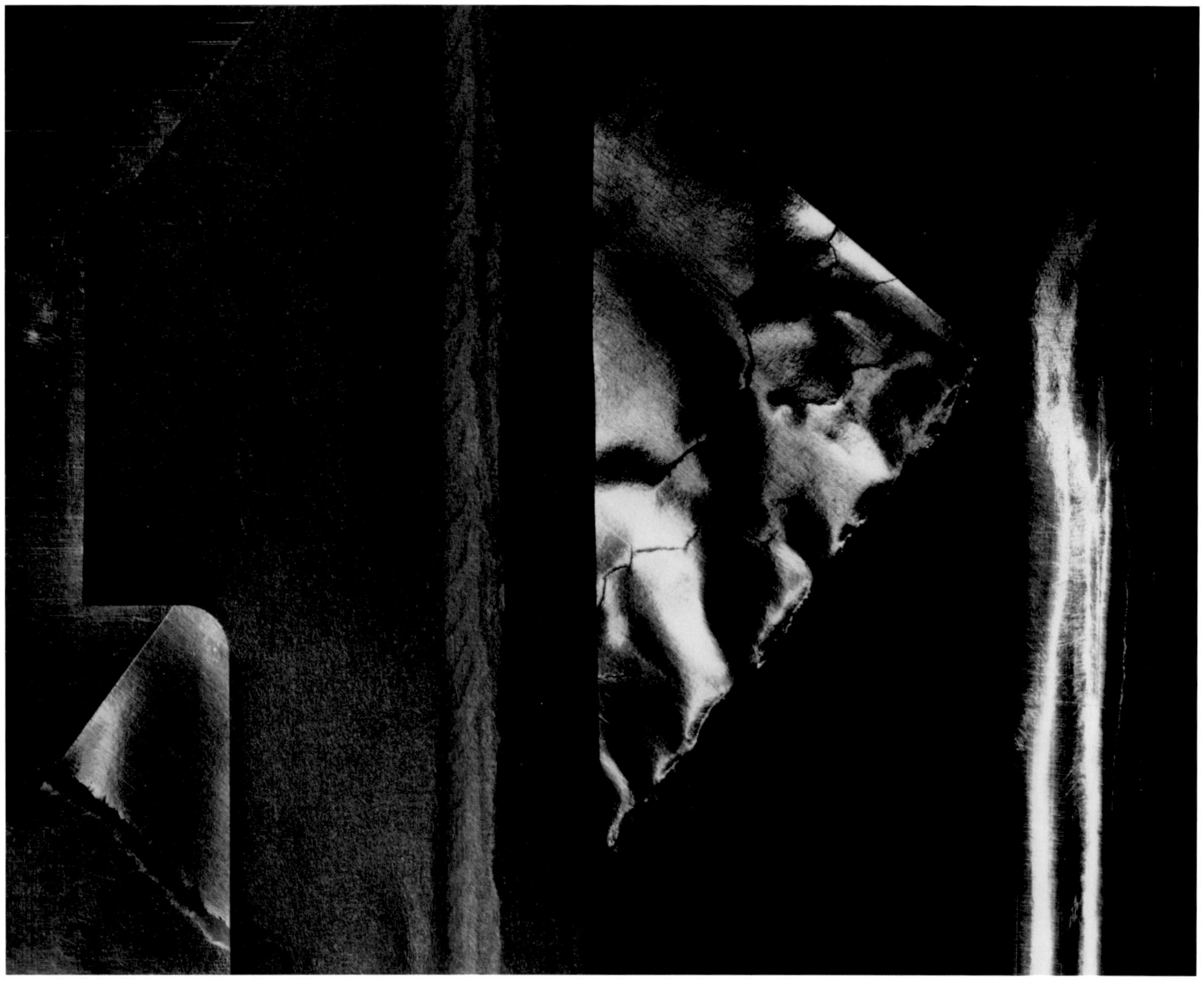

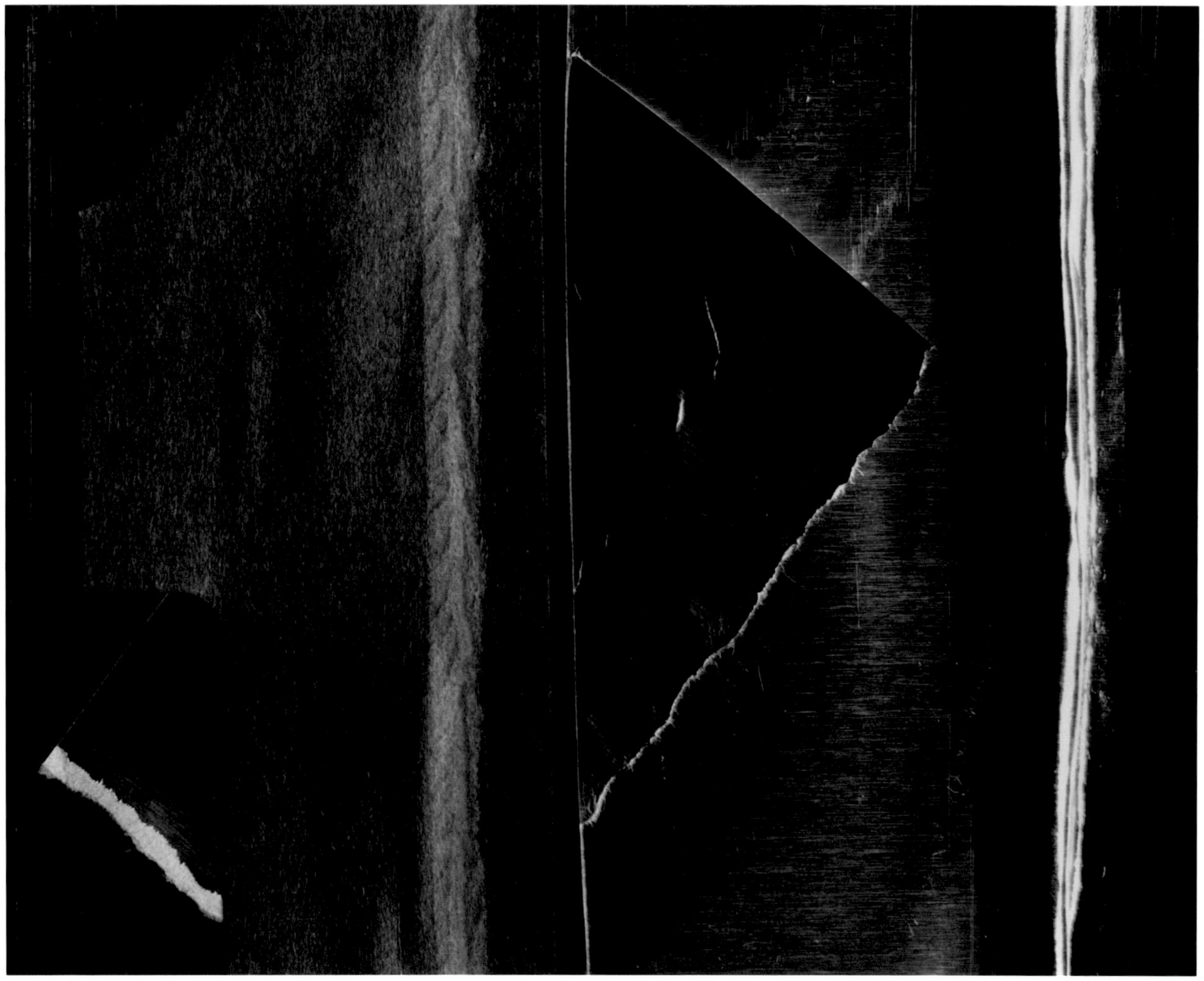

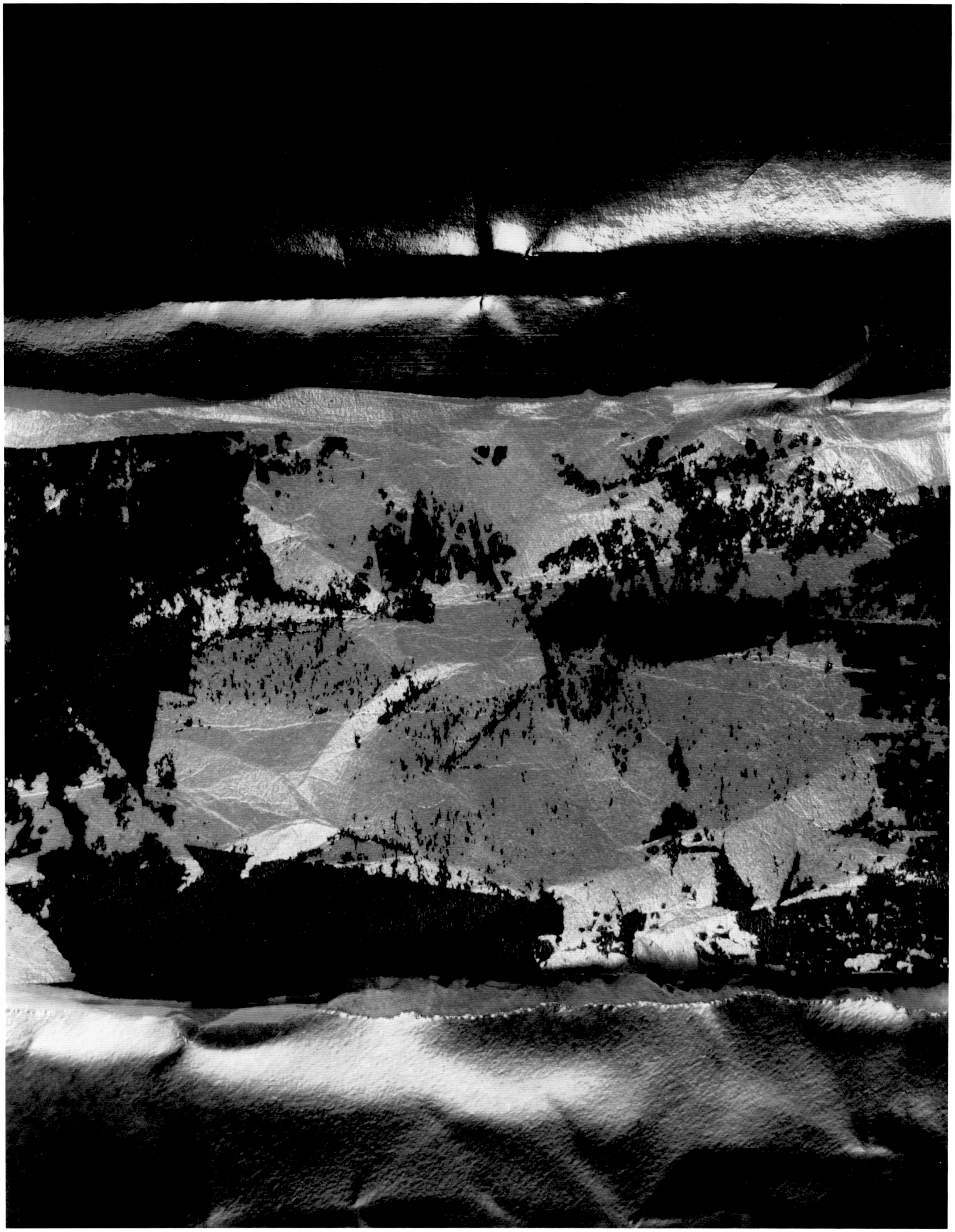

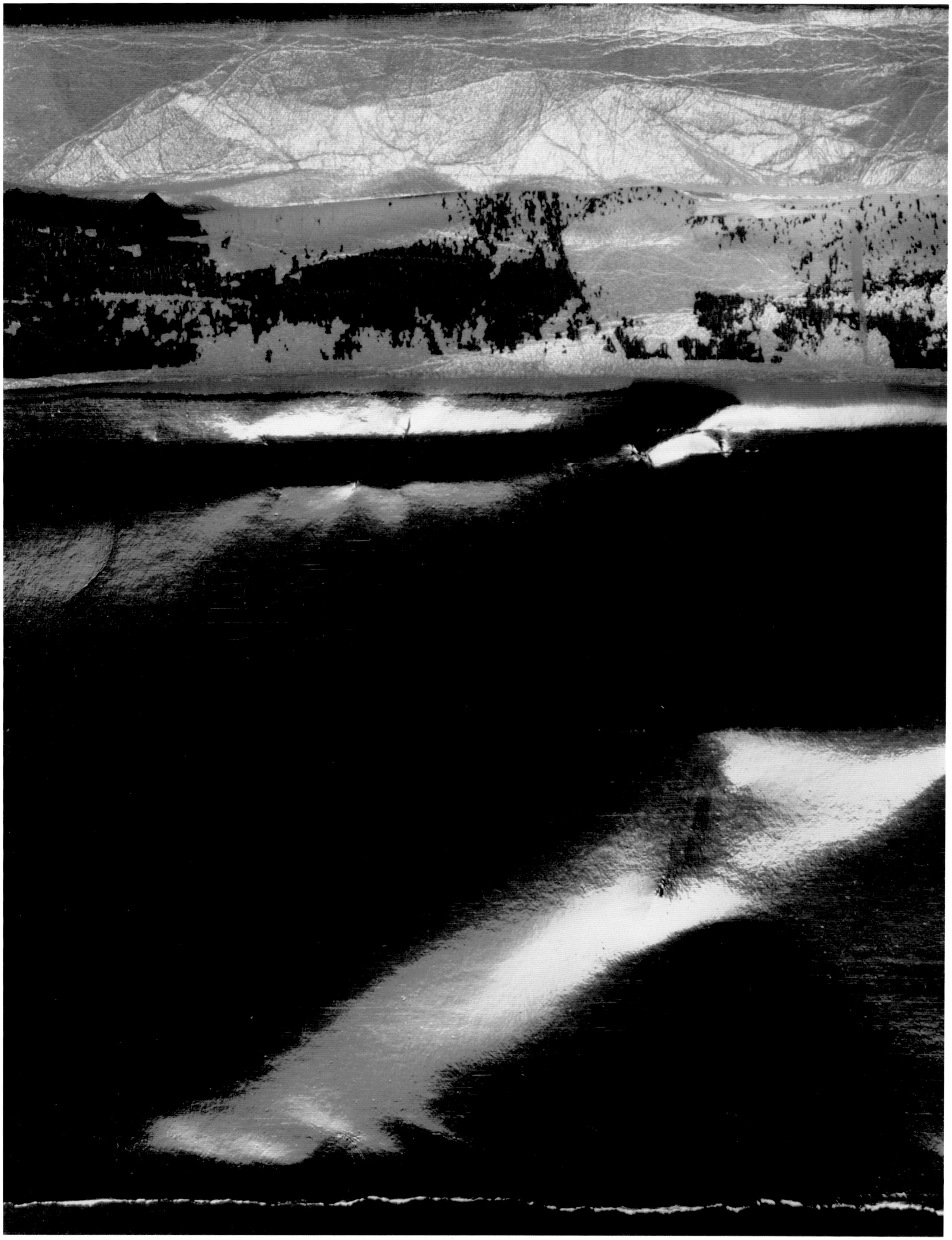

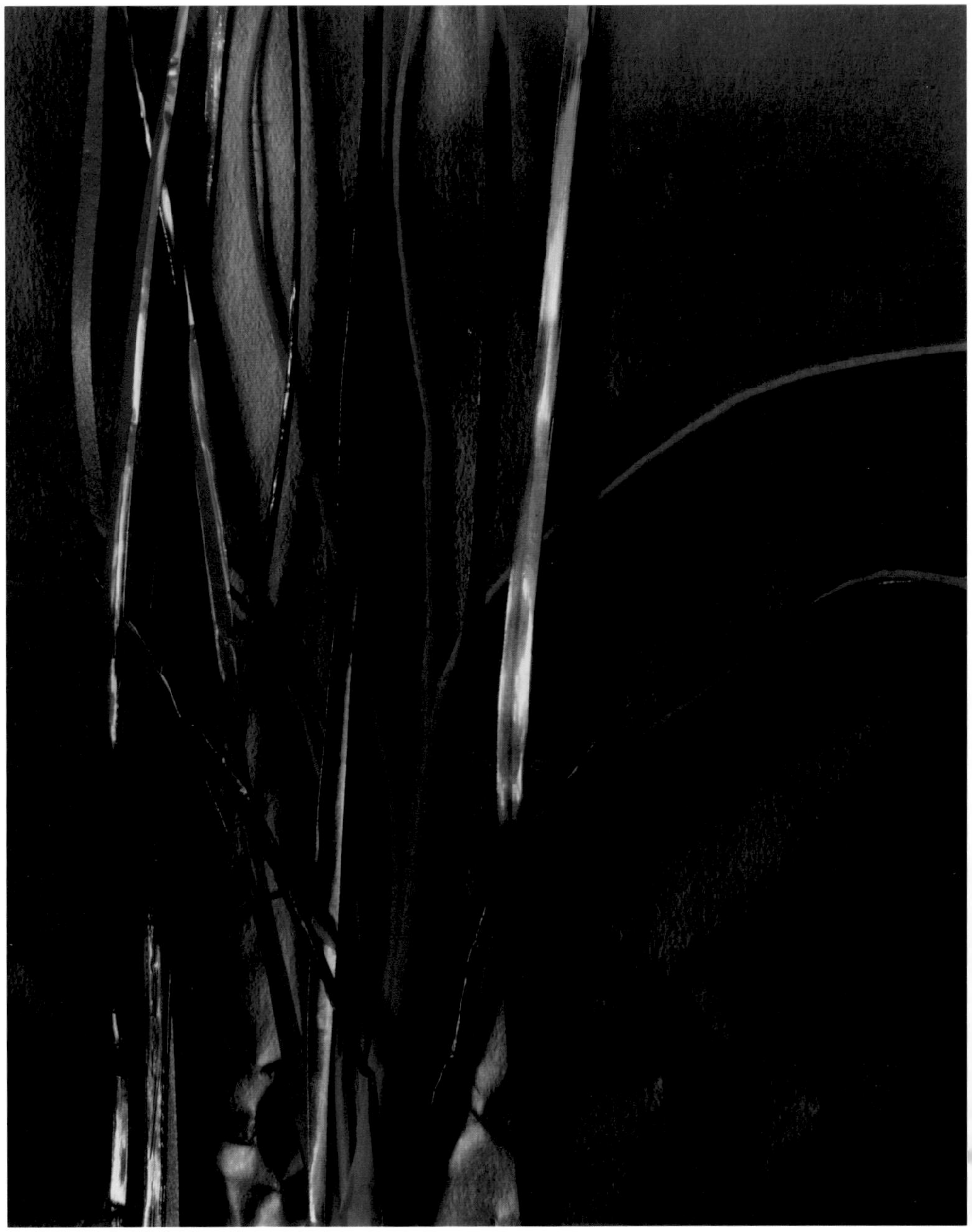

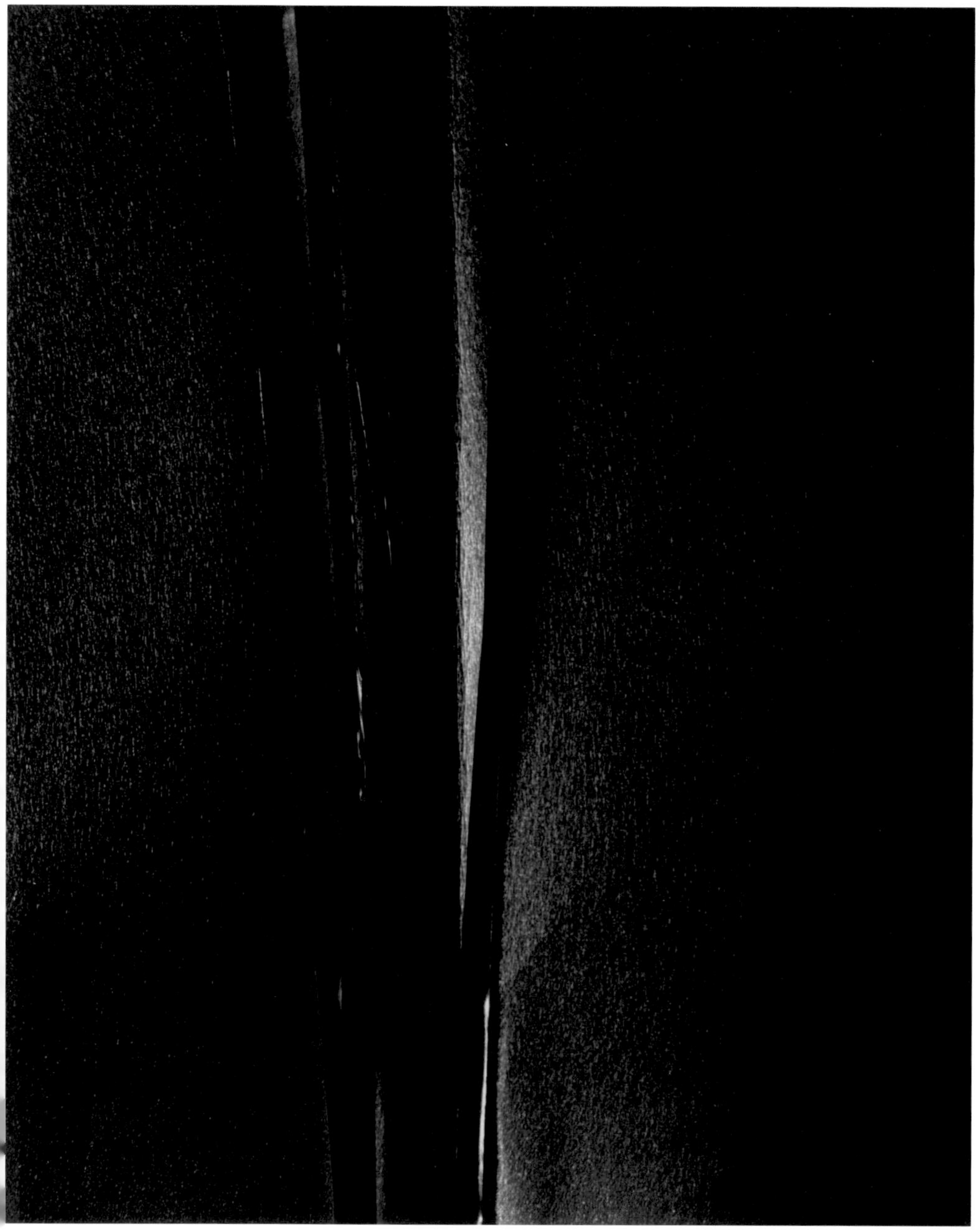

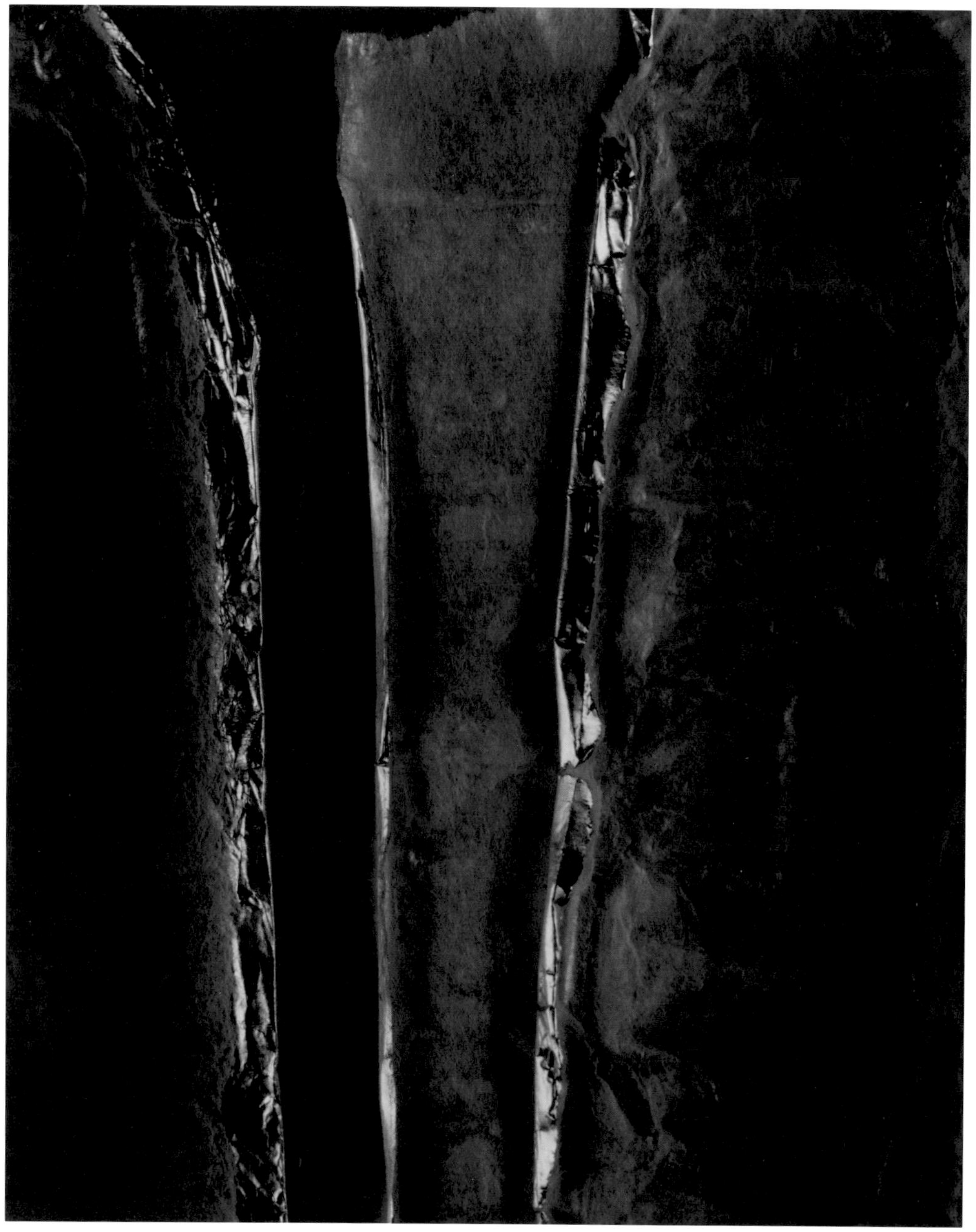

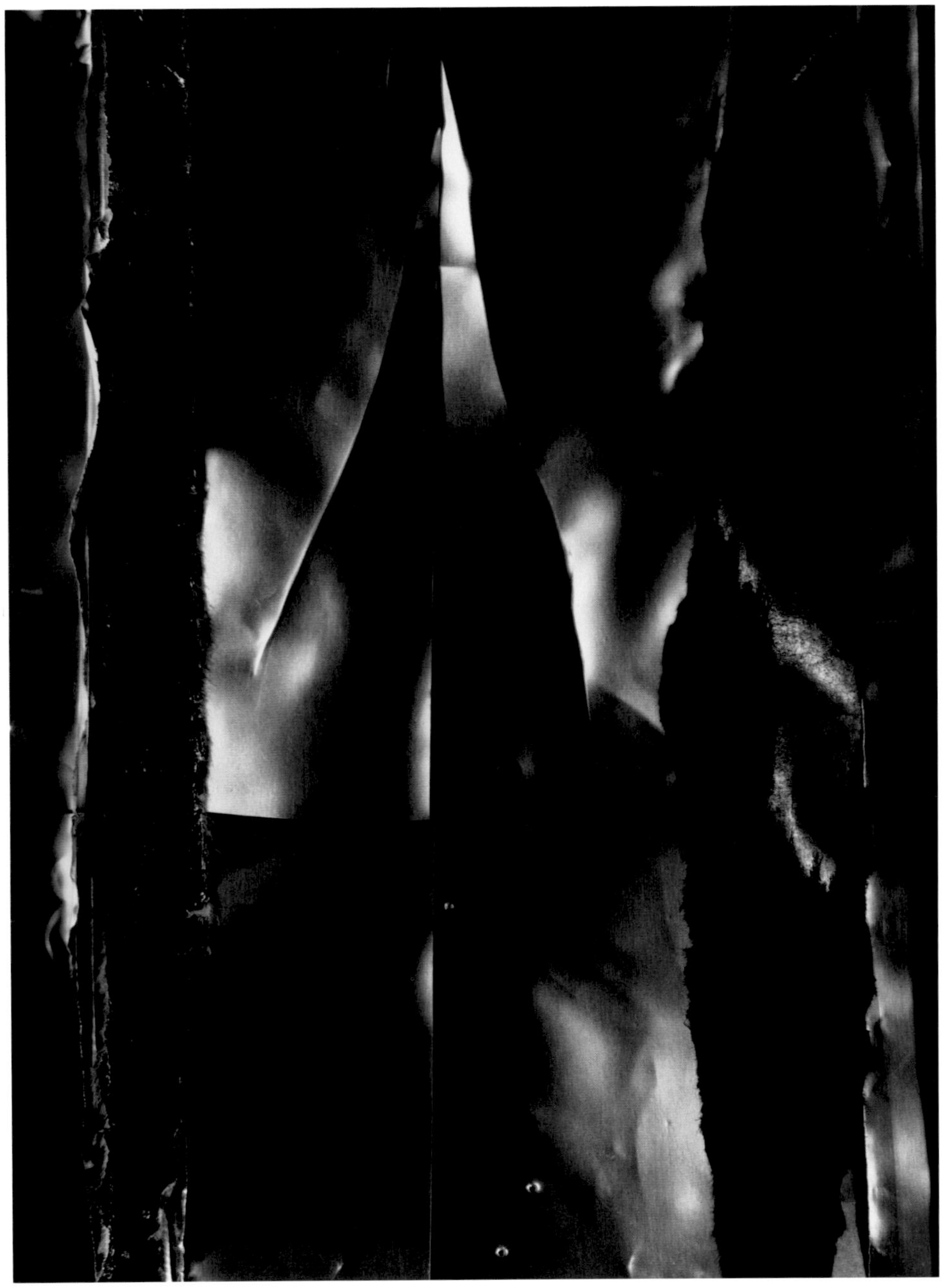

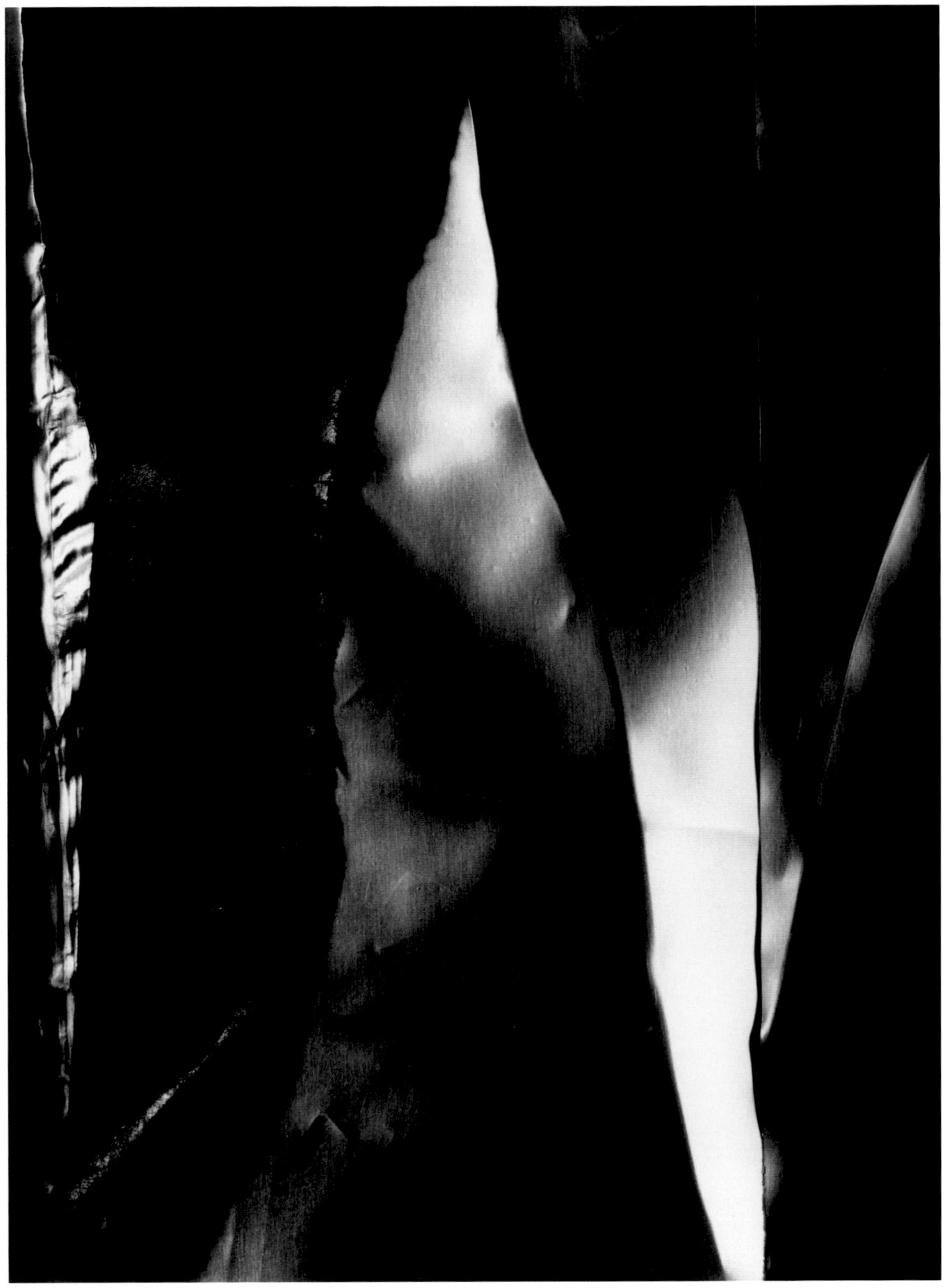

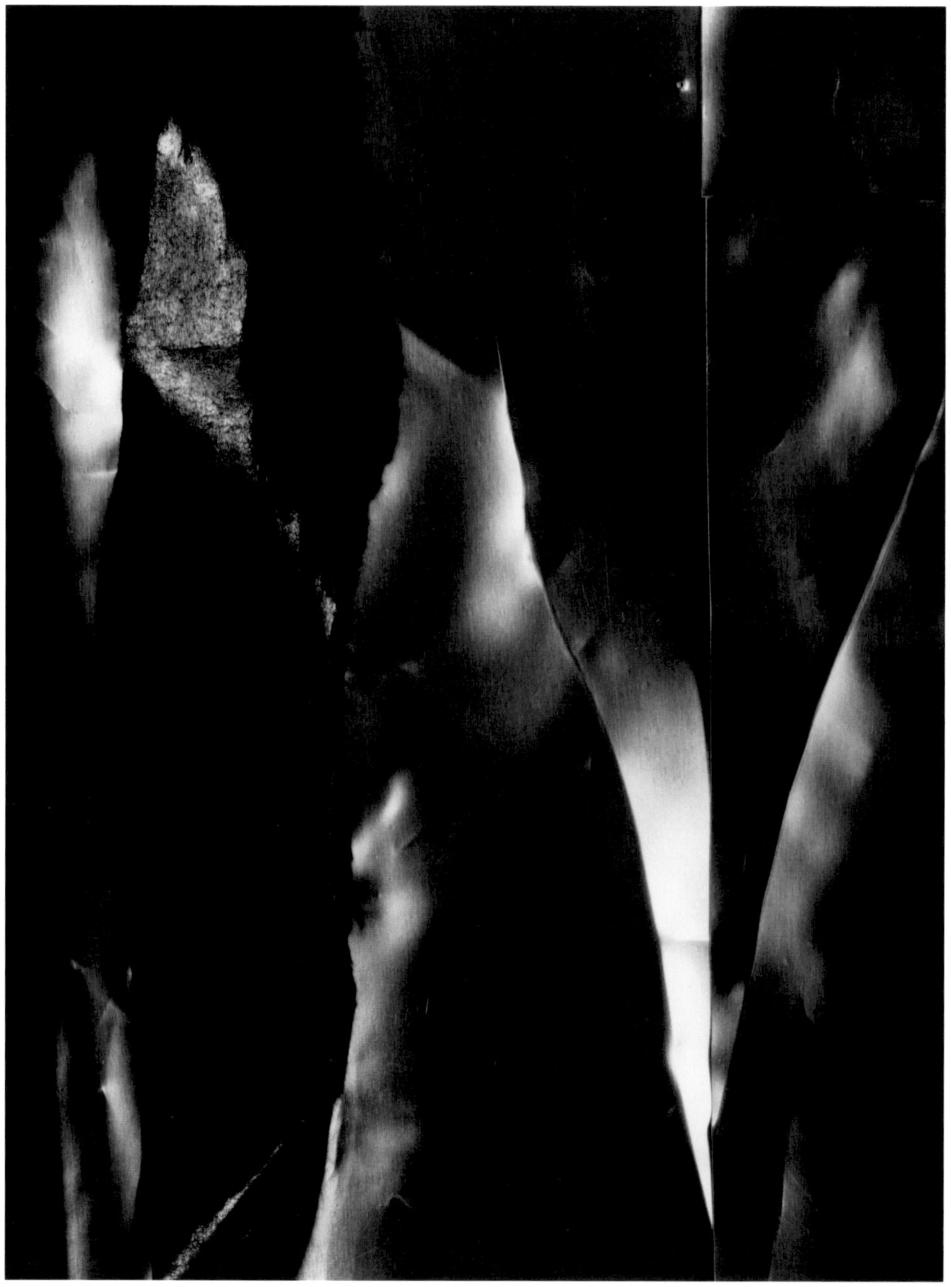

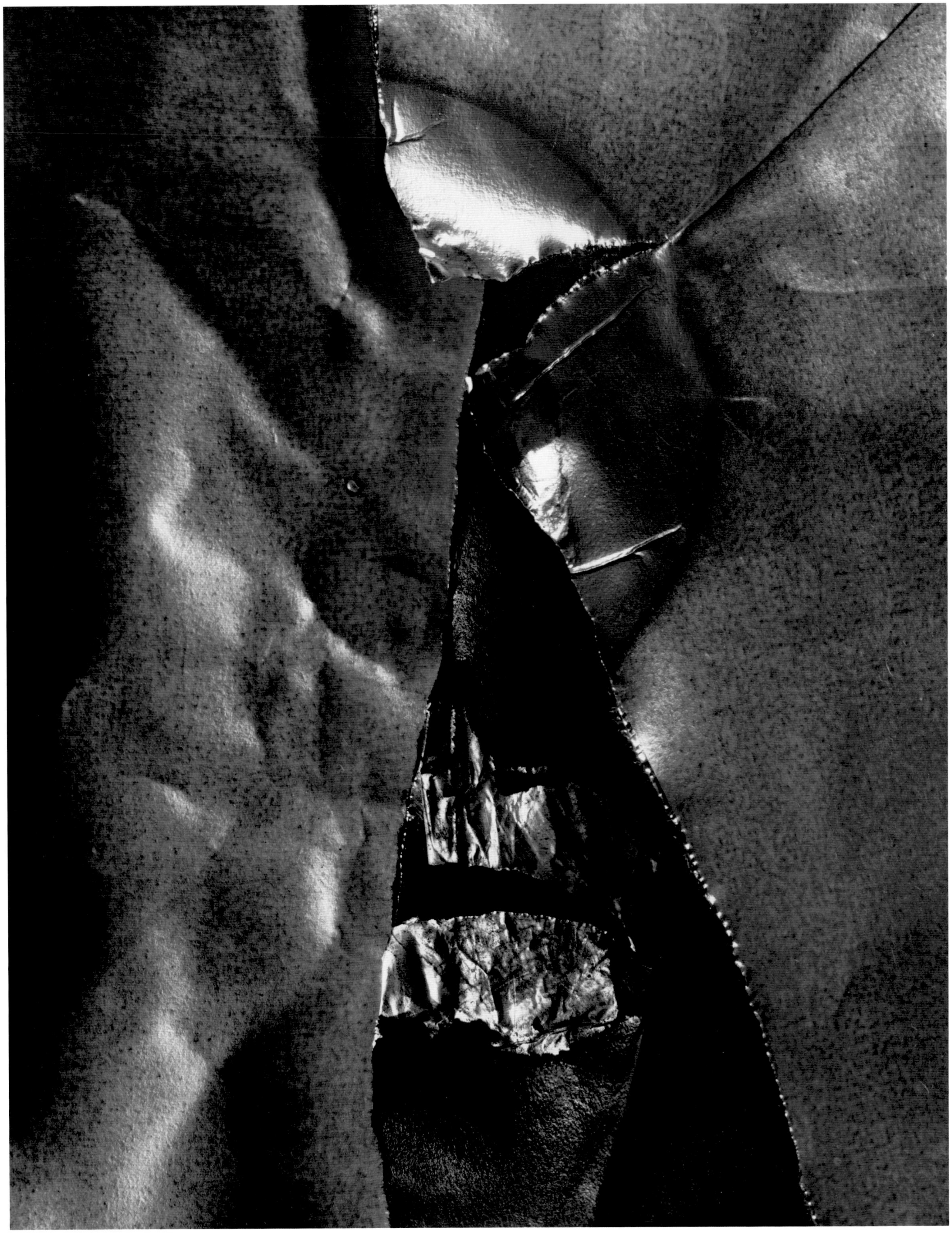

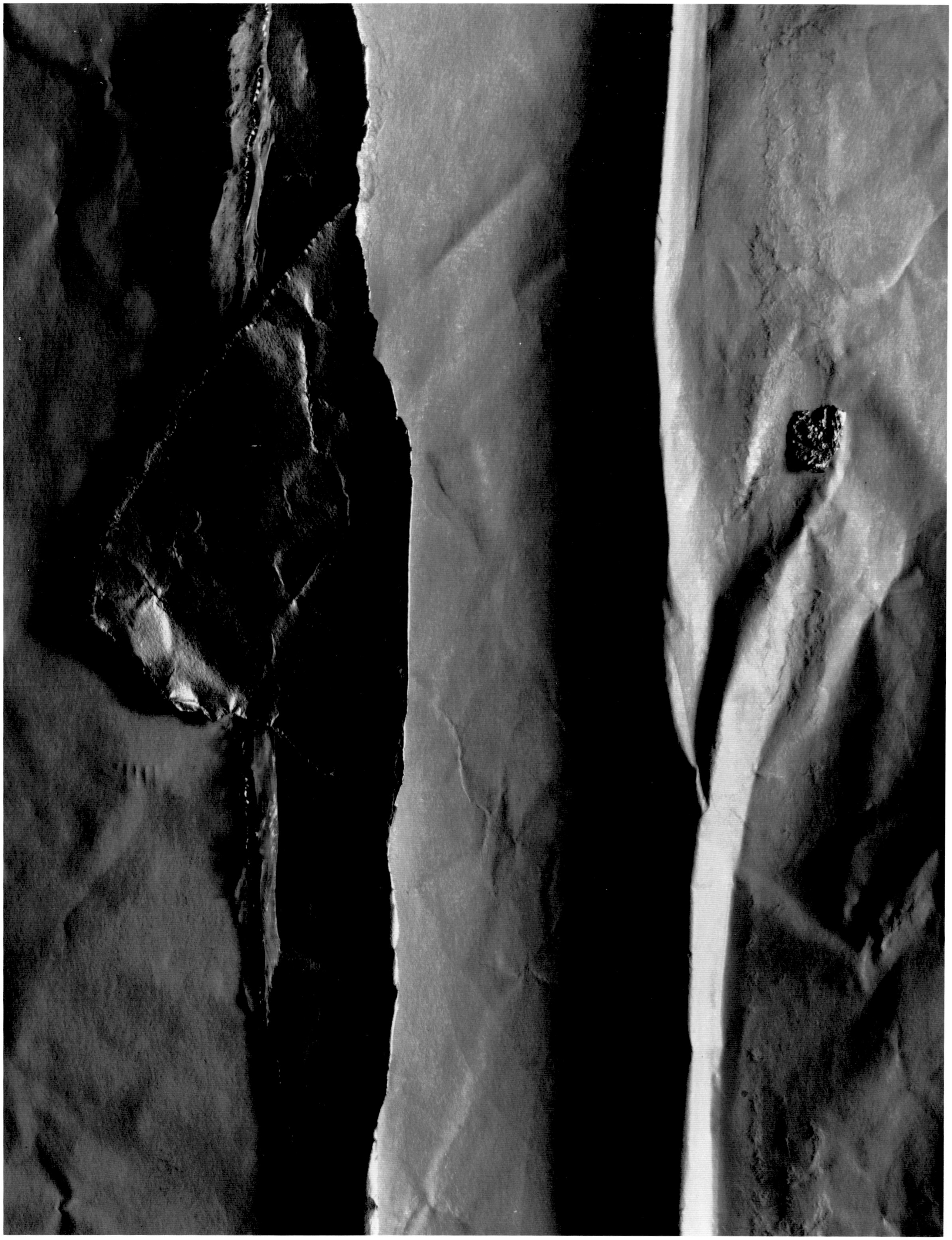

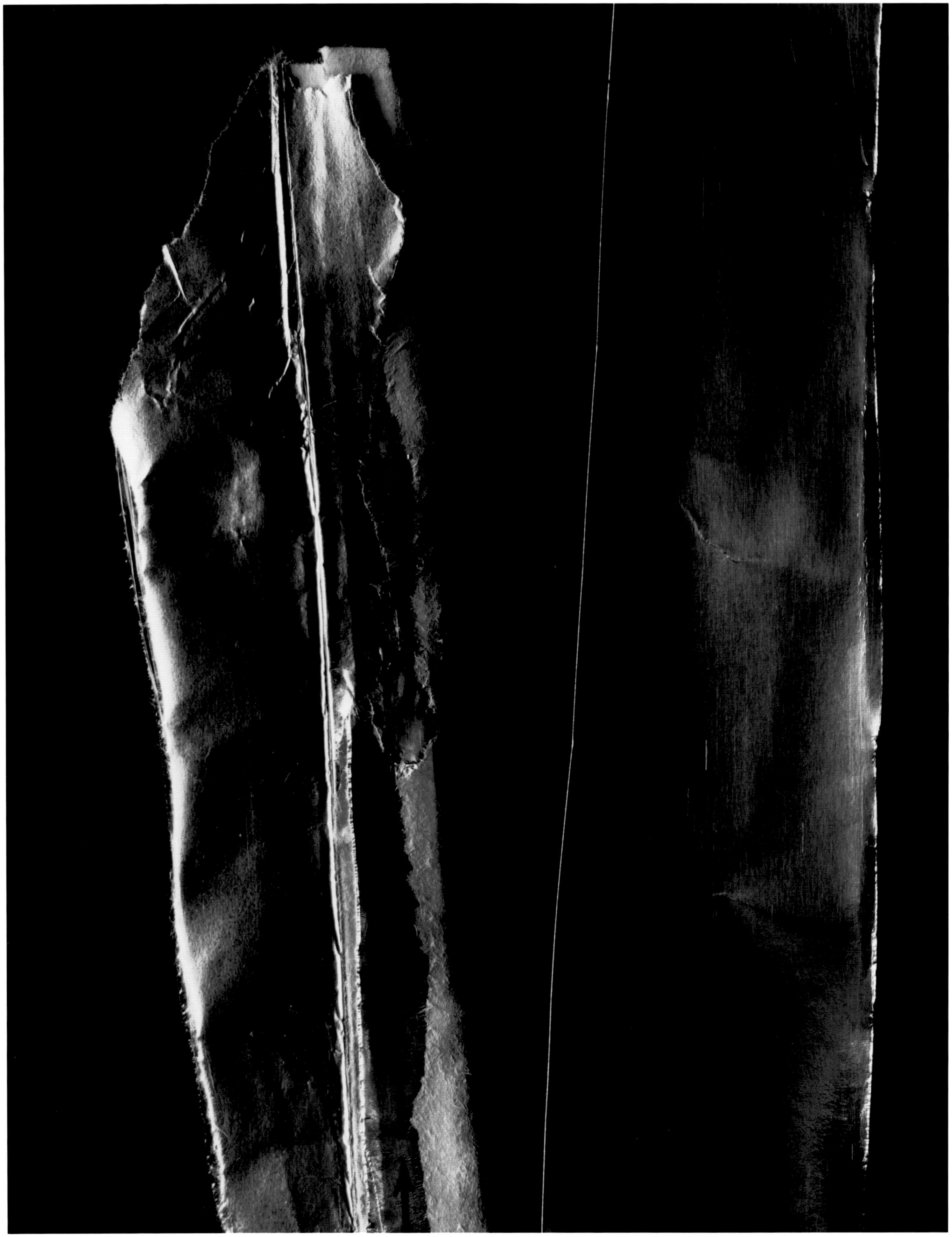

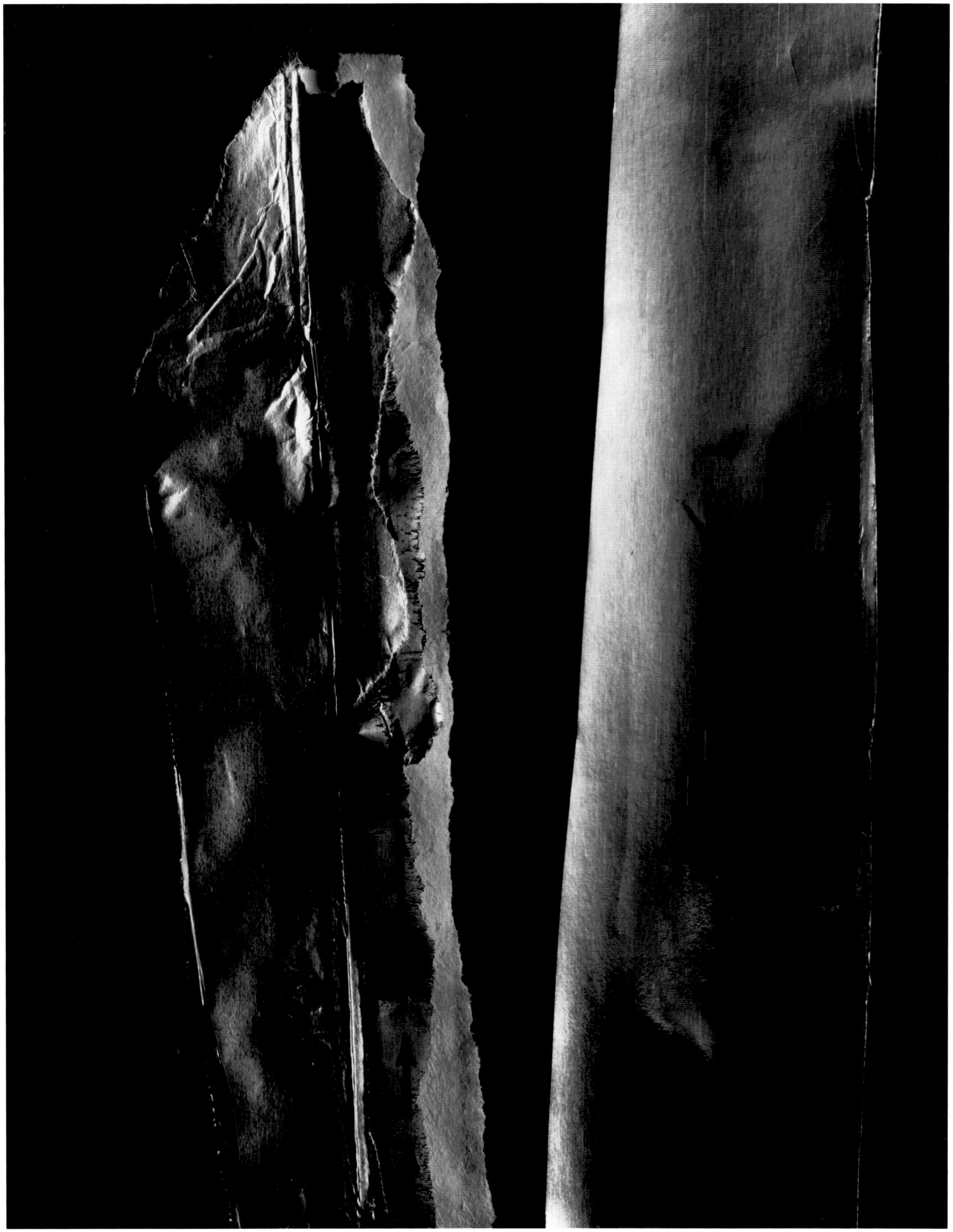

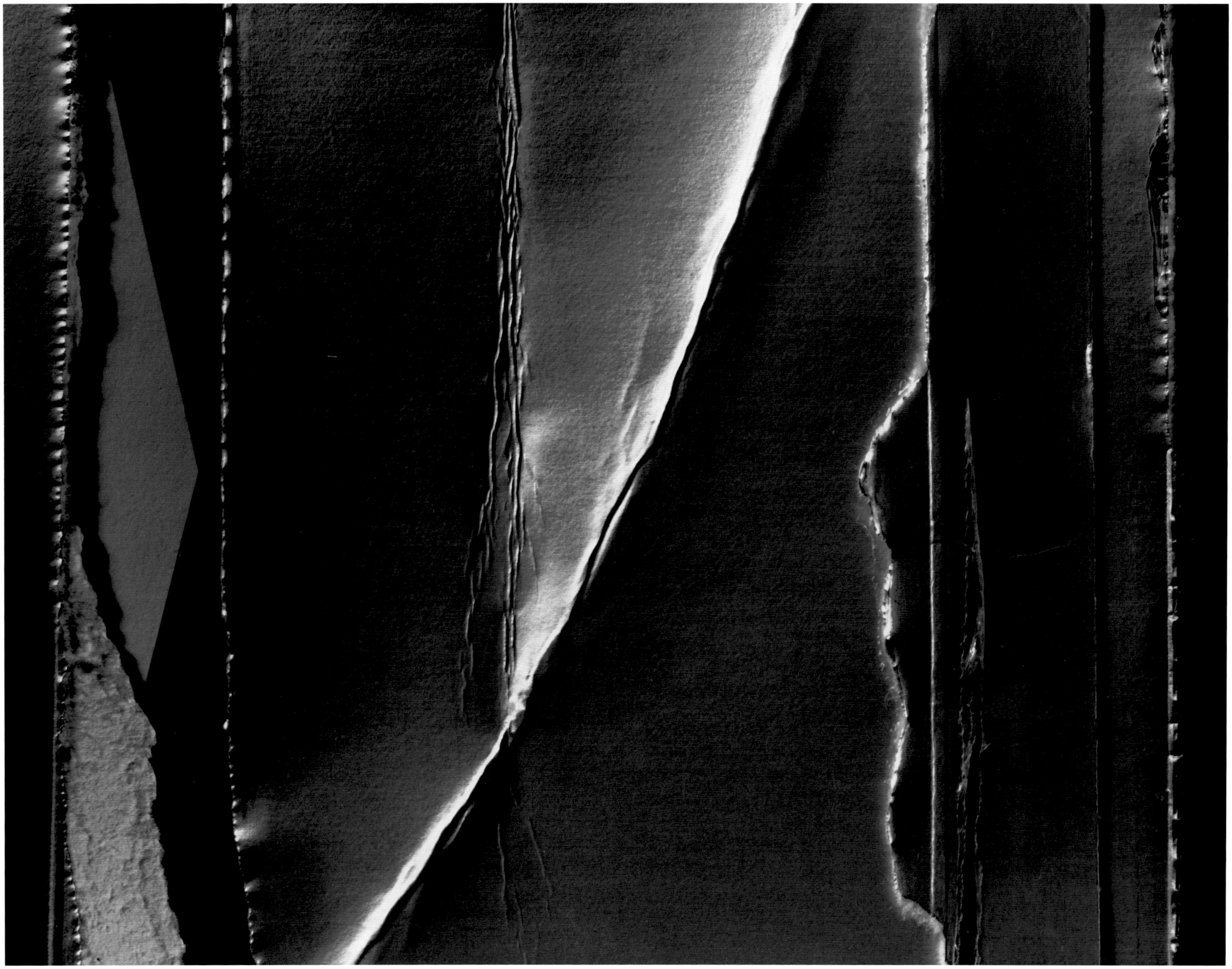

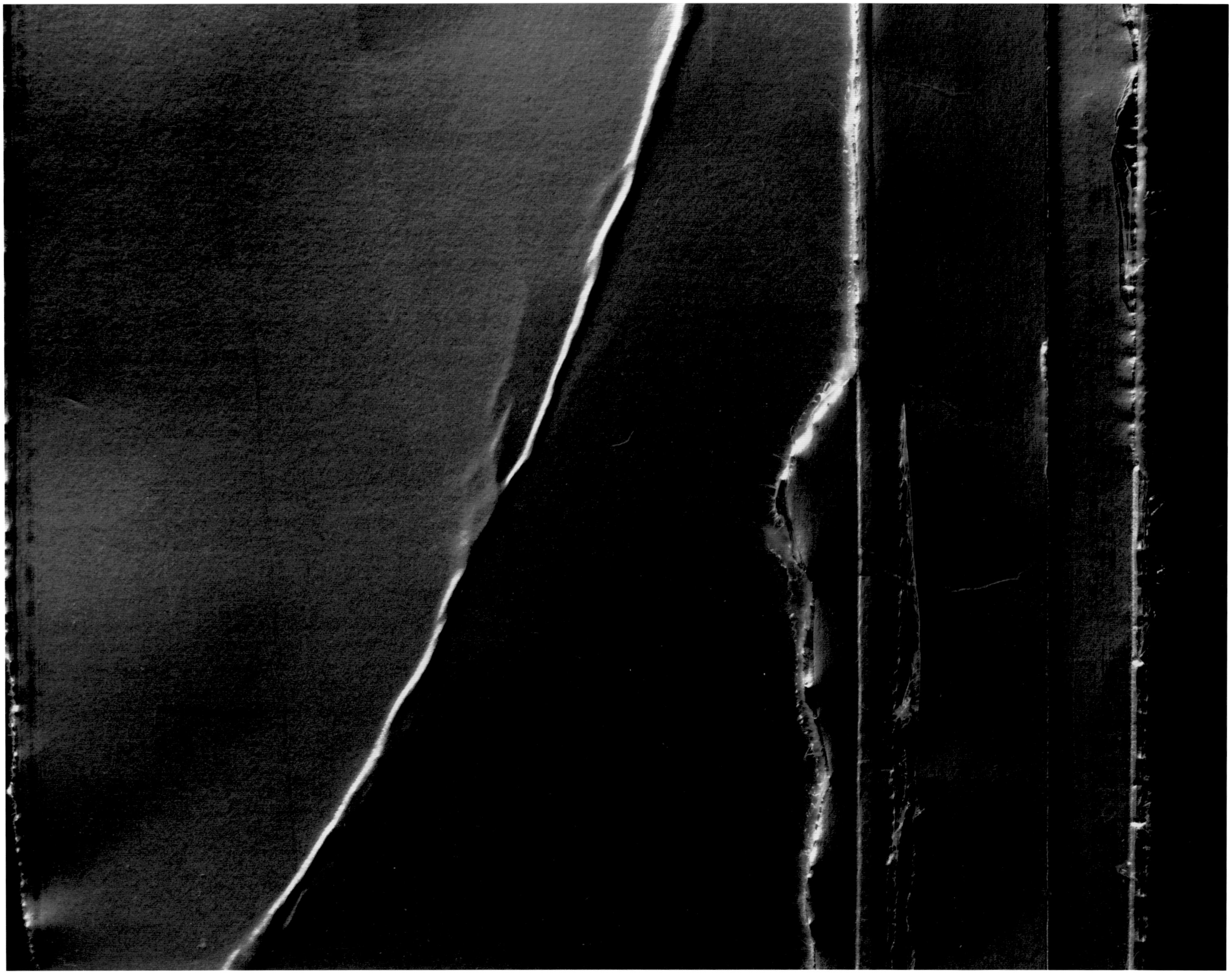

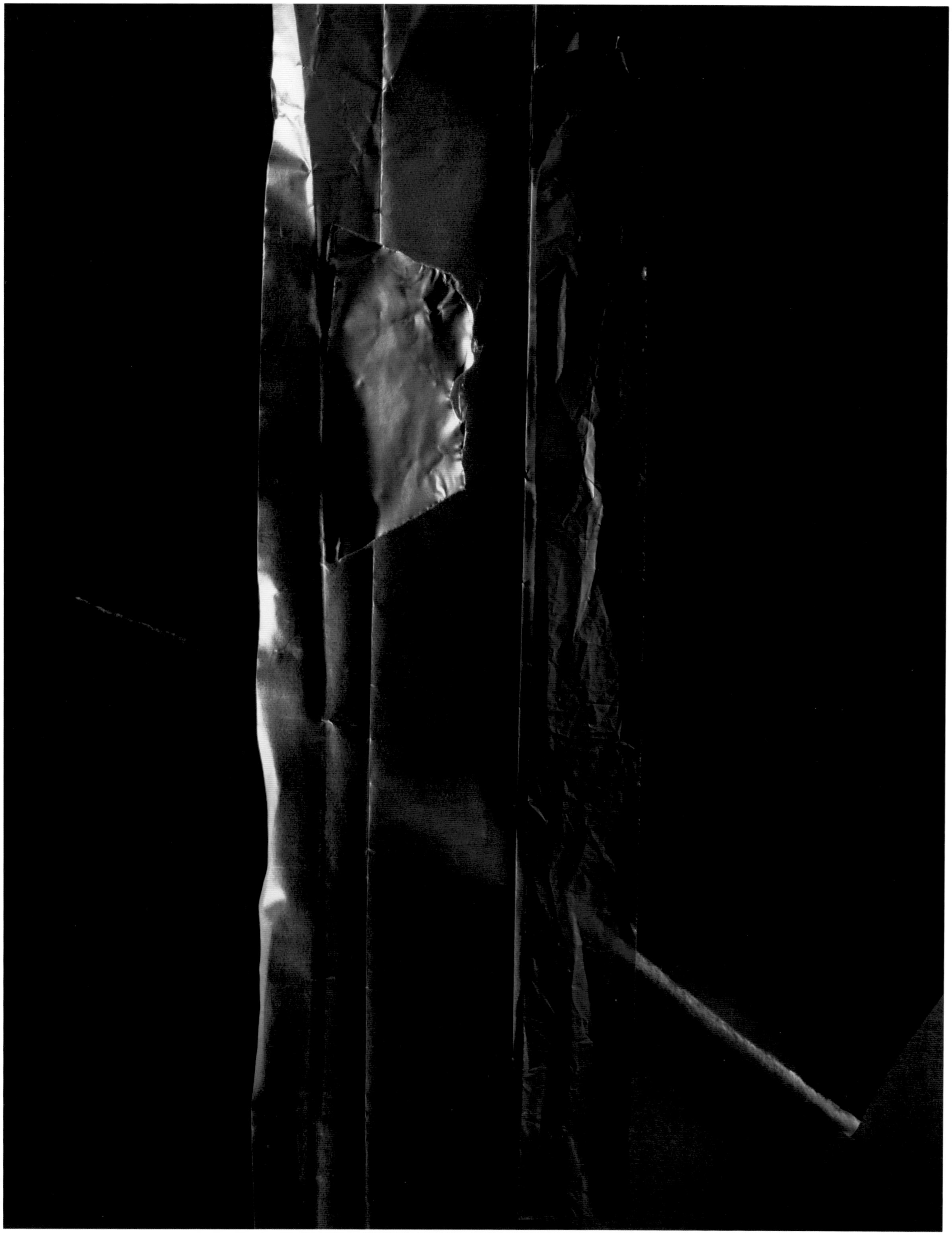

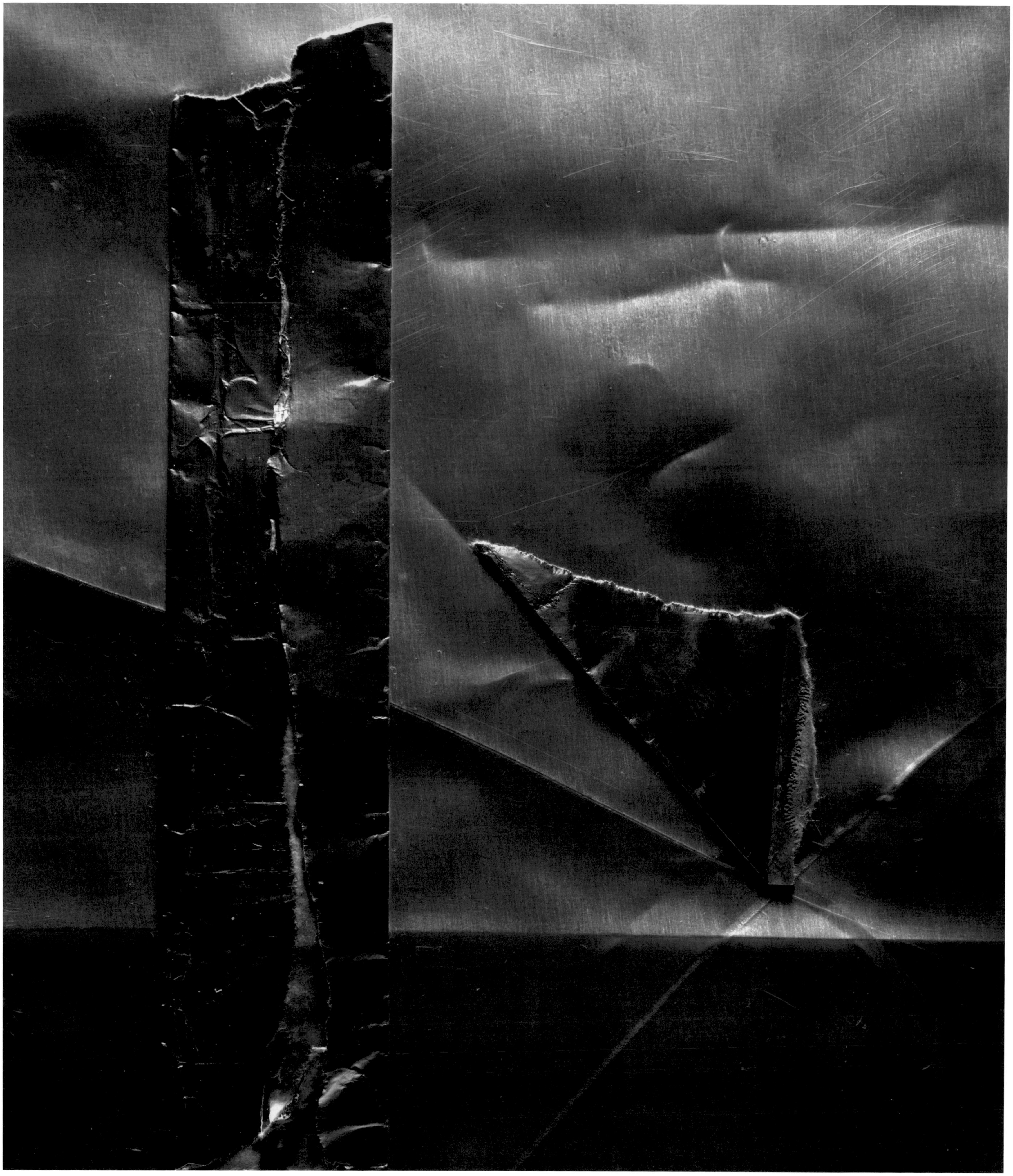

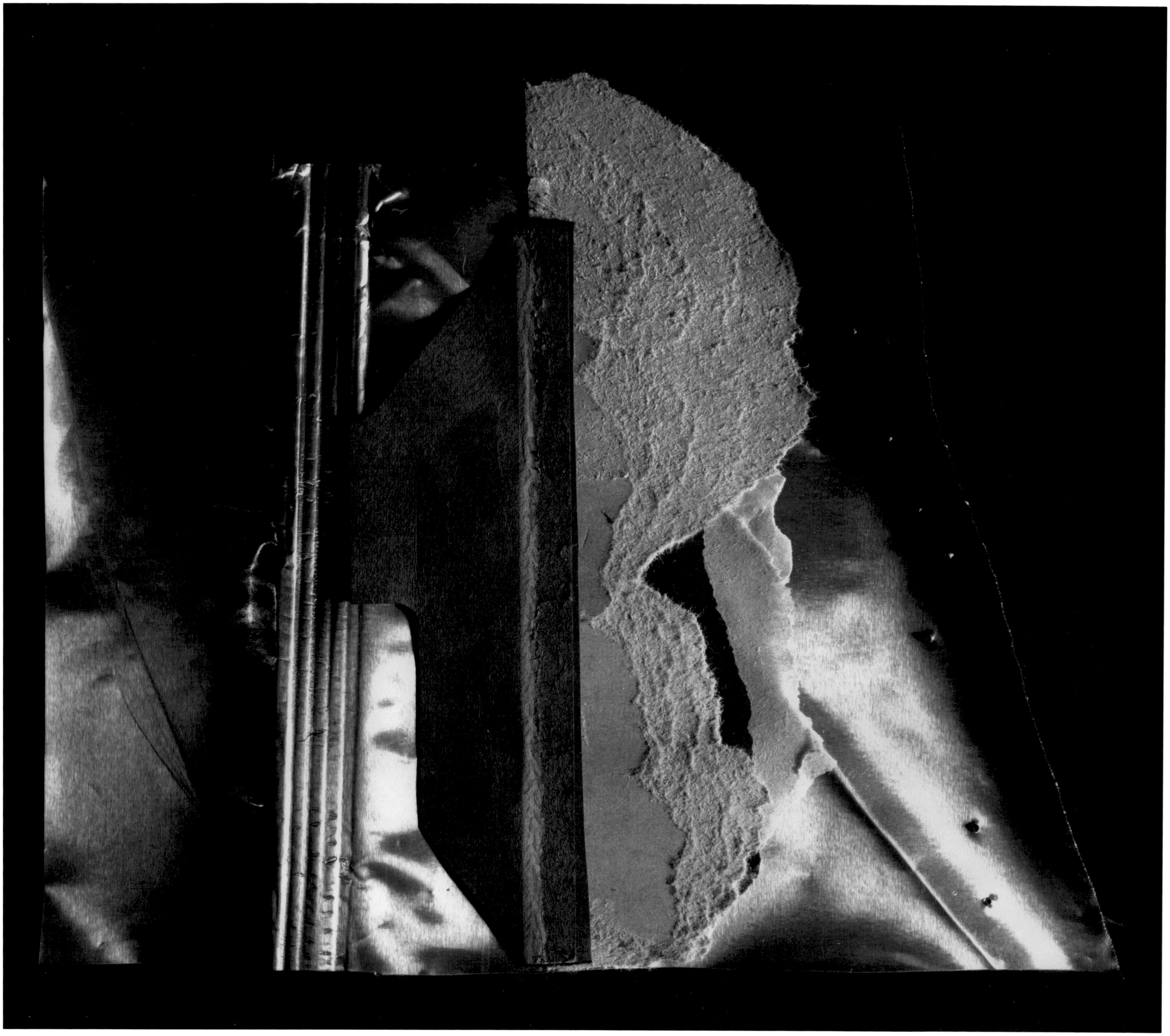

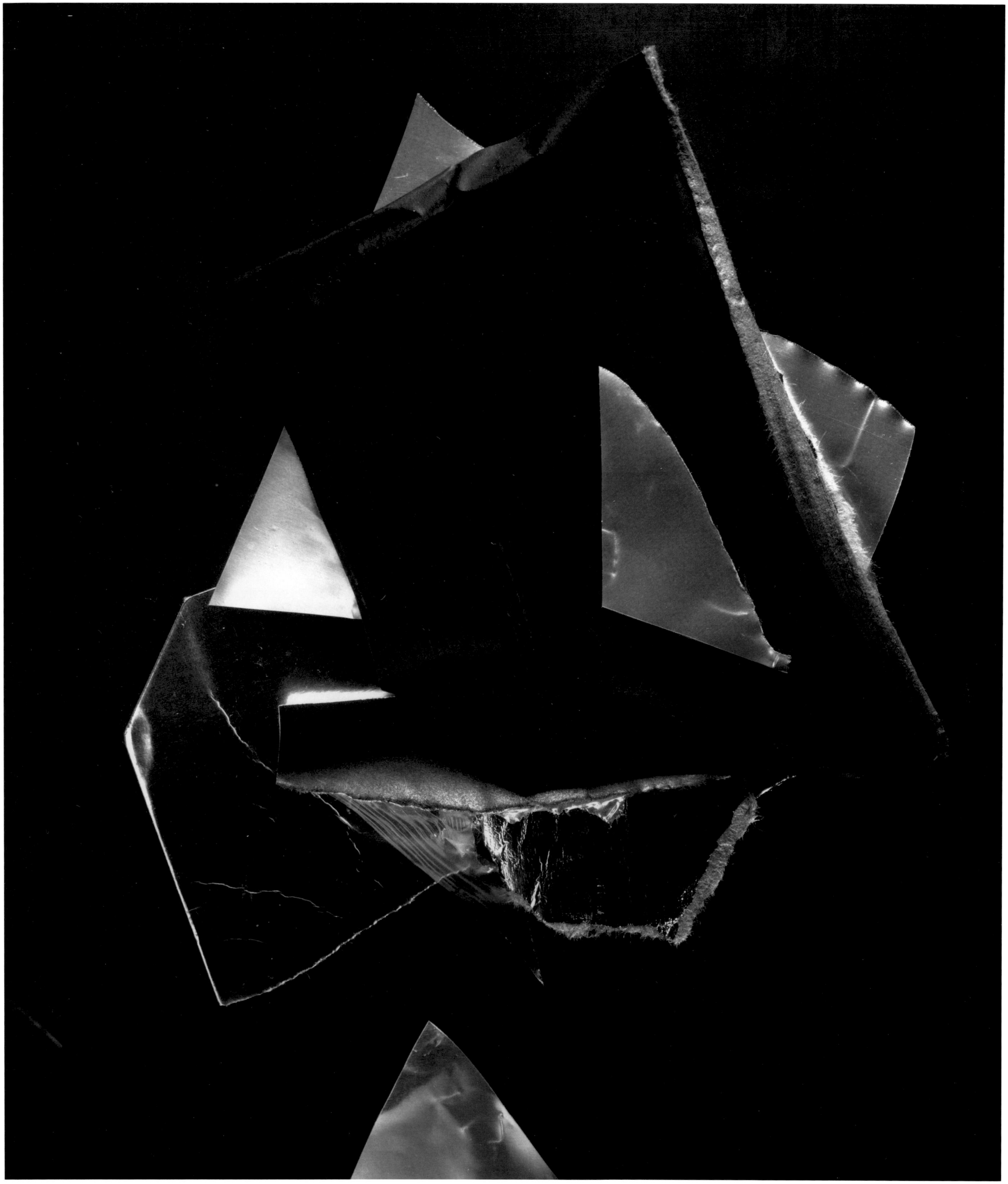

AFTERWORD

Carl Chiarenza's photography, considered as a whole, has been characterized by the consistency and unity of vision that often typifies the work of profoundly serious artists. There are no sudden and dramatic shifts of emphasis or changes of style. Rather, there is slow and steady maturation, a refining and perfecting of means, that constitutes the flowering of a remarkable art.

That flowering is in some sense the ontogenetic recapitulation of the progress of abstraction in all the arts, a progress which has taken some 150 years. The end of that progress – the sustained achievement of a monumental and thoroughgoing abstraction – is a more recent development than is sometimes imagined. It depends in each medium on a few artists of rigorous vision and high ideals. Painting has, for example, its Olitski and sculpture its Caro. Increasingly, it looks as if the analogous position in photography is occupied by Carl Chiarenza.

Historically, Chiarenza's art is situated in the noble tradition of American photography stemming from Stieglitz and flowing through Weston, Adams, and Siskind. The visual precision and intensity of these masters ripens in Chiarenza's work into something that if not unexpected is at least fresh and striking, as artistic quality always is. Seen in somewhat narrower perspective, Chiarenza's pictures affiliate clearly with those of Minor White, and at times with Caponigro's, as well as with those of such photographers as Nicholas Dean and Paul Petricone with whom Chiarenza was associated in Boston around 1960. To name these names is to create a context within which Chiarenza's work can be situated, to evoke its look and sensibility as a means of coming to grips with it. It is also to see it through the eyes of others, not for what it is in itself.

During the second half of the 1950s, Chiarenza's subjects were often similar to those of Ansel Adams – nature and worn or aged human artifacts. If, however, these subjects were sometimes seen as Adams might have seen them, they were differently felt. Adams found visual drama in the objects he photographed, and his images were both theatrical and stylish. (Neither of these words is pejorative in relation to Adams' work, any more than "decorative" is pejorative in relation to Matisse's painting.) Chiarenza eschewed the dramatic in favor of the declarative. His value range was far narrower than Adams' and was used more to structure his images than to dramatize them. Reticence was, and is, one of the most salient characteristics of Chiarenza's images. A reticence underlain by an immense reserve of power.

If Chiarenza's early repertoire of subjects recalls Adams, his love of black brings Weston to mind. Here again, the comparison is more apparent than real. Weston's rich, velvety blacks are used as local color and for contrast. Chiarenza's suffuse the whole image and are its very subject. There is a meaningful sense in which his entire accomplishment can be said to be a set of variations on the theme of black. Nor is Chiarenza interested in the tension produced in Weston's photographs by the transformation of sensuous subjects into abstract objects and of objects into sensuous subjects. His visual material is baldly presented. Its emotional richness and complexity are projected uniquely by the esthetic entity – the photograph – and not at all by what it represents.

By the early 1960s, Chiarenza had largely abandoned recognizable subject matter in favor of photographs of crystalline structures. This subject, which had been explored by Minor White around 1960, was also favored at the time by Dean and others. It offered a bridge to total abstraction that was used to advantage by Chiarenza. Although it not infrequently produced images that could be interpreted as referring to other natural phenomena – some of them so blatant that Chiarenza cannot have missed them – it just as often resulted in luminous abstraction. Sharper in value contrast than the work of the '50s, these pictures moved away from discrete internal elements toward more unitary and larger-scaled images. Their apparent suggestion of White's work is, like the earlier suggestions of Adams', more in terms of appearance than of substance. Like Adams, White projected drama in his images, a lyrical and poetic drama rather than a monumental one, a drama capable of resonating even the most abstract-seeming pictures.

Chiarenza discovered his mature voice in the mid-1960s, and has strengthened and deepened that voice ever since. By then, he was creating large-scaled totally abstract pictures that neither looked nor felt like the photographs of any other artist. Their closest affinities were with the work of Aaron Siskind, and it is no accident that Chiarenza should respect that work and devote his scholarly efforts to it. Siskind, more than any other major photographer of his time, has uncompromisingly followed his art, and art in general, into abstraction, a feat that has been more difficult in photography than in other media. Like Pollock, Siskind has never totally abandoned figuration but, like Pollock, he has accepted a Cubist-derived space that tends to identify image and picture plane, and has shifted the burden of emotion from the photographic subject to the photographic object. Inspired by Siskind's example, Chiarenza has chosen to imitate neither his effects nor his space. In the work of the last 20 years, he has created an indeterminate space that is at once flat – although not identified with the picture plane – and infinitely yielding. It is structured by inflections of black, ranges of gray, and occasional accents of muted white into unified entities of tremendous suavity.

The armatures around which these tonal variations have been constructed, particularly during the later 1970s, have tended to be spare linear patterns, often involving a line that runs through the composition and disappears at both edges. Together with their general compositional simplicity and overall tonal unity, this gives these pictures remarkable amplitude of scale. These formal effects are enhanced by Chiarenza's ability to produce prints of extraordinary beauty of surface and technical perfection. He is certainly among the finest printers photography has produced.

Recently – in the '80s – Chiarenza has chosen to disrupt the suavity, although not the scale, of his pictures by abrupt internal shifts in pattern or texture. These unexpected and apparently disjunctive transitions suggest an artist who, having thoroughly internalized the laws of his art, feels free to break those laws for expressive purposes. The harmonious disunity of this recent work has led Chiarenza to experiment with two or three separate images juxtaposed in one frame – diptychs and triptychs. The resulting freedom recalls work such as the late Degas sculpture, a rough and uncanonical art of great intellectual complexity and complete self-possession.

The question that naturally arises in confronting a body of work as impressive and as beautiful as Chiarenza's is, how can it remain so little known? In part, its obscurity results from Chiarenza's own reticence and the inevitable devotion of a dedicated artist to his art and not to its dissemination. In part, it results from the fact that it shares the fate of all contemporary art. The best work in every medium is today relatively undervalued, in every sense, because, like all good art, it is complex both emotionally and intellectually and difficult of access. The artist may not want it to be that way, but insofar as he is a good artist it is almost inevitably so. The situation is doubly difficult for the abstract artist and for photography, which is generally expected to look like the work of, for example, Walker Evans or Diane Arbus. In a perverse way, the fact that Chiarenza's pictures are relatively little known is, given the milieu in which they exist, an assurance of their quality as well as of the fact that their power and beauty will survive and be noticed long after most of what is now generally admired has disappeared.

CHARLES W. MILLARD

January 1987

CHRONOLOGY

Compiled by Susan E. Cohen and William H. Johnson

1935-1949

Carl was born in Rochester, New York on September 5, 1935, the third of four sons of Charles and Mary Chiarenza, Sicilian immigrants to the United States. Following the Depression his mother worked as a seamstress and his father worked as a cabinet maker. The family was interested in the arts; his father and uncle were amateur painters, his brothers played musical instruments. Carl obtained his first camera and began voice and clarinet lessons when he was about eight years old. A playground director converted a sports equipment locker into a darkroom and his uncle helped Carl build his first enlarger.

During high school Carl was active in all vocal and instrumental classes and groups. He added the tenor and baritone saxophone to his repertoire and played in dance and jazz ensembles throughout the city. He also took a photography class in high school and photographed for the school newspaper and yearbook.

1953-1957

Carl entered the two-year program in photography offered at the Rochester Institute of Technology, where he was exposed to all aspects of the medium and encouraged by C. B. Neblette, William Shoemaker, Leslie Stroebel, and Hollis Todd. In 1955 he obtained the A.A.S. degree, then continued in the newly-formed B.F.A. program. It was a stimulating atmosphere – his teachers were Charles Arnold, Frank Clement, Ralph Hattersley, Robert Koch, Beaumont Newhall and Minor White. Peter Bunnell, Bruce Davidson, Kenneth Josephson, Pete Turner and Jerry Uelsmann were among his classmates. Carl was strongly drawn to creative photography and began to learn the history and contemporary practice of the medium, studying at the George Eastman House, then traveling to Chicago and New York, where he visited The Museum of Modern Art and the Limelight Gallery. He continued to meet people, including Walter Chappell, Nathan Lyons, Nancy Newhall, and Franz Wildenhain – and was introduced to the work of Richard Avedon, Harry Callahan, Irving Penn, and Aaron Siskind. He also studied the magazines: *Life* and *Infinity* and *Image* and *Aperture.* At this time Carl was torn between photojournalism and creative photography, feeling that Henri Cartier-Bresson and W. Eugene Smith, on the one hand, and Alfred Stieglitz and Edward Weston, on the other, were major influences on his work. During his final year at RIT, he worked as an assistant instructor, thus beginning a long and distinguished teaching career. Carl also began to show his photographs in exhibitions and some of his photographs or brief writings were published in *Aperture* and other magazines.

1957-1962

In 1957 Carl moved to Boston, Massachusetts, to enter the graduate program in journalism at Boston University. He obtained a Graduate Assistantship in Photojournalism under Harris G. Smith. A *Reader's Digest* Research Grant allowed Carl to produce a photo-essay on the LaSalette Seminary and to generate his thesis book, *City Hospital,* another extended photographic essay. He received his M.S. in Journalism in 1959. During these years he shared an apartment with David C. Kelly, also a Boston University student and R.I.T. graduate.

However, throughout this time his interests in "creative" photography also continued to grow and Carl founded and directed the Image Study Gallery at Boston University where he presented monthly exhibitions of contemporary photography. His work was published in *Aperture, Editor and Publisher,* and *Modern Photography* and his photographs were included in the important "Photography at Mid-Century" exhibition at the George Eastman House in 1959. At this time a small circle of creative photographers in the Boston area was beginning to find a focus and coalesce into a loosely-formed group. Carl joined John Brook, Paul Caponigro, Marie Cosindas, Nicholas Dean, Chester Michalik, Irene Schwachman, Stephen Trefonides, and others in regular meetings at the Carl Siembab Gallery and at George Lockwood's Impressions Workshop.

After graduation Carl worked as a free-lance writer and photographer with the Sickles Agency. He also continued the periodic photographic field-trips with Paul Caponigro, Walter Chappell, Nicholas Dean and Paul Petricone that were personally meaningful to him. He shifted to the large-format camera for his personal photography. His work continued to attract critical recognition, and was shown in The Museum of Modern Art's "Sense of Abstraction" exhibition in 1960 and in his first one-man show at Boston University during the same year.

At the end of 1959 Carl was drafted into the United States Army, where he worked as an editor on military publications, reading art history and art criticism in his spare time. In September, 1961, he married Anne Spencer Thurman. Carl completed his military service in December of that year and entered Boston University again in January, this time in the Art History program.

1962-1970

Inspired and encouraged by professors William Jewell and George Levitine, Carl studied to receive his M.A. in Art History. In the course of this program he earned several Graduate Assistantships, then a part-time lecturer's position in Art History at Boston University in 1963, and in 1964, after receiving his Master's degree, he became an Instructor in Art History there. In that year he taught his first course on the history of photography.

Throughout this period Carl also continued his personal photography. Between 1962 and 1970 he exhibited in more than seventy group exhibitions and had twelve one-man shows. In 1962, Carl used Polaroid materials for the first time, when he served as a Consultant for the company. He made close-up abstractions from nature, photographing in towns along the New England coast as well as abstractions made by photographing the crystallized chemicals in his darkroom.

Carl was also extending his commitments to the growing community of creative photographers. The evolving sense of community among Boston photographers led to the formation of the brief-lived but important Society of Heliographers in 1963, and Carl was both a co-founder and member of that group. There were strong connections between Boston, New York, and Rochester during this time through individuals associated with this organization. In 1963 Carl accepted the regional editorship of the magazine, *Contemporary Photographer*, then being edited by Lee Lockwood in New York. *Contemporary Photographer* was an independent quarterly journal devoted to creative photography, one of the few vehicles for that position published at that time. In 1965 Carl became the Associate Editor, and he assumed the Editorship for 1966 to 1969. During those final years of the magazine Carl provided, in spite of many financial and administrative difficulties, one of the few forums then available for scholarly and serious critical responses to the medium of photography.

In 1964 Carl also joined the newly formed Society for Photographic Education, where he renewed contacts with the small community of photographer/educators who had begun to surface throughout the American university system. Here, among others, he met Robert Heinecken and found a significant, life-long friendship.

In 1966 Carl entered the Ph.D. program in Art History at Harvard University, where he studied primarily with Professors James Ackerman, Agnes Mongan, and Seymour Slive. While in the program Carl co-curated, with Davis Pratt, the exhibition "The Portrait in Photography, 1848-1966" at the Fogg Art Museum, Harvard University, in 1967. This popular show was the first major exhibition of creative photography held at the Fogg Museum. At Harvard Carl met Clifford Ackley, Marjorie B. Cohn, William Johnson, Bruce MacDonald, and Charles Millard, who became important collegues and friends.

In 1967 Carl and his wife adopted a daughter, Suzanne Mari.

During the next few years, as well as meeting the requirements for the doctoral program, Carl continued his already active professional educational role, teaching at Boston University, where he was promoted to Assistant Professor in 1968. In addition to his continuing role as editor of *Contemporary Photographer* Carl served as Director of the New England Region of the Society of Photographic Education from 1967 to 1973, and from 1968 to 1973 he served as a Member of its National Board of Directors. He was also a member of the National Conference Committee of that organization from 1968 to 1971, when he organized a series of lectures and a symposium on criticism and photography for the 1969 national meeting. From 1966 to 1968 he also was a member of Artists Against Racism and War. Between 1966 and 1970 Carl participated in over twenty-five public lectures and seminars around the country. And as a consultant and curator for the Itek Corporation in Boston, he organized a series of photography exhibitions throughout 1968-69. In 1970 he was listed in *Outstanding Young Men in America.*

1971-1975

Carl decided to write his Ph.D. dissertation on the life and work of the still active artist/photographer Aaron Siskind, a choice of topic which was then unusual for any Ph.D. dissertation and unprecedented at Harvard. Only the unusual liberality of those times made Carl's choice possible and the strength of his work made it acceptable. In 1971 and 1972 Carl worked on his dissertation, with assistance from a Harvard University Research Grant, a Boston University Summer Research Stipend, and a Kress Foundation Research Grant. He also functioned as a consultant and member of the selection committee for the International Fund for Concerned Photography, established by Cornell Capa.

In the Spring of 1971, after discussions with photographer Warren Hill and businessman Don Perrin, Carl called a weekend conference in his home to discuss the formation of an independent center for creative photography and related media in the Boston area. Photographers and educators from around the country responded, and the meeting was attended by Peter Bunnell, Cornell Capa, Paul Caponigro, Warren Hill, Robert Heinecken, William Johnson, Nathan Lyons, Chester Michalik, William Parker, Carl Siembab, Jerry Uelsmann, and Minor White, among others. This meeting generated support and suggestions for the formation of the Imageworks Center and School, which was founded in the Fall of 1971, and which functioned as a school, workshop, and gallery, before closing in 1973. Carl helped to provide a necessary focus for this organization during its formation, even though he had temporarily moved to California to be with his wife, who had moved there to follow her own career as a lawyer. However, Anne and Carl obtained a divorce in 1972.

In 1971, Carl met Professor James Hullett and formed another important friendship. Together they taught a seminar on philosophy and photography at Boston University. In 1972 Carl also participated, with Peter Bunnell, Allan Dutton, Jonathan Green, Robert Heinecken, Jerome Liebling, Frederick Sommer, Jerry Uelsmann, Jack Welpott, and Minor White, in a five-day retreat at Sippewisset, on Cape Cod, which was personally important to him.

In 1972 Carl was nominated as a University Professor for the Year at Boston University, an award granted for superior teaching. In 1973, the year he finished his dissertation, he was appointed Associate Professor of Art History. In 1973-74 he served as acting chairman of the department, while also traveling to Rochester, New York, each month to conduct graduate seminars as Adjunct Visiting Professor at the Visual Studies Workshop. His students at the Workshop included Skip Atwater, Thomas Southall and Alex Sweetman. Carl has introduced the concepts and history of creative photography to hundreds of students over the years and he has helped direct the interests of a new generation of art historians toward that discipline. Mary Goodwin Bataille, Susan E. Cohen, Alicia Faxon, Eleanor Hight, Deborah Irmas, Patricia Johnston, Debi Martin, Sandra Olsen, Mary Panzer, Lesley Spiro, Maren Stange and Jennifer Todd are among those who studied with Carl recently and who are now contributing to the field.

In 1974 Carl joined the Advisory Council of the newly-formed International Center of Photography in New York City, a position he still holds. In the Fall of 1974 Carl taught, with Robert Heinecken and Jerry Uelsmann, at the Ansel Adams Workshop at Carmel, California. There he met Heidi Katz. During 1974 Carl also met Jon Holmes, and later, Sam Yanes. Both were to become friends and major supporters of Carl's photography, and through their association with Polaroid, they made it possible for Carl to work extensively with Polaroid materials. From 1971 to 1975 Carl continued to photograph, and amid all his other activities exhibited in more than twenty-five shows.

1975-1985

In 1975-76 Carl took a sabbatical and, with support from a Massachusetts Arts and Humanities Foundation Artist's Fellowship, spent his first year as a full-time working artist. Carl and Heidi Katz lived on an old farm owned by his friends Jerry and Martin Cohn in Richmond, New Hampshire during that year, which was one of the most productive periods of his career as a photographer. Carl made some nature studies and many photographs in the scrapyards and in worn and damaged structures found in industrial areas around New England. Carl also traveled to New Mexico, where he and Paul Caponigro photographed together, and to Arizona, where he photographed with Harold Jones. Through Carl Siembab and Ted Hartwell, Carl met Hall Peterson, who became a friend and a patron.

Returning to Boston University in 1976, Carl was elected to the position of Chairman of the Department of Art History by his fellow faculty. He held the position until 1981.

In 1976 Carl assisted in the second attempt to establish an independent center for creative photography in the Boston area, by advising his friend Chris Enos, then becoming a member of the Board of Directors when she established the Photographic Resource Center. During 1978-1979, Carl played an instrumental role in affiliating the Center with Boston University and during 1984-1985, he helped establish the new physical facility, with exhibition galleries, library, and lecture spaces, at the University.

In 1975 Carl was also elected to the Board of Trustees of the Visual Studies Workshop in Rochester, New York, a position he still holds. He also served on the Advisory Board of the Texas Center for Photographic Studies during 1975-76. From 1976 to 1978 he served on the Advisory Committee of the Center for Creative Photography at the University of Arizona in Tucson. And in 1977 he was a consultant/evaluator of educational programs at the International Center of Photography for the New York State Education Department of the State University of New York. In 1978-79 he served as consulting evaluator of the Environmental Photography Program and of the Center of Visual Studies at Unity College, Unity, Maine. In 1979, he served on the nominating panels for *American Photographer* and for the "U.S. Eye" exhibition. In 1980, Carl juried the Traveling Scholarship Grants for the School of the Museum of Fine Arts in Boston and he served on the Regional Task Force on the Photography Program of the National Endowment for the Arts. From 1980 to 1983 he also served as an Advisory Trustee for the Friends of Photography in Carmel, California.

Carl received an Artist's Fellowship from the National Endowment for the Arts in 1977-78, and built his first professional darkroom in his home in Arlington, Massachusetts. Carl met Eelco Wolf through their mutual connection to the Photographic Resource Center, and through Eelco's assistance, was invited to experiment with the new Polaroid 20 x 24 camera in 1979. Carl's experience of working within the studio conditions imposed by that system provided a major turning point in his photography. He found the experience of collaging materials and being able to control his compositions and lighting, along with the interaction available during each photographic session through the immediate development of the prints, to be an exciting direction to follow, and during his sabbatical year 1979-1980 he pursued this method with 4 x 5 Polaroid positive/negative materials.

From 1975 to 1985 Carl exhibited in more than fifty-five group exhibitions and thirteen one-man shows in the United States and Europe. In 1979, Ted Hartwell at the Minneapolis Institute of Arts, curated a retrospective exhibition of about fifty of Carl's photographs (November 25, 1979 – January 4, 1980). The entire exhibition was then purchased for the Museum's permanent collection.

Carl's critical essays on Aaron Siskind, Robert Heinecken, and other topics which were published throughout the second half of the 1970s, helped bring a measure of solid scholarship and authority into a discipline that was still very new and unformed. In 1979 Carl published his important theoretical paper in historiography, "Notes Toward an Integrated History of Picturemaking" in *Afterimage.* And in 1980 he began the work necessary to translate his doctoral thesis on Aaron Siskind into a monograph.

Heidi Katz and Carl married in 1978. Their son Jonah Katz was born in 1980, and their daughter Gabriella Christine was born in 1983.

In 1981, Carl was promoted to the rank of Professor of Art History at Boston University. He curated the exhibition "A Photographic Patron: The Carl Siembab Gallery" at the Institute of Contemporary Art, Boston, honoring Siembab's long commitment to creative photography in Boston. During the same year he joined the New England Advisory Committee for the Archives of American Art, a post he held until 1986. He served as a juror on the New Works Projects for the Massachusetts Council on the Arts and Humanities and the Photographic Resource Center and Consultant to the Steering Committee for the Society for Photographic Education. In

1982 he served on the Photography Fellowship Panel for the National Endowment for the Arts.

Carl's book, *Aaron Siskind: Pleasures and Terrors,* was published by Little, Brown & Co., in 1982. The book received many favorable reviews and a Merit Award from the American Photographic Historical Society in 1983.

During 1983-84, Carl was appointed Harnish Visiting Professor of Art at Smith College and he received an Artist-in-Residence Grant from the Massachusetts Council of the Arts and the Museum of Fine Arts, Boston to work with the Polaroid 20 x 24 camera once again, this time using black and white materials.

Beginning in 1985, Carl has served as an Editorial Consultant for *History of Photography* magazine and served as a juror, with Vicki Goldberg and Lou Dorfsman, for the International Center of Photography International Awards. In 1986 he served as Juror/Curator for the "Northlight/Southwest Juried Group Exhibition" held at the Northlight Gallery, Arizona State University, Tempe.

1986 - 1988

In 1986 Carl was appointed the Fanny Knapp Allen Professor of Art History and Acting Chairman for the Department of Art and Art History at the University of Rochester where he will develop a graduate program in the history of photography in collaboration with the International Museum of Photography at George Eastman House. After thirty years of functioning as a catalyst, consultant, critic, administrator, educator, and artist in the Boston area, Carl returned to Rochester.

Landscapes of the Mind, tracing Carl's invaluable contributions to photography over the past three decades was published by David R. Godine, Boston, in March of 1988, to coincide with a comprehensive retrospective of his work at the International Center of Photography in New York.

BIBLIOGRAPHY & EXHIBITIONS

Books and Portfolios

Interaction – Verbal/Visual, privately published, limited handmade edition with original prints, Rochester, 1957.

City Hospital, privately published, limited handmade edition with original prints, Boston, 1959.
[Discussed by Chiarenza in "Honesty and Patience Beget Picture-Story in a Hospital," *Editor and Publisher* (September 12, 1959): 15, 60.]

"Carl Chiarenza: A Portfolio," introduction by Lee Lockwood. *Contemporary Photographer* 5:2 (1965): 37-59; 14 photographs and a poem.

Landscapes of the Mind, David R. Godine, Publisher, Boston, MA, 1988.

Selected Discussions and Reproductions of Chiarenza's Photographic Work

(See List of Exhibitions for Catalogs and Reviews)

Patricia Caulfield, "Discovery No. 35: Carl Chiarenza," *Modern Photography* 22:6 (1958) : 76-77; text and two photographs.

Aperture 9:1 (1961) ; one photograph on back cover.

Aperture 9:3 (1961) : one photograph on front cover; statement inside back cover.

Photography Yearbook, London (1962): 162.

Ralph Hattersley, "Carl Chiarenza," *Infinity* 11:9 (1962) : 21-25; essay and several photographs.

"The Heliographers: A New Photographic Movement," *U.S. Camera* (May, 1964): 61-65.

Jacob Deschin, "Contemporary Photographer is Back," *New York Times,* November 12, 1967.

Stephen Perrin, "Boston Photographers," *Boston After Dark,* October 16, 1968, pp. 10-11, one photograph.

Boston Review of Photography, 1:5 (1968); two photographs.

Joy Zweigler, *Man in the Poetic Mode: 5,* McDougal, Littell & Co., Evanston, IL, 1970, p. 17; one photograph.

Joy Zweigler, *Man in the Poetic Mode: 6,* McDougal, Littell & Co., Evanston, IL, 1970, pp. 3, 46, 105; three photographs.

"Synoptic Catalog of the George Eastman House Collection," *Image* 14:5 & 6 (1971) : 35; catalog entry and one photograph.

Arnold Gassan, *A Chronology of Photography,* Handbook Co., Athens, OH, 1972, p. 204.

Elton M. Davies, *Arts and Cultures of Man,* Intext Educational Publishers, London, 1972, pp. iv, 586: citation and one photograph.

Camera (Lucerne), 53:10 (October, 1974): 38; one photograph.

David R. Weimer and Joan M. Weimer, *America: 20th Century Poetry: Landscapes of the Mind,* McDougal, Littell & Co., Evanston, IL, 1975, pp. 12, 74, 180; three photographs.

George M. Craven, *Object and Image*, Prentice-Hall, Englewood Cliffs, NJ, 1975, p. 178; text and photograph.

Jessica Alonso, "Photos that Last in Visual Memory," *The Boston Globe*, January 3, 1977, p. 17.

Lee Ewing, "The Fire and its Offering," *Parabola* 3:2 (May, 1978): 48-53; one photograph.

Marnie Samuelson, "Very Large Format Photography: Experimenting with the 20 x 24 Polaroid Color Camera," *Close-up* 10:1 (Winter 1979) : 8-9.

Videotape interview with Alex J. Sweetman, School of the Art Institute of Chicago, Art Data Bank, Chicago, IL, April 1979.

Lee D. Witkin and Barbara London, *The Photograph Collector's Guide,* Boston, New York Graphic Society, 1979, pp. ix, 235, 302, 307, 336.

Ken Winokur, "Boston's Photographic Resource Center. . . ," *The Boston Phoenix,* May 1979, Special photo section, p. 9.

Three videotape interviews with William Johnson, Center for Creative Photography, Tucson, AZ, 1979.

Lee Lockwood, "Carl Siembab," *American Photographer* 3:6 (December 1979) : 57-63.

Jessica Bethoney, "A Guide to Galleries in and Around Boston," *The Boston Globe Calendar*, January 17, 1980, pp. 10-11; text and two photographs.

Skip Atwater, "Carl Chiarenza: Contemporary American Photography Since 1945," *Views* 1:3 (Spring 1980) : 4-5.

Skip Atwater, "Interview with Carl Chiarenza," *Views* 1:3 (Spring 1980) : 5-6.

Carol Goldfarb, "Idealism vs. Pragmatism: Four Photo Groups of the '70s," *Views* 2:1 (Fall 1980) : 8-9.

Turner Browne and Elaine Partnow, *The Complete Book of Photographers,* MacMillan & Co., London and New York, 1981.

Lee Lockwood, "The Carl Siembab Gallery," in *A Photographic Patron: The Carl Siembab Gallery*, Institute of Contemporary Art, Boston, MA, 1981.

Ken Winokur, "A Photographic Patron: The Carl Siembab Gallery," *The Real Paper*, Cambridge, MA, April 2, 1981, pp. 43-44.

"Where Photography Has Friends," *Camera 35* (June, 1981): 42-43, 77.

James L. Enyeart, *Jerry N. Uelsmann: 25 Years, A Retrospective,* Little, Brown & Co., Boston, 1982, pp. 52, 226.

Kelly Wise, "There's a feast for the eyes," *The Boston Globe*, December 19, 1982, p. A39.

Gerald Peary, "Boston Photography," *Boston Magazine* 75:12 (December 1983) : 152-157, 188-194.

Alex J. Sweetman, *Center of the Eye,* Aspen Center for the Visual Arts, 1983, passim.

Kelly Wise, "Some of the finest photographs found in small galleries,"*The Boston Globe,* December 26, 1983, pp. 66-67.

David Robinson, "Q & A: Carl Chiarenza," *American Photographer* 11:6 (December 1983) : 86-94.

Jean Caslin, "The Polaroid Collections," *The Polaroid Newsletter for Photographic Education*, (Fall 1984): 9-10.

Kelly Wise, "Photography," *The Boston Globe*, December 30, 1984.

Turner Browne and Elaine Partnow, *The MacMillan Biographical Encyclopedia of Photographic Artists and Innovators,* MacMillan, London and New York, 1984, pp. 109-110.

C. T. Hartwell, *The Making of a Collection,* Aperture, New York, 1984, p. 67.

Statement and two reproductions in "Minor White: A Living Remembrance," *Aperture* no. 95 (Summer 1984) : 44 and back cover.

Kelly Wise, "The Highs and Lows: 1985 Photography," *The Boston Globe*, December 29, 1985, p. A12.

Estelle Jussim and Elizabeth Lindquist-Cock, *Landscape as Photograph,* Yale University Press, New Haven, 1985, pp. 128, 131.

Kelly Wise, "Very few negatives in 1986," *The Boston Globe*, January 3, 1987.

Jim Stone, *A User's Guide to the View Camera*, Little, Brown and Co., Boston, 1987, pp. 2-3.

William E. Parker, "Considerations for Observers of Post-Darkroom-Altered Photographic Prints," *INsight* (Fall, 1987): 15.

Estelle Jussim, "The Art of Carl Chiarenza," *Polaroid Newsletter for Photographic Education* (Spring, 1988).

William E. Parker, lecture on the photographs of Chiarenza, International Center of Photography, New York, NY, March 9, 1988.

One-Person Exhibitions with major reviews

1960
Image Gallery, Boston, MA.

1962
Carl Seimbab Gallery, Boston, MA.
[Reviewed: Nicholas Dean, "Chiarenza at the Siembab," *Boston Herald,* October 21, 1962. Harris Smith, "An Exhibition by Carl Chiarenza," *Contemporary Photographer*, 4:1 (1963).]
School of the Art Institute, Chicago, IL.

1963
Fitchburg Museum, Fitchburg, MA.
Harvard University, Cambridge, MA.
Paul Art Center, University of New Hampshire, Durham, NH.

1965
Gallery 216, New York, NY.

1966
Arizona State University, Tempe, AZ.

1967
Museum of Art, University of Oregon, Eugene, OR.
[Reviewed: "Artist-Editor Exhibits at UO," *Eugene Register-Guard, Emerald Empire*, January 22, 1967, p. 8.]

1968
Carl Siembab Gallery, Boston, MA.
[Reviewed: Robert Taylor, "Gallery Preview," *Boston Arts* (February, 1968): 48, 50.]
Focus Gallery, San Francisco, CA.
[Reviewed: Michael E. Bry, "Gallery Snooping," *Modern Photography* 33:3 (March 1969) : 34, 36.]

1970
Phoenix College, Phoenix, AZ.

1973
Cary Memorial Library, Lexington, MA.
University of Massachusetts, Boston, MA.

1976
Carl Siembab Gallery, Boston, MA.
[Reviewed: Jessica Alonso, "Carl Chiarenza Displays Mastery of Non-Realism," *Boston Globe,* February 25, 1976, p. 43. Martin Fishkin, "Seeing is Believing," *The Real Paper*, Cambridge, MA., March 3, 1976.]
The Cronin Gallery, Houston, TX.
[Reviewed: Mimi Crossley, "New Purity in Abstract Photography," *The Houston Post,* May 23, 1976; text and photograph.

John Scarborough, "Chiarenza Walks Thin Line Between Words, Photographs,"*The Houston Chronicle,* May 26, 1976. John Scarborough, "Eruptions of Art in Photos," *The Houston Chronicle,* May 29, 1976.]

1977

Art Gallery, Western Carolina University, Cullowhee, NC.
[Catalog: Ray Menze, *Carl Chiarenza Photography Portfolio.* Text, portrait, 3 photographs. Reviewed: Steve Brady, "Photographer Reveals Mysterious;" and Tom West, "Chiarenza Photographs are Impressive," *The Western Carolinian*, February 8, 1977.]

1978

Carl Siembab Gallery, Boston, MA.

1979

The Minneapolis Institute of Arts, Minneapolis, MN. (traveled).
[Reviewed: Don Morrison, "They'll Give us Life from Varied Angles," *The Minneapolis Star*, November 26, 1979, p. 3C.]

1980

Carl Siembab Gallery, Boston, MA.
[Reviewed: Jessica Bethoney, "Carl Chiarenza at the Siembab Gallery," *Boston Globe,* February 21, 1980, p. 63. Charles Giuliano, "Local Artists Carry Realism into New Decade," *Boston Ledger*, February 29, 1980, p. 21.]
St. Mary's College, Winona, MN.

1982

Carl Siembab Gallery, Boston, MA.
[Reviewed: Dan Ranalli, "Carl Siembab Gallery: Carl Chiarenza," *Art New England*, (January 1983) : 13.]

1984

"Moment to Moment: The Photographs of Carl Chiarenza," Palazzo Reale Museum, Milan, Italy. (traveled).
"Chiarenza: New Photographs," Vision Gallery, Boston, MA.
[Reviewed: Kelly Wise, "Photographs by Carl Chiarenza,"*Boston Globe,* February 21, 1984, p. 55.]
School of Art, Portland, ME.
[Reviewed: Nicholas Dean, "Photographs by Carl Chiarenza," *Views* 5:3 (Spring 1984) : 14.]

1987

"Carl Chiarenza," Hartnett Gallery, University of Rochester, Rochester, NY.

1988

"Chiarenza: Landscapes of the Mind," International Center of Photography, New York, NY.
"Chiarenza: New Work," Vision Gallery, Boston, MA.

Invitational Group Exhibitions

Exhibition catalogs and major reviews are cited with the exhibitions to which they refer. Unless otherwise noted, catalogs have the same title as the exhibition and are published by the exhibiting institution.

Annually at Carl Siembab Gallery, Boston, MA., 1960-1983

1957

Rochester Institute of Technology, Rochester, NY.
State Teachers College, Geneseo, NY.
Albright-Knox Gallery, Buffalo, NY.

1959

"Photography at Mid-Century," George Eastman House, Rochester, NY. (traveled).
[Catalog, one photograph, p. 33.]

1960

"The Sense of Abstraction," The Museum of Modern Art, New York, NY.
[Catalog: *Contemporary Photographer* 1:2 (July/August 1960) ; issue devoted to "Sense of Abstraction" exhibition but not all participants included. Reviewed: Minor White and Nathan Lyons, "The Sense of Abstraction," *Aperture* 8:2 (1960) : 90, one photograph.]
"Fotografia della Nuova Generazione," Pescara and Galleria d'Arte Moderna, Milan, Italy.
[Catalog.]
Museum of Fine Arts, Boston, MA.
DeYoung Museum, San Francisco, CA.

1961

"Tenth Boston Arts Festival," Boston, MA.
[Catalog, pp. 45-47.]

1962

"Photography USA," DeCordova-Dana Museum, Lincoln, MA.
[Catalog, p. 4.]
Addison Gallery of American Art, Andover, MA.
The Groton School, Groton, MA.

1963

"Photography in the Fine Arts IV," Metropolitan Museum of Art, New York, NY. (traveled).
[Catalog, one photograph. Reviewed: A. Hyatt Mayor, "How to Bake an Exhibition," *Photography in the Fine Arts Bulletin* (Fall 1964) : 13, one photograph. Bartlett H. Hayes, "Notes for an Essay on Photography," *PSA Journal,* 1964, text and one photograph.]

"8 Major Photographers, 1963: Ansel Adams, Ruth Bernhard, Nathan Lyons, Carl Chiarenza, Brett Weston, Paul Caponigro, Minor White, Walter Chappell," Edward Cain Galleries, Denver, CO.
[Catalog, one photograph.]
"Fine Photographs," Kalamazoo Institute of Arts, Kalamazoo, MI.
"Three Photographers," George Eastman House, Rochester, NY.
[Curator's statement: Nathan Lyons, "Three Photographers Exhibition," *Image* 12:1 (1963) : 2-3, text and one photograph.]
VII Photographers Gallery, Provincetown, MA.
"Heliography," Lever House, New York, NY.
[Catalog, pp. 8-9, 18; two photographs and biography. Reviewed: Murray Deitz, "The Association of Heliographers," *Infinity* 12:10 (October 1963) : 22-23; text and one photograph. Ralph Hattersley, "The Heliographers at Lever House," *Contemporary Photographer* 4:4 (1963) : 60-61.]
"Photography 63," George Eastman House, Rochester, NY. (traveled).
[Catalog, pp. 20, 87; one photograph and biography.]
" Turn Toward Peace," Community Church (?), Boston, MA.

1964

Museum of Fine Arts, Boston, MA.
"Boston Arts Festival: Photographs, A New England Invitational Exhibition," Boston, MA.
[Catalog, p. 59.]
"Two Photographers," (with John Brook), Pine Manor College, Wellesley, MA.
El Mochuelo Gallery, Santa Barbara, CA.
"Four Photographers," Community Church, Boston, MA.
"In Honor of Carl and Marie Siembab," Grover Cronin, Waltham, MA.
"Nature, Man and Remnants" (with Nicholas Dean and Paul Petricone), Hicks Street Gallery, Brooklyn Heights, NY.
[Reviewed: Jacob Deschin, "Brooklyn Show," *New York Times,* August 23, 1964, p. 20x.]
Cosindas Gallery, Vineyard Haven, Martha's Vineyard, MA.
Gallery 216, New York, NY.
"Six Photographers," Trinity College, Hartford, CT.
Long Beach Museum of Art, Long Beach, CA.
Institute of Design (IIT), Chicago, IL.
Indiana University, Bloomington, IN.
Association of Heliographers Gallery, New York, NY.

1965

"Six Photographers," George Eastman House, Rochester, NY. (traveled).
University of Illinois, Urbana, IL.
"Contemporary Photographs from the George Eastman House Collection, 1900-1964," George Eastman House, Rochester, NY. (traveled).
Institute of Design (IIT), Chicago, IL.
Purdue University, Lafayette, IN.
London Public Library and Art Museum, London, Canada.
"Voices of the City," City Hall Gallery, Boston, MA.
[Brochure, one photograph. Reviewed: Jules Aarons, "A City Venture," *Photography* (London), 20:2 (1965): 26-27; text and one photograph.]
"Exhibition I," M.I.T., Cambridge, MA.
"Reality in Painting, Abstraction in Photography," Slater Memorial Museum, Norwich, CT.
"Photography in America: 1850-1965," Yale University Art Gallery, New Haven, CT.
[Catalog, by Robert M. Doty; one photograph.]
Indiana University Museum of Art, Bloomington, IN.

1966

Arlington Street Church, Boston, MA.
"American Photography: The Sixties," Sheldon Memorial Art Gallery, University of Nebraska, Lincoln, NB.
[Catalog, pp.7, 13; one photograph and biography.]
"Winterfest," Boston, MA.
Cambridge Art Association, Cambridge, MA.
"Faculty Show," Boston University, Boston, MA.
Regis College, Newton, MA.

1967

LaSalle Junior College, Auburndale, MA.
"Professors of Photography," University of Oregon, Eugene, OR. (traveled).
"Ten in Focus," Smithsonian Institution, Washington, D.C. (traveled).
"Photography in the Twentieth Century," George Eastman House, Rochester, NY, with the National Gallery of Canada. (traveled).
[Catalog, by Nathan Lyons, Horizon Press; p. 101, one photograph.]
"Contemporary Photographers I," George Eastman House, Rochester, NY. (traveled).
"CRIA," Carpenter Center for the Visual Arts, Harvard University, Cambridge, MA.
"Photography Invitational," San Jose State College, San Jose, CA.
"Photography USA 1967," DeCordova-Dana Museum, Lincoln, MA.
[Catalog, one photograph and biography.]

University of New Mexico, The Museum of Art, Albuquerque, NM.

1968

Minneapolis Institute of Arts, Minneapolis, MN.
Jewish Community Center, Washington, D.C.
"Artists Against Racism and the War," Boston Common (?), Boston, MA.
Rhode Island Arts Festival, Providence, RI. [catalog.]
Smithsonian Institution Photography Exhibition and Sale, Washington, D.C.
"Contemporary Photographs," UCLA Art Galleries, Los Angeles, CA.
[Catalog, one photograph and biography.]
"Light 7," Hayden Gallery, MIT, Cambridge, MA.
[Catalog, by Minor White, MIT Press, two photographs; reprinted as *Aperture* 14:1 (1968).]
Focus Gallery, San Francisco, CA.
"Focal Point," Paul Art Center, University of New Hampshire, Durham, NH.
Juniata College, Huntington, PA.

1969

"Young Printmakers," Jewett Arts Center, Wellesley College, Wellesley, MA.
"Siembab Gallery Photographs," Minneapolis Institute of Arts, Minneapolis, MN.
"Photographs from the Siembab Gallery," Museum of Fine Arts, Boston, MA.
"Eight Photographers," Harvard University, Cambridge, MA.
Carr House, Rhode Island School of Design, Providence, RI.

1970

Fogg Art Museum, Cambridge, MA.
Photographic Studies Workshop Travelling Exhibition, Carl Siembab Gallery, Boston, MA.
[One of several group exhibitions organized to raise funds for the Visual [Photographic] Studies Workshop.]
Bristol Art Museum, Bristol, RI.

1971

"Ansel Adams, Carl Chiarenza, Richard Faller, Chester Michalik, Aaron Siskind, and Minor White," SUNY, Cortland, NY.
Scituate Arts Festival, Scituate, MA.
"Photographic Invitational," University of Florida, Gainesville, FL.
St. Francis College, Biddeford, ME.
Imageworks, Cambridge, MA.

1972

"Six Photographers," Brockton Art Center, Brockton, MA.
"Photovision '72," (Invitational Section), Boston Center for the Arts, Boston, MA. (traveled).
[Catalog, one photograph.]
"Octave Of Prayer," Hayden Gallery, MIT, Cambridge, MA.
[Catalog, by Minor White, Aperture Books, p. 44, one photograph; also issued as *Aperture* 17:1, (1972).]
"New England Photographers," The Johnson Gallery, Middlebury College, Middlebury, VT.
"Contemporary American Photographers," Fogg Art Museum, Harvard University, Cambridge, MA.

1973

University of California, Riverside, CA.
"From 1839: Revolution in a Box," Pomona College, Pomona, CA.
Museum of Art, Portland, ME.
Hopkins Center, Dartmouth College, Hanover, NH.
"By SX-70," Light Gallery, New York, NY.
"Seen and Unseen," Fogg Art Museum, Harvard University, Cambridge, MA.
Stonehill College, North Easton, MA.
Brown University, Providence, RI.
Treat Gallery, Lewiston, ME.
Provincetown Art Association, Provincetown, MA.
Currier Gallery, Manchester, NH.
Museum of Art, Bowdoin College, Brunswick, ME.
University of Connecticut, Storrs, CT.

1974

"Celebrations," Hayden Gallery, MIT, Cambridge, MA.
[Catalog by Minor White, Aperture Books, p. 41, one photograph; also issued as *Aperture* 17:2 (1974).]
"Photographic Directions," College Art Gallery, SUNY New Paltz, NY.
Art 74, Framingham, MA,
"5 Fotografos Americanos: Carl Chiarenza, Kipton Kumler, Nathan Lyons, Brett Weston, Minor White," Galeria da Emenda, Lisbon, Portugal.
[Catalog, by Hellmut Wohl; text, biography, one photograph.]

1975

"The Polaroid Print," Lamkin Gallery, Fairfax, CA.
"Recent Photographs by Ten Visiting Artists," Frederic S. Wight Art Gallery, UCLA, Los Angles, CA.
"In Just Seconds: A Polaroid Color Survey," International Center of Photography, New York, NY.

"International Invitational of Photography" (Auction Exhibition for Volunteer Service Photographers), Union Carbide Exhibition Gallery, New York, NY.
"Contemporary Art: Italian Heritage," Boston City Hall Gallery, Boston, MA.
[Catalog, biography and one photograph.]
Cronin Gallery, Houston, TX.
Art Institute of Chicago, Chicago, IL.

1976
"Contemporary American Photography, The UCLA Collection," Frederic S. Wight Art Gallery, UCLA, Los Angeles, CA.
[Catalog, p. 65, biography.]
"12 East Coast Photographers," Cornell University, Ithaca, NY.
" Work by Recipients of Massachusetts Arts and Humanities Foundation Fellowships," Enjay Gallery, Boston, MA.
[Reviewed: Ann Parsons, "Don't Take these Images for Granted," *The Boston Phoenix,* January 11, 1977, section 2, p. 3.]

1977
"The Target Collection of American Photography," Museum of Fines Arts, Houston, TX.
[Catalog, ed. by Anne Tucker, p. 58; text and biography.]
"Four Directions/Photography," Worcester Craft Center, Worcester, MA.

1978
"Art of the State/State of the Art." Vision Gallery, Boston, MA.
[Catalog, ed. by Susan R. Channing, introduction by Estelle Jussim (Addison House, Danbury, NH); pp. 8, 11-12, 16-19; text, biography, four reproductions.]
"New Presences in the Fogg Museum," Fogg Art Museum, Harvard University, Cambridge, MA.

1979
"New Acquisitions," Center for Creative Photography, Tucson, AZ.
"Attitudes: Photography in the 1970s," Santa Barbara Museum of Art, Santa Barbara, CA.
[Catalog, ed. by Fred Parker.]
"Master Class Teachers," Maine Photographic Workshop, Rockport, ME.
"The Anthony G. Cronin Memorial Collection," Museum of Fine Arts, Houston, TX.
[Catalog, by William C. Agee and Anne Tucker.]

1980
"Aspects of the 70s: Photography, Recent Directions," DeCordova Museum, Lincoln, MA.
[Catalog, by James Sheldon. Reviewed: Michael Pretzer, "Scrambling the '70s," *Afterimage* 8:3 (October 1980) : 15, one reproduction.]
"Photographs from the Collection: 35 Photographs by Chiarenza, Giacomelli, Kasebier, King, Ranalli, Schwachman, Sheeler, Steiner, Stieglitz," Worcester Art Museum, Worcester, MA.
"Finnphoto International Photographic Event," Satakunta Museum, Pori, Finland.
"A Moment of Vision," MFA Gallery, Rochester Institute of Technology, Rochester, NY
[Catalog, by J. Hafey, et. al, eds. Dark Sun Press, Rochester, NY; one reproduction and text.]
"Recent Polaroid Photographs in Historic Perspective," Bell Gallery, List Art Center, Brown University, Providence, RI.

1981
"Photo Facts and Opinions," Addison Gallery of American Art, Andover, MA.
[Catalog, by Kelly Wise, ed., text and biography. Reviewed: Edward Earle, "Photo Facts and Opinions at the Addison Gallery," *Views* 2:3 (Spring 1981) : 16-17.]
"The First Twenty-five Years," Carl Siembab Gallery, Boston, MA.
Madison Art Center, Madison, WI.
"Photographs from the Collection," International Museum of Photography at George Eastman House, Rochester, NY.
"The Permanent Collection: Photographs Acquired 1969-80," Minneapolis Institute of Arts, Minneapolis, MN.

1982
"Sixteen Photographers," Montserrat Gallery, Beverly, MA.
"Landscape Photographs: Robert Adams, Paul Caponigro, Carl Chiarenza, Linda Connor, Jim Dow, Richard Misrach," Jorgenson Gallery, University of Connecticut, Storrs, CT.
[Catalog.]
"New England's Teaching Photographers," Carlson Gallery, University of Bridgeport, Bridgeport, CT.
[Catalog: *First They Wrought: New England's Teaching Photographers.*]
"Art in Support of Art," Symphony Hall, Boston, MA.
"Re-Views: Carl Chiarenza, Linda Conner, Judy Dater, Roy DeCarava, Anne Noggle, Gilles Peress, Aaron Siskind," Boston University Art Gallery, Boston, MA.
[Reviewed: Kelly Wise, "Group show is more than meets the eye," *The Boston Globe*, December 1, 1982, p. 43.]

1983
"Four Photographers," JEB Gallery, Providence, RI.

"Jurors," Art Association of Newport, RI.
"The Last Picture Show," Creative Photography Laboratory, MIT, Cambridge, MA.
"Treasures from the Collection: Permanent Survey of the History of Photography," International Museum of Photography at George Eastman House, Rochester, NY.
"Arboretum," Schwader Art Gallery, University of Denver, Boulder, CO. (traveled; slide set).
"Shared Views, Views Shared," RIT Photography Gallery, Rochester Institute of Technology, Rochester, NY.
"Rare Photographs," Yale University Art Gallery, New Haven, CT.

1984
"Local Abstraction: Works in Photography and Sculpture," Project Arts Center, Cambridge, MA.
"20th Century Art," Smith College Museum of Art, Northampton, MA.
Yale University Art Gallery, New Haven, CT.
Rhode Island School of Design Museum of Art, Providence, RI.
DeCordova Museum, Lincoln, MA.
"Selections 2," Photokina, Cologne, Germany. (traveled).
[Catalog: Verlag Photographie, Schaffhausen, West Germany; two full page reproductions.]
"Twelve on 20 x 24," School of the Museum of Fine Arts Gallery, Boston, MA. (traveled).
[Catalog, by Jon Holmes, The New England Foundation for the Arts; p. 2. Reviewed: N. Stapen, "Artists' Giant Camera Work Intrigues," *The Boston Herald*, November 14, 1984, p. 31.]

1985
Museum of Contemporary Photography, Chicago, IL.
Museum of Art and History, Fribourg, Switzerland.
Joan Whitney Payson Gallery, Portland, ME.
Vision Gallery, Boston, MA
"Boston Now: Photography," Institute of Contemporary Art, Boston, MA
[Catalog, by David A. Ross, et. al; pp. 33, 35, 41-42. Reviewed: Nancy Stapen, "ICA's 'Boston Now: Photography,' " *The Boston Herald* (July 4, 1985). Kelly Wise, " 'Boston Now' Offers Dazzling Treats at ICA," *The Boston Globe* (July 7, 1985) : B1-2. William Parker, "Uneven *Spectrums*/Neglected *Operators*," *Views* 7:1 (Fall 1985) : 12-14; citation and reproduction. David Herwaldt, "ICA Documents Boston Now," *Art New England* 6:10 (October 1985): 9, 24. Charles Giuliano, "Photographic Feast at ICA," *The Patriot Ledger, Boston, MA, July 6, 1985, pp. 13-14. Cliff Garboden, "Photography: Recent Developments," The Boston Phoenix*, July 23, 1985, Section 3, pp. 1, 10.]
"Boston Arts Festival: Invitational Section," Boston, MA.
"Photography from the Permanent Collection," National Museum of American Art, Washington, D.C.
"Works of Art on Paper," Smith College Museum of Art, Northampton, MA.

1986
"Nature Observed: Sculpture, Painting & Photography by Contemporary Artists," Danforth Museum of Art, Framingham, MA.
"Three Photographers," (with Chester Michalik and Dan Ranalli), Temple Gallery, Tyler School of Art, Temple University, Philadelphia, PA.
"Photo-Synthesis: An Informational Survey of Photography Resources in the Valley," Smith College Museum of Art, Northampton, MA.
[Reviewed: L. Muench, "'Photo-synthesis: An Informational Survey of Photography . . .'" *Views* 7:5 (Fall 1986): 14.]
"Selections 3," Photokina '86, Cologne, Germany (traveled).
[Catalog: Verlag Photographie, Schaffhausen, West Germany.]
"Masterworks of Contemporary Photography," Atrium Gallery, University of Connecticut, Storrs, CT.
"Commitment to Vision," Museum of Art, University of Oregon, Eugene, OR. (traveled.)
[Catalog, by David D. Featherstone.]

1987
"Work from Two Decades," Pollard Gallery, City Hall, Lowell, MA.
"A Panorama of Photography: 150 Years Since Daguerre," Worcester Art Museum, Worcester, MA.
"Legacy of Light," International Center of Photography, New York, NY. (traveled).
[Catalog, ed. by Constance Sullivan, Alfred A. Knopf, New York, NY, pp. 196-197.]
"Photography and Art: Interactions Since 1946," The Los Angeles County Museum of Art, Los Angeles, CA. (traveled).
[Catalog, by Andy Grundberg and Kathleen McCarthy Gauss, Abbeville, New York, NY, pp. 55, 72.]

1988
"Art Networks, 1950-1970," Transco Art Gallery, Houston, TX.
"Evocative Presence: 20th Century Photography in the Permanent Collection," Museum of Fine Arts, Houston, TX.

Works in Public Collections:

Addison Gallery of American Art, Andover, MA.
Amherst College, Mead Museum of Art, Amherst, MA.
Artists Foundation, Boston, MA.
Atlantic-Richfield Corporate Art Collection, Los Angles, CA.
Bibliotheque Nationale, Paris, France.
Boston Center for the Arts, Boston, MA.
DeCordova Museum, Lincoln, MA.
Glendale College, Glendale, AZ.
Harvard University, Fogg Art Museum, Cambridge, MA.
International Center of Photography, New York, NY.
International Museum of Photography at George Eastman House, Rochester, NY.
International Polaroid Collection, Offenbach, Germany.
Massachusetts Institute of Technology, Cambridge, MA.
Minneapolis Institute of Arts, Minneapolis, MN.
Museum of Fine Arts, Boston, MA.
Museum of Fine Arts, Houston, TX.
Museum of Fine Arts, St. Petersburg, FL.
National Museum of American Art, Washington, D.C.
New Orleans Museum of Art, New Orleans, LA.
Phoenix College, Phoenix, AZ.
Polaroid Collection, Cambridge, MA.
Princeton University Art Museum, Princeton, NJ.
Princeton University, Minor White Archives, Princeton, NJ.
Rhode Island School of Design, Museum of Art, Providence, RI.
Smith College Museum of Art, Northampton, MA.
University of Arizona, Center for Creative Photography, Tucson, AZ.
University of California, The Grunwald Collection, Los Angeles, CA.
University of Colorado, Denver, CO.
University of New Hampshire, Durham, NH.
University of North Carolina, Ackland Art Museum, Chapel Hill, NC.
Visual Studies Workshop, Rochester, NY.
Worcester Art Museum, Worcester, MA.
Yale University Art Gallery, New Haven, CT.

Lectures and Workshops

1969
Printmaking workshop with Nicholas Dean, Portland School of Fine Arts, Portland, ME.

1972
Participant, five-day retreat at Sippewisset (Cape Cod) with Peter Bunnell, Allan Dutton, Jonathan Green, Robert Heinecken, Jerome Leibling, Frederick Sommer, Jerry Uelsmann, Jack Welpott, and Minor White.

1974
Ansel Adams' Yosemite Contemporary Creative Photography and History Workshop, with Jerry Uelsmann and Robert Heinecken, Yosemite, CA. (August).

1975
Workshop for Advanced Photography Students, University of California, Los Angeles, CA. (July).

1977
Visiting Photographer, Western Carolina University, Cullowhee, N.C. (January-February).
Radio discussion/interview with Frank Belski, Multiversity, WBUR, Boston, MA. (June).

1979
"A Master Class with Carl Chiarenza: The Abstract Landscape," Maine Photographic Workshops, Rockport, ME. (July).
"Carl Chiarenza, Photographs, 1954-1979," Minneapolis Institute of Arts, Minneapolis, MN. (November).
Artist-in-Residence, Center for Creative Photography, University of Arizona, Tucson, AZ. (November).

1983
"Carl Chiarenza: A Life in Photography," Art Institute of Boston, Boston, MA. (February).

1986
"My Work as a Photographer," University of Arizona, Tuscon, AZ. (Spring).

1988
Lecture, Art Networks Symposium, Museum of Fine Arts, Houston, TX. (Spring).

Awards and Honors

1975-76
Artist's Fellowship, Massachusetts Arts and Humanities Foundation

1977-78
Artist's Fellowship, National Endowment for the Arts

1981
Nominated without solicitation for AVA National Visual Artist Fellowship

1983-84
Museum of Fine Arts, Boston; Polaroid Corporation; and Massachusetts Council on the Arts and Humanities Grant (20 x 24), Artist in Residence Project

PROFESSIONAL ACTIVITIES

Publications by Chiarenza on Aaron Siskind

Aaron Siskind: Pleasures and Terrors, Little, Brown and Company (A New York Graphic Society Book), Boston, MA, 1982.
[Reviewed: Andy Grundberg, "Photography Books," *The New York Times Book Review,* December 5, 1982, p. 58. Estelle Jussim, "The Art of Aaron Siskind," *Boston Review* 8:4 (August 1983) : 24-25. Henry Holmes Smith, *Print Collector's Newsletter* 14:5 (November-December 1983) : 182-183. Janice Felgar, *Umbrella* 6:4 (September, 1983): 116. David L. Jacobs, "Notes Toward a New Biography," *Afterimage* 12: 1/2 (Summer 1984) : 18-20. Gerry Badger, "The Photographic Collector Library,"*The Photographic Collector*, 5:2 (1985): 239-40.].

"Aaron Siskind's Photographs of Bucks County," (review of *Bucks County: Photographs of Early Architecture,* text by William Morgan), *Afterimage* 2:8 (February 1975) : 4-5.

"Siskind's Homage to Kline (1972-1975)" in *Photographs by Aaron Siskind in Homage to Franz Kline,* The David and Alfred Smart Gallery, University of Chicago, IL, 1975. Reprinted (with extensive illustration) as "Aaron Siskind's Photographs in Homage to Franz Kline,"*Afterimage* 3:6 (December 1975) : 8-13.

"Siskind's Critics: 1946-1966," *Center for Creative Photography* (University of Arizona) nos. 7/8 (September 1978) : 1-47.

"Form and Content in the Early Work of Aaron Siskind, *The Massachusetts Review* 19:4 (Winter 1978) : 803-833. Reprinted in Jerome Liebling (ed.), *Photography: Current Perspectives,* Light Impressions, Rochester, NY, 1979.
[Discussed: Ben Lifson, "Siskind Re-revisited," *The Village Voice,* December 18, 1978, p. 95. Ronald J. Hill, "Aaron Siskind: Ideas in Photography," *Record of the Art Museum, Princeton University 1980* 39:1 & 2 (1981) : 4-27.]

Consultant, film on Aaron Siskind, produced by Edgar B. Howard, The Checkerboard Foundation, 1980-81.

"Aaron Siskind: A Biographer's Short View, *The Nineteenth St. Botolph Club Foundation Award* (brochure), St. Botolph Club, Boston, MA, 1982.

"Siskind in the Sixties," *Views* 4:3 (Spring 1983) : 9-12.

"Aaron Siskind: A Portrait," *Arts Quarterly* (New Orleans Museum of Art) 7:2 (April-May-June 1985) : 12-15.

"The Chicago Facades," essay for limited edition portfolio, *Chicago Facades* by Aaron Siskind, Palm Press, Littleton, MA, 1985.

Lectures by Chiarenza on Aaron Siskind

1976
"Siskind's Critics," paper delivered at the 20th Century History of Photography Symposium, University of New Mexico, Albuquerque, NM. (October).

1980
"Conversation: Aaron Siskind and Carl Chiarenza," Israeli Cultural Center, Boston, MA. (November).

1982
"Aaron Siskind and His Work," Photographic Resource Center, Boston, MA. (November).
"The Art of Aaron Siskind," St. Botolph Club, Boston, MA. (December).

1984
"Aaron Siskind: Choices and Relationships," Minneapolis Institute of Arts, Minneapolis, MN. (March).

1985
"Continuity and Change in the Photographs of Aaron Siskind," National Museum of American Art, Washington, D.C. (February); Museum of Fine Arts, Boston, MA. (September) ;
Arizona State University, Tempe, AZ. (November).
[Reviewed: William Johnson, "Carl Chiarenza: 'Continuity and Change in the Work of Aaron Siskind,' " *Views* 7:2 (Winter 1986) : 24.]
"Aaron Siskind Master Seminar," International Center of Photography, New York, NY. (February).
"Aaron Siskind Before and After the Depression," New Orleans Museum of Art, New Orleans, LA. (June).

1986
"From Social Representation to Abstraction: The Photography of Aaron Siskind," Wadsworth Athenaeum, Hartford, CT. (January).
"Aaron Siskind: Continuity and Change," The Museum of Contemporary Photography, Chicago, IL. (October).
[Previewed: Abigail Foerstner, "Siskind's abstract view a challenging opening to [lecture] series," *Chicago Tribune,* September 26, 1986, section 7, pp. 57-58.]
"Aaron Siskind: Life and Work," (with commentary by Aaron Siskind) Des Moines Art Center, Des Moines, IA. (October).

1987
"Aaron Siskind: Fifty Years of Photography," Memorial Art Gallery, Rochester, NY. (September).
"Continuity and Change in the Work of Aaron Siskind," Spencer Museum of Art, University of Kansas, Lawrence, KA. (September).

Journal articles and essays for exhibitions, catalogs, brochures, and portfolios

Untitled poem and statements used by Minor White in "An Experiment in 'Reading' Photographs," *Aperture* 5:2 (1957) : 56, 65, 67.

"Stereotypes: Barriers to the Experience of Photographs," *Aperture* 6:2 (1958) : 90-91.

"The Closing of the Siembab" (with Anne Chiarenza) *Contemporary Photographer* 4:4 (1963) : 9-11.

Untitled poem, *Contemporary Photographer* 5:2 (1964-1965) : 58.

"Who Cares? – Concern, Protest and Action in Photography," *Contemporary Photographer* 6:2 (1969) : 2-4. Reprinted in *America Illustrated* (1972) and in *Elliniki Fotografia* (Athens, 1974).

"Manet's Use of Photography in the Creation of a Drawing," *Master Drawings* 7 (1969) : 38-45.

"Chiarenza Summary: Some Recollections," *Exposure* 11:1&2 (May 1973) : 21-22

Dru Shipman, "Implications of Sontag's View of Photography Panel: Summaries of Intended Comments by Chiarenza, Garver, Jay and Shipman," Society for Photographic Education National Meeting (1975) : 2-4. (Mimeographed brochure).

Excerpt from unpublished article on Robert Heinecken, Exhibition brochure, Light Gallery, New York (October 1973). Reprinted as

"Statement," in *18 UCLA Faculty Artists,* Frederick S. Wight Gallery, Los Angeles, CA. (1975).

"Notes on Aesthetic Relationships Between 17th Century Dutch Painting and 19th Century Photography," in Van Deren Coke (ed.), *One Hundred Years of Photographic History,* University of New Mexico Press, Albuquerque (1975) : 18-34.
[Reviewed: Alex Sweetman, "One Hundred Years of Photographic History: A Review," *Afterimage* 3:9 (March 1976) : 8-9].

"The View Camera Experience," essay for Burleigh Brooks Optics, Inc. (1976). Reprinted as "Revelations in the Ground Glass," *The Professional Photographer* no. 104, 1976 (November 1977) : 67-68.

"From cliche-verre to Vary Cliche," critical text published with suite of lithographs by Robert Heinecken, Light Gallery, New York (1979), edition of 20.

"Notes Toward an Integrated History of Picturemaking," *Afterimage* 7:1&2 (Summer 1979) : 35-41. Reprinted in Thomas F. Barrow, et. al. (eds.), *Reading Into Photography: Selected Essays, 1959-1980,* University of New Mexico Press, Albuquerque, 1982.
[Reviewed: David L. Jacobs, "Of Cretans and Critics: In Search of Photographic Theory," *Afterimage* 10:7 (February 1983) : 9-14. Judy Siegel, "Reading Into Photography," *Exposure* 21:1 (1983) : 44-47.]

"Some Notes on Robert Heinecken," in James Enyeart (ed.), *Heinecken,* The Friends of Photography, Carmel, CA. and Light Gallery, New York, 1980.
[Reviewed: Dinah Portner, "Heinecken," *Obscura,* 1:4 (March-April 1981) : 46-48].

Introduction by Carl Chiarenza, essay by Lee Lockwood, *A Photographic Patron: The Carl Siembab Gallery,* Institute of Contemporary Art, Boston, MA., 1981.
[Reviewed: Jean Caslin, "A Boston Tradition,"*Afterimage,* 11:1&2 (Summer 1981) : 36-37.]

Untitled essay in Kelly Wise (ed.), *Photo Facts and Opinions,* Addison Gallery of American Art, Andover, MA., 1981.

"Eye and Mind: The Seriousness of Wit," in *Kenneth Josephson,* Museum of Contemporary Art, Chicago, IL., 1983.
[Reviewed: David Miller, "Fathers and Sons: Kenneth Josephson's Chicago Retrospective," *Afterimage* 11:4 (November 1983) : 14-16].

"Ansel Adams: American Artist," Exhibition brochure, Boston University Law School, Boston, MA., 1983.

"Ansel Adams, 1902-1984," *Views* 5:4 (Summer 1984) : 20.

"Bibliography for Historical Photography and the History of Photography," in *Books for College Libraries* 3rd edition, forthcoming 1988, from the American Library Association.

Reviews of Books and Exhibitions

"Notes from Boston: Three recent Shows at the Carl Siembab Gallery," *Contemporary Photographer* 4:2 (1963) : n.p.

"Paul Strand and Basil Davidson. *Tir A'Mhurain – Outer Hebrides,*" *Contemporary Photographer* 4:2 (1963): 63-65.

"Total Picture Confusion: Andreas Feininger," (review of Feininger's *The World Through My Eyes*), *Contemporary Photographer* 5:1 (1964) : 43-45.

"Letter from Boston," *Contemporary Photographer* 5:2 (1964-1965) : 60-62.

"Whither Go We, John Brook?" *Boston Review of Photography* 1:3 (1967) : 2-3.

"Aaron Scharf, *Art and Photography,*" *Art Journal* 31:3 (1972) : 338-344.

"Richard Rudisill, *Mirror Image, The Influence of the Daguerreotype on American Society,*" *Art Journal* 31:3 (1972) : 344-350.

"James Baker Hall, *Minor White: Rites and Passages,*" *Print Collector's Newsletter* 11:2 (May-June 1980) : 59-63.

From 1981 to the present, Chiarenza has reviewed over forty books with photographic subjects including monographs, biographies and histories for *Choice: The American Library Association.*

Lectures, Workshops, Symposia and Juries

1966

Series of four lectures on the history of photography, Rhode Island School of Design, Providence, RI.
[Reviewed: Pete Meserol, "Chiarenza Lecture," *Blockprint* (RISD) 9:18 (1966)]

Leader, Seminar on Photography, Danforth Teacher Conference, Danforth Foundation, Danforth Camp, MI.

1967

Lecture, "The Portrait in Photography, 1848-1966," in conjunction with exhibition of the same title, curated with Davis Pratt, Fogg Art Museum, Harvard University, Cambridge, MA.
[Reviewed: Mark L. Rosenberg, *The Harvard Crimson*, April 17, 1967, p. 3]

Lecture, "Religion and Art," Charles Street Meeting House, Boston, MA.

Lecture, "The Seeing Eye," Boston College, Newton, MA.

Lecture, "You Ain't Seen Nothing Yet," University of Massachusetts, Boston, MA.

Panel discussion, "The Arts Today," Boston College, Newton, MA.

1968

Eight-week seminar, "Connoisseurship in Photography," Worcester Art Museum, Worcester, MA.

Guest critic, Boston Camera Club, Boston, MA.

Three-day symposium, "Focal Point," University of New Hampshire, Durham, NH. (Sidore lecture series).

Designed and produced a series of one-person exhibitions for Itek Corporation, Lexington, MA., continuing monthly through 1969.

1969

Panelist, discussion on photographic publications, Society for Photographic Education National Conference, Oakland, CA.

Five-day seminar on the history of photography, Department of Art, University of Utah, Salt Lake City, UT.

Lecture, "Photography: Some Contemporary Points of View," Museum of Fine Arts, Boston, MA.

Workshop, Boston Camera Club, Boston, MA.

Lecture, "Interaction: Verbal/Visual," Massachusetts College of Art, Boston, MA.

Chairman, Regional meeting, Society for Photographic Education, University of Connecticut, Storrs, CT.

1970

Chairman and participant, Criticism symposium, Society for Photographic Education National Conference, University of Iowa, Iowa City, IA.

Lecture, "The Picture as Subject," for *Celebration, A Festival of the Arts,* University of Florida, Gainesville, FL.

Seminar, "Photography Now," for art history students, University of Florida, Gainesville, FL.

Seminar, "The Picturesque Subject," for photography students, University of Florida, Gainesville, FL.

Lecture, "Pictures within Pictures and Albums," for history of photography students, Harvard University, Cambridge, MA.

1971

Panelist, "What is an Original Print?" DeCordova-Dana Museum, Lincoln, MA.

Lecture, "On the Nature of Photographic Representation," Harvard University, Cambridge, MA.

Seminar, "The Tools of Art," Boston University Student Union Spring Arts Festival, Boston, MA.

Organized and chaired three-day seminar of 20 nationally prominent teachers and museum people to discuss the possibility of establishing a center and school in the Boston area for the study of photography and related media. Resulted in the later formation of Imageworks, in Cambridge, MA.

Inaugural lecture, "What Does the Picture Mean?" Imageworks, Cambridge, MA.

1973

Lecture, "Problems in Art and Visual Perception," Boston University, Boston, MA.

Lecture, "Aspects of 20th Century Photography Seen in the Work of Five American Photographers," University of Massachusetts, Boston, MA.

Monthly graduate seminars on the history of photography and visual perception, Visual Studies Workshop, Rochester, NY., (SUNY Buffalo), continuing through Spring 1974.

Juror, Newman Club Photography Competition, Boston University, Boston, MA.

Commentator, Print discussion group, Boston Camera Club, Boston, MA.

Panelist, "Various Approaches to the Teaching of Photographic History in a Studio Situation," Society for Photographic Education National Conference, University of New Mexico, Albuquerque, NM.

1974
Lecture, "History and Special Effects of the Still Image," at symposium, "The Future of Special Effects and Animation," Museum of Fine Arts, Boston, MA.
Panelist, "What's Happening in Photography?" Hampshire College, Amherst, MA.

1975
Paper given and panelist for discussion, "Implications of Sontag's View of Photography," Society for Photographic Education National Conference, Asilomar, Pacific Grove, CA.
Juror, Greater Hartford Civic and Arts Festival, Hartford, CT.
"Carl Chiarenza Weekend: Workshop on History and Criticism," Sun Valley Center for the Arts and Humanities, Sun Valley, ID.
Lectures, "On International Trends in Photography in the 1920s and 1930s," University of California, Los Angeles, CA.

1976
Moderator of panel discussion with Thomas Barrow, A. D. Coleman and Alex Sweetman, "Important Aesthetic Problems in 20th Century Photography," J.B. Speed Art Museum, Louisville, KY.

1977
Lecture, "Photography and Representation in the History of Art," School of the Museum of Fine Arts, Boston, MA.
Lecture, "From the Cave Paintings to the Photograph," Museum of Fine Arts, Houston, TX and University of Texas, Dallas, TX.

1978
Juror, Marblehead Arts Festival, Marblehead, MA.
Panelist, "Art History for Studio Artists," School of The Museum of Fine Arts, Boston, MA.

1979
Paper, "Notes and Questions in Search of an Integrated History of Picturemaking," Art Institute of Chicago, Chicago, IL.
Symposium moderator and participant, "Toward the New Histories of Photography," School of the Art Institute of Chicago, Chicago, IL.

1980
Juror, Traveling Scholarship Grants, School of the Museum of Fine Arts, Boston, MA.
Moderator, "Treasures of the Royal Photographic Society: Research in Context," A Conference on Victorian and Edwardian Photography, Boston University and the Photographic Resource Center, Boston, MA.

1981
Curator, "A Photographic Patron: The Carl Siembab Gallery," Institute of Contemporary Art, Boston, MA.
Juror, Massachusetts Council on the Arts and Humanities and the Photographic Resource Center: New Works Project.

1982
Moderator, "Landscape: In Position/Imposition," Minneapolis Institute of Arts, Minneapolis, MN.
Photography Fellowship Panel, National Endowment for the Arts.

1983
Juror, Alumni Traveling Fellowships, School of the Museum of Fine Arts, Boston, MA.

1985
Lecture, "The Move to Abstraction in American Photography," History of Photography Class, Wellesley College Art Department, Wellesley, MA.
Juror, with Vicki Goldberg and Lou Dorfman, International Center of Photography International Awards.

1986
Paper, "Manet's *Rue Mosnier* Drawings of 1878 and Stereo Photography," Society for Photographic Education National Conference, Baltimore, MD.
Paper, "Further Notes Toward an Integrated History of Picturemaking," University of Rochester, Rochester, NY.
Seminar for graduate students of Columbia College, The Museum of Contemporary Photography, Chicago, IL.
Juror/curator, "Northlight/Southwest Juried Group Exhibition," Arizona State University, Tempe, AZ.

1987
Seminar for advanced history of photography students, University of Kansas, Lawrence, KA.

1988
Co-curator, "On Time in Photography," Hartnett Gallery, University of Rochester, Rochester, NY.
Panelist, Art Networks Symposium, Museum of Fine Arts, Houston, TX.

Grants and Awards

1957-59; 1962-64
Graduate Assistantships, Boston University, Boston, MA.

1958-59
Reader's Digest Research Grant

1962
Howard Thurman Educational Trust Fund Fellowship

1966-67; 1967-68
Harvard University Fellowships (declined)

1966-67; 1967-68
Danforth Teacher Grants

1968
Harvard University Travel Fellowship

1970-71
Kress Foundation Research Grant

1970
Harvard University Research Grant

1970
Boston University Summer Research Stipend

1983
Merit Award for *Aaron Siskind: Pleasures and Terrors,* Photographic Historical Society

Professional Memberships

American Association of University Professors, 1972-82.
Archives of American Art, New England Advisory Committee, Boston, MA., 1981-86.
Artists Against Racism and the War, Boston, Ma., 1966-68.
Artists Foundation, Boston, MA., Artists Advisory Panel, 1977-1980.
Association of Historians of American Art, 1979-.
Cambridge Multicultural Arts Center, Advisory Panel, 1984-85.
Center for Creative Photography, University of Arizona, Tucson, AZ., Advisory Committee, 1976-78.
Center for Photographic Studies, Louisville, KY., 1976-78.
College Art Association, 1963-75; Committee, Films on Art, 1970-71.
Committee for the Rescue of Italian Art, 1969.
Friends of Photography, Carmel, CA., 1973-; Advisory Trustee, 1980-83.
Harvard University, Subcommittee of Harvard Overseers' Committee to Visit the Fine Arts, 1969-71.
History of Photography, Editorial Consultant, 1985-.
International Center of Photography, New York, NY., International Advisory Council, 1974-.
International Museum of Photography at George Eastman House, Rochester, NY., Academic Coordinating Committee, 1986-.
National Endowment for the Arts, New England Regional Task Force on the Photography Program, 1980.
Photographic Heritage Association, Rochester, NY., Board of Directors, 1986-.
Photographic Resource Center, Boston, MA., Board of Directors, 1977-.
Polaroid Higher Education Project, Board of Advisors, 1982-.
Society for Photographic Education, 1964-; Board of Directors, 1968-73; Director, New England Region, 1967-73; National Conference Committee, 1968-71; Committee for Grant-in-Aid, 1971-72; Steering Committee, 1973-74; Nominating Committee, Northeast Region, 1976-77; Nominating Committee, National, 1978-79; Consultant, Steering Committee, 1981-82; 1989 National Conference Advisory Committee.
Texas Center for Photographic Studies, Dallas, TX., Advisory Board, 1975-76.
Visual Studies Workshop, Rochester, NY., 1969-; Board of Trustees, 1975-.

Professional Listings

Biography International, Delhi, India, 1984.
Contemporary Authors, 1983.
Contemporary Photographers, London, 1987.
Dictionary of International Biography, 1973-.
International Authors and Writers Who's Who, Cambridge, England, 1985.
International Contemporary Arts Directory, London, 1984-85.
International Who's Who of Contemporary Achievement, 1984.
MacMillan Biographical Encyclopedia of Photographic Artists and Innovators, 1984.
Men of Achievement, England, 1983.
The New York Art Review, 1987.
Notable Americans of the Bicentennial Era, 1976.
Outstanding Young Men of America, 1970.
Personalities of America, 1984.
Photo Diary, Milan, Italy, 1985, 1986.
Photographers Encyclopedia International, 1839 to the Present, Geneva, Switzerland, 1985.
Who's Who in America, 1981-.
Who's Who in American Art, 1980-.
Who's Who in Society, 1986.
Who's Who in the East, 1974, 1981-.
Who's Who in the United States, 1986.